Baseball's
Greatest
Moments
1860-1990

Baseball's Greatest Moments 1860-1990

by
Harold "Stu" Southworth

WINDSOR HOUSE
PUBLISHING GROUP INC.

Windsor House Publishing Group
Austin, Texas

Baseball's Greatest Moments
1860-1990

796.357
Southworth

This is a work of fiction. All similarties to other than known
events and historical figures are unintended and coincidental.

PRINTING HISTORY
First Edition November, 1998

ISBN: 1-881636-24-0
Library of Congress Card Number: 98-61085

Published by:
Windsor House Publishing Group, Inc.,
11901 Hobby Horse Court, Suite 1516
Austin, Texas 78758

The name "Windsor House" and the logo are trademarks belonging to
Windsor House Publishing Group, Inc.

PRINTED IN THE UNITED STATES OF AMERICA
10 9 8 7 6 5 4 3 2 1

Dedication

This collection of baseball's adventures and misadventures of the 1860 to 1990 era is dedicated to my wife, Thelma Southworth, for her countless hours of attentive listening. The many yarns of the great national pastime, dug up from the four corners of the baseball world, Thelma shared with her husband, enjoyed, and critiqued. Not only am I certain Thelma has memorized each of these stories, but I was constantly inspired to continue with my work on this collection of anecdotes from her hearty laughter and wise counsel.

Foreword

It is with great pleasure that I have the opportunity to comment on an extremely entertaining collection of baseball stories and a talented author. Stu Southworth was the first coach I ever had at an organized level and in many ways the best coach I ever had. His attention to detail and his tough training methods have stayed with me all through life as I've worked my way to being a NCAA Division I head beaseball coach at California State University, Northridge. You too will benefit from his expertise and insight.

Occasionally a book comes along which captures the spirit and flavor of its subject from a unique perspective. This is such a book. Baseball has earned the status of being America's national pastime, because, like no other sport, it reflects the varied human diversities that make up our culture. The game is played by all ages, body sizes and types and races and therefore mirrors all of society. It is literally a playing out of the human drama on a unique stage – the baseball diamond.

A natural result is an opportunity for humor, strange twists, and extraordinarily unusual happenings – the stuff of life.

This book is about such stories. You will experience an array of unbelievable anecdotes that will leave you wondering how these could be true, but believe me, they are. In fact, I lived through one of them with the author myself as a high school baseball player, so I can personally attest to the validity of the "sprinkler" story.

If you have had the pleasure and educational experience of reading the previous books of Stu Southworth, you have obtained the nuts and bolts of how the game of baseball is played successfully. Now you can see the color and dynamic that have made it more than just a great ball game. These stories will help you understand why baseball has endeared itself to the American people and then the world. You will see why it is a game that is not just played – it is lived and loved.

Whether you have played extensively or watched baseball as a rabid fan or just "had a catch" with your dad as a kid, you will be thoroughly entertained by this collection of a century's worth of baseball's amazing but true stories. Read it with a friend and relive your own unforgettable memories about the greatest game ever invented.

– Bill Kernen
Head Baseball Coach, Cal State Northridge

Acknowledgments

So many people and so many sources are responsible for this work of humorous incidents from the countless games of baseball played in America. A hearty thanks to all the characters playing their parts in their many roles as these stories unfold to test the reader's imagination. It took every one of these unusual and zany characters in the great sport of baseball to accomplish this history of baseball through a parade of adventures and misadventures.

A special thanks to both my wife, Thelma, to whom I dedicated this volume, and my daughter Kathy, both of whom, in our weekly coffee sessions, would eagerly await the next unbelievable baseball tale to share with the author.

A great expression of gratitude to my close friend Wendell Young, living in Angelus Oaks, California, at the time of these book's writings, who, likewise, endured and enjoyed many of the baseball tales, old and new, laid upon him at our weekly gatherings. His kind comments, bursts of laughter, and critiques were always greatly appreciated.

Special thanks to the author's granddad Samuel Southworth and his dad William Dallas Southworth. They provided the oldest tales, recounting them with great memory, from 1860 to 1900, and from the 1900 to 1940 era.

This collection would not have been possible without a cartooned sketch for each baseball story. The 53 wonderful sketches provided by John Evanko, commercial artist and supervisor of Graphic Arts for the Altoona, Pennsylvania School District have made each story come alive for the reader. His work illustrating the incidents of various eras has been remarkable.

The works of the following authors and their publishers were helpful in providing four tales from each of the thirteen decades of baseball: Donald Honig and The St. Martin's Press; Fred Leib and the firm of Coward, McCann, and Geoghegan; Joe Reichler and The Crown Publishers; Ira Smith and H. Allen Smith with McGraw-Hill Publishers; Jules Tygiel with The Oxford University Press; Tristam Potter Coffin with Herder and Herder Press; Harry Ellard, The Ohio Bookstore of Cincinnati, Ohio; Katherine Burns, Permissions Editor *Reader's Digest*, for a reprint of the story in the June, 1989 issue; *The Philadelphia Inquirer Sunday Magazine*, for the story of October 16, 1988; Head Coach Ron Fraser, Baseball Coach at the University of Miami, Florida, for his creation and use of "Trick Pickoff Play" used in the College World Series at Omaha, Nebraska; Jackie Mason, Permissions Department, periodicals "The Country Gazette" sections August 1989 issue; to Ted Williams, Hall of

Fame home run slugger for the Boston Red Sox for his permission to use the story of "The Well-Trained Home Run" of 1937; and Bill Kilmer, former high school superstar and quarterback for the New Orleans Saints and The Washington Redskins professional football teams.

Preface

The baseball reader will find this work to be an unusual journey through our national game of baseball, in the form of a series of the most varied and hilarious incidents recorded to date. Truly, that is a unique collection of misadventures.

There are 53 humorous incidents written in chronological order, beginning with the year 1860 and carrying on through the 13 decades of baseball. In 1869 the game became professional.

The interesting fact to note about these many stories is that in practically every case any one of these happenings could have occurred within the past 100 years.

This volume is not only a book containing various forms of humor on the diamond, but it's so interesting for the reader to follow three master storytellers of baseball yarns. The three narrators are or were all intensely interested in the game, the players, events, and oddities so characteristic to baseball. Our three tellers of tales are successive generations of the Southworth family having its roots in St. Louis, Missouri, and the adjacent farming area of the State of Illinois across the Mississippi River. Granddad Samuel, Dad William, and Son Stuart, three will bring you games and game moments heretofore never written in baseball literature.

With humorous stories is usually also taught a hard lesson, often moral examples, and each of these tales reveal the "dos" and the "don'ts" of this great pastime.

Lean back and enjoy the extraordinary events which players, coaches, managers, spectators, umpires, and anyone remotely involved in baseball can cause himself to experience, or have thrust upon him unexpectedly.

Special Notes to the Readers

Some of the names and places of the 53 baseball tales have been changed to prevent any embarrassment to towns, teams, players or umpires involved. In any collection of humorous baseball stories, there are basically three elements: the story tellers, the listener or readers, and the target of the humor. It is not the intention of the author to target any persons, teams, towns, umpires, fans, etc. by name. These people do become victims of jokes and rare happenings purely by uncontrollable circumstances.

Several towns and teams and players have been given fictitious titles, either to avoid embarrassment to them, or because we could not find them through research.

In some cases, dates of events have been changed.

It was our intention to bring to the reader exactly four zany tales from each of the thirteen decades from 1860-1990, so some dates were changed to fit into the decade time slot. The chronological flow was necessary for the reader to sit there and imagine he was progressing through the years as the game changed very little.

An interesting note about unusual occurrences on a baseball diamond.

Any player, manager, umpire, fan may feel that he witnessed such an extraordinary feat or unorthodox play or occurrence one day while watching an inning of baseball, what he saw and heard could never occur again on any diamond as he saw it unfold. Right here and now let the author assure any viewer of baseball antics that (1) what was observed probably occurred in exactly that same manner in the years past, who knows how many times and (2) your bizarre tale which you tell to willing listeners will surely happen again in the future. There are simply too many people playing too many games of ball for it not to occur again.

Each of the stories in this collection are unbelievable but true, except the one entitled "The Best Seat In The House" which is an imaginary adventure of a Cuban from Havana, come to Cleveland, Ohio, to see his childhood buddy, Minnie Minoso, play in the big leagues. That story was included in this repertoire, because it has now become a standard part of baseball lore. Somewhat likened to "Casey at the Bat," the poems, or the 7th inning stretch song, "Take Me Out To The Ballgame."

Finally, the author must explain the first four stories, 1860's decade. I must add my apologies to the St. Louis, Missouri, Chapter of the Society of American Baseball Research, that great national group of which the author has been a member in the past. Story Number 1 and Story Number 2 have some elements of fantasy introduced to make the tale set in St. Louis emphasize the importance of the Civil War in spreading baseball popularity. The third and fourth tales are as accurate in time settings and details as it was possible to recall – from stories told to a 13-year-old boy by a very elderly grandfather who saw the first few ball games ever played in St. Louis. We hope that the St. Louis Chapter of the SABR will get a few laughs and additions to the lore of their great baseball city.

Narrators
In Order Of Appearance

GRANDFATHER   Samuel Southworth
St. Louis, Missouri
Born – Jerseyville, Illinois
October 12, 1849

Narrator of baseball periods:
1860-1870
1870-1880
1880-1890
1890-1900

FATHER   William D. Southworth
San Diego, California
Born – St. Louis, Missouri
June 12, 1895

Narrator of baseball periods:
1900-1910
1910-1920
1920-1930
1930-1940

SON   Harold Stuart Southworth
San Bernardino, California
Born – Dallas, Texas
April 19, 1925

Narrator of baseball periods:
1940-1950
1950-1960
1960-1970
1970-1980
1980-1990

THE GREAT
LEWIS AND CLARK
MEMORIAL ARCH

DOWNTOWN ST. LOUIS, MISSOURI
NEAR THE MISSISSIPPI RIVER

IN THE VICINITY OF THE
BIRTHPLACE OF BASEBALL IN ST. LOUIS

Contents

Introduction

These are a collection of over 50 baseball incidents, a potpourri of the most diverse kinds of experiences involving players, coaches, management, umpires and some of the fans in attendance. The earliest of these are four recollections of baseball as recalled from the Civil War years, in the city of St. Louis, Missouri, 1861-1865 told by the author's Granddad Sam who then continues to spin the unusual tales of the 1870s, the 1880s, the 1890s up to the 20th century.

The reader will look at the modern news photo of downtown St. Louis, Missouri, and imagine the earliest baseball fields laid out between the tall buildings and the great river. Where did these early accounts take place? Was it near one of the bases of the great Modern Memorial Arch? We certainly know that several were very near the river front, from all accounts.

This humorous collection has attempted to show baseball readers those kinds of experiences which they had not realized could occur on the main baseball diamonds of America. These recount the story of the origins and development of baseball from a child's game into a highly organized business and social institution.

In politics subtle jokes and humor are defined as "tiny revolutions." So let it be with humor for our great national pastine. The 20th century has seen a lot of laughs. In one small and hardly redeeming sense it has produced such an array of humor. This has always been a striking out at strict rules and tyranny of one kind or another.

Freud said that in making jokes there are three participants: the teller, the listener, and the target. As with politics, humor in baseball is a form of "coping." The game of baseball is guided by a strict set of rules which has been changed and sometimes upgraded by a rules committee.

These rules are undeniably enforced by the "men in blue," who can instantly recall and enforce any one of them. Exceptions to this code are often amusing to all.

One of the reasons that baseball humor is so popular is that it depicts and glorifies the unusual as well as the ordinary players, umpires, decisions, strategy, chicanery at all levels, scandals, rowdyism and even violence.

Certainly the baseball humor set down in this volume, more than anything else, shows the reader the wide cross-section of people who have competed against others on the field of play, such a set of "characters" as no other sport has ever seen.

In the 150 years since its humble birth, baseball has shown an infinite capacity for producing exhilarating triumphs, heart breaking losses, amusing blunders, and really awe-inspiring feats. The author has "touched all bases," capturing the whole human dream of baseball in a cascade of stories that offers a nostalgic feast.

The *Ball* once struck off,
Away flies the *Boy*
To the next destined post
And then Home with Joy

reprinted from *Country Home Magazine*

Batter Up!

Sometimes a story spreads over the miles and years until it becomes a cherished legend. George Washington didn't really chop down a cherry tree then declare that he couldn't lie about it. And Abner Doubleday, a major-general who fought bravely at the Battle of Gettysburg and died seven years before the beginning of this century, didn't invent the great American pastime of baseball. NO ONE ACTUALLY "INVENTED" BASEBALL. It evolved from the British game of "rounds" or "rounders" and references to it go back to the 16th century. Even in colonial America, New England children played variations of a game they called "one old cat" and "two old cat," depending upon how many bases they used. After hitting the ball with a stick, batters ran to a post scoring if they could get back to home without getting stuck ("soaked") with the ball they were playing with. With each out, fielders moved up to the plate for their turns at bat, and anyone who caught a fly ball changed places with the batter. It is the older version of our school and playground game called "workup." In towns where large groups played, the game was called "town ball." Eventually more bases and batters were used and pitchers wanted everyone to connect with the ball so that others got a chance to bat. Village rivalries became intense, and competition often ended in brawls ever the game's casual rules.

The person with valid claim to the title "FATHER OF BASEBALL" was Alexander Cartwright.

At 6 feet 2 inches and more than 200 pounds he was an avid ball player and an original member of the Knickerbocker Club of New York City, one of the first organized teams. In 1845 he made an effort to systematize the rules of this new game, creating virtually the same game we know today, excepting a few rules changed in the 1895-1905 era.

Cartwright placed four flat bases 90 feet apart with the batter at home base, established the positions of basemen and shortstop, decided that a regular batting order should be announced before the game, eliminated the "soaking," or striking the runner with the thrown ball, and instituted the three out inning. He did not establish the nine inning game, though. In his day, a game ended when one team scored more than 21 aces (runs). Yogi Berra would have been right at home there, too, in philosophizing that "it ain't over 'til it's over." Cartwright's new rules spread rapidly, and this new "baseball" became the "New York game." Organized, but not yet professional ball clubs, sprang up everywhere. By 1858 there were 25 of them taking the field.

"ROUNDERS"

1589

Be it Proclaimed that on Saturday the 20th of
May, at half past the hour of eleven, there shall
be a game open to the public to join in.

And at half past four on that same day the Guild of
St. Ives' (Merchants) is to be challenged by the Guild of
St. Michael's (Military).

On Sunday the 21st of May at half past the hour
of Eleven, there shall be a game open to the public to join in.

At half past four on that same day HCSB Bark
Star to be challenged by Ricky Rangers.
Market and the visit of our most beloved Queen,
Elizabeth Glorianna

It being that many folks amongst us at the time of our Faire are foreign unknowing of our village and the common things of England, we herein do endeavor to explain our favored sport known as Rounders.

In our shire there are eight players to a side. Each striker must be made out before those in the field may take to the bat. A player may be made out if his knock is caught in the air, upon a single bounce with a single hand, or the Runner is plugged fairly by an opposing Scout. A fair plug is one wherein a Scout both hit the Runner with the ball thrown directly, not upon the bounce nor upon the ground. Each runner hopes to race around the course set by the three stakes and to touch the talley stake to score for his side. The Feeder doth endeavour to deliver the ball to the place the Striker has shown him. The Striker need never swing unless the ball is thrown to his liking and he doth swing until he has knocked the ball.

Any contact between bat and ball is a knock. Any knock which lands within the boundaries of the Horse Tourney is fair to be played. If a Runner must stop along the course he may claim any stake for safety — one time each. When the ball is again struck he may advance again to the next stake: or to his victory or defeat.

If you be of a curious nature, know that the good folk with beribboned arms are most glad to answer your questions.

PART ONE

Baseball's Greatest Moments 1860 - 1990

Narrator of Baseball Tales:

SAMUEL SOUTHWORTH
(1849 - 1950)

THE FIRST MEETING OF THE BASEBALL NARRATORS JUNE, 1938

HE WAS AN OLD GENTLEMEN of 89 that year, this white haired man who sat in the old oak rocker near the first story bay window at 3669 Shenandoah Avenue, one of many identical two story post-Civil War red brick homes lined up like dominoes in St. Louis, Missouri. At that moment one would observe his anxiety as he peered down the street in the direction of the great river. It was Summer, June of 1938.

Today Samuel Southworth was not only to be visited by his eldest son, William (Will), but, he'd been promised, finally meet the only one of his six grandchildren he had never seen, Harold Stuart, Will's only child. Not only meet Stuart, who had been named for Sam's other son, but have a visit several afternoons of that week. Samuel hadn't seen Will for over two years, and his eyes lighted up when he saw the 1937 green Plymouth sedan drive up and park at the curb. Sam saw Will get out of the car with a tall blonde boy following quickly into the front entrance of the old brick house. The grandfather noted that the young man was almost as tall as his son, William, but he did resemble his namesake, Stuart.

Samuel Southworth was born in Jerseyville, Illinois, some forty miles northeast of this teeming metropolis, on a farm in 1849. On Columbus Day, in fact. His entire life had been spent working in the St. Louis-Jerseyville-Alton, Illinois region. As a man in his middle years he had taken Emma McKinney, a Scottish beauty, as his wife, in Jerseyville. From that union were born three children - William, Hazel, and Stuart, in that order. The terrible flu epidemic of 1918 - 1919 claimed Emma as a victim, among tens of thousands more throughout the USA. The heartbroken father had, some years later, remarried a St. Louis woman whose name was Mae. She was a very loving person who cared for Sam now in these advancing years. Samuel Southworth would reach his 90th birthday in another four months.

Dear Mae ran to the door to admit Will and the young grandson in. My, what an embrace she did give the 13 year old and his dad, as she announced from the entryway, to Sam in the next room, "It's Will, and your grandson Stuart, come to see you." Mae led the two visitors into the huge Victorian looking living room of the old home. Will and Sam embraced, and a few tears flowed from his blue eyes as Will faced his blonde son and proudly said to the granddad, "Pop, I want you to meet your grandson, Stuart." Stu stepped up and shook hands with the old fellow, his grandfather about whom he had heard so much, but had seen only when he was 1 year old. Sam hugged him for quite a while from his sitting position in the rocking chair.

Will then handed Mae a package that sure smelled fishy. "Got us some channel cat down at the big fish market on the river (Mississippi) on the way over here. I knew you two liked catfish, and I think Stuart does." Stu heartily nodded approval, rubbing his stomach a few times. Will turned to his son and remarked, "Boy, Mae is a fine cook. Just you wait and see." Soon Mae was in the old kitchen preparing the catfish for the evening meal.

Within a half hour after meeting Granddad Southworth, Stuart noted talk turned from their trip from Amarillo, Texas, to St. Louis, on to the hot weather they were suddenly having, a lot of politics, some nice comments about Uncle Stuart and Aunt Hazel and their wonderful families. It didn't take long for the topic at hand to be our great national game – good old baseball. Presently Dad and Granddad were talking and debating heatedly about, it seemed to young Stu, every team in the major leagues. "Well, the Cards are doing mighty good, but those poor Browns are near the bottom of the American League again. I sure hope they get better pitching soon." Sam's comments were followed by, "Hope those Cards take it this season. They just might."

With a real twinkle in his eye, Grandpa Sam turned to the boy and questioned him, "Ya play baseball yet, Stuart?" Stu offered a shy "No" explaining that his home town, his home from age six months to the present, Liberal, Kansas, had never had a "hardball" team that he had ever known about. "Oh, we play softball at recess time at school in Liberal, and in our gym classes in junior high school, but no one ever uses a baseball." Sam looked in amazement after Stu's remarks were finished, and Will just shook his head in disbelief as he blurted out, "A town with no baseball in it?" (It should be explained to the reader that this was the case in Liberal in the 1920 - 1940 period. Shortly after Stu left Liberal, Kansas, moving to San Diego, California, to live with his mom and dad there, the town of Liberal has steadily risen in baseball prowess, until its town team, of Semi-pro level, won National championships at the 53 year old NBC World Series in Wichita, Kansas. In fact, Liberal won the USA title once each in the 1960's, 1970's, and 1980's. Recently that town has been voted the outstanding baseball community in the nation, for its size.)

Stuart told the older men another tale about Liberal. "When I was a little kid in grade two, Mother and I saw a softball game between men at a big Lion's Club picnic on Labor Day. A batter hit the softball so hard, the bat split in two. Half of the wood sailed out to the mound and ran itself right into the stomach of the pitcher, and it was sticking out the back of him. They took him to the hospital, and pulled the piece of bat out. He lived and has been fine ever since." the two old ball fans cringed at these gory details, but the grandson told it "matter of factly."

Granddad Sam then instructed Will, "Ya gotta teach this guy how to play baseball when you get him back to San Diego. I'll bet they play it there aplenty." "Why, this kid says he's never seen a baseball game." It was hard for either of the men to imagine as they talked to Stu.

This sudden display of disbelief rather unnerved the grandson, and he suddenly realized that, indeed, he had never witnessed such a contest in the sport. Oh, the radio carried all of the World Series games in October, and so did the local paper. People got mildly excited about the results, but the sports interest quickly turned back to high school football in Liberal. Stuart further remembered that he had never even seen a hardball tossed around by anyone, had never seen a baseball mitt or glove in Liberal. Neither balls or gloves were sold in any of the Liberal stores. On the softball field, the kids never used a glove.

"Did you play baseball when you were young?" young Stuart quizzed grandpa, then asked the same question of his father. Granddad Samuel spoke first. "You see, young man, we moved into St. Louis from the farm in 1860, when I was barely eleven years old. Just a month before that move my daddy hitched up the best farm wagon we owned to a good team of horses, out at Jerseyville. He drove the entire family to Springfield, Illinois, a four day trip, in time to see Abe Lincoln mount the observation platform on the last car of that railroad train that took him to his Presidential Inauguration. When we got there, I was so small, and there so many people at that train depot area, my big dad lifted me up by my legs and hoisted me up on his shoulders to see old Abe in his funny high stovepipe hat. That's a day I'll never forget."

Sam Southworth changed the bright reminiscent expression on his face to one of sadness when he added. "Yes, son, and there are a few other days that I'll not forget that year of 1860, and the next ones, too." The old gentleman with long gray hair continued the sad tale of his first early losses in life. "Dad moved the family from the farm down into the middle of St. Louis, down close to "Ole Muddy," the Mississippi. Steamboats were tied up, side by side, for miles, when we moved in there."

When April, 1861, rolled around, we were in the Civil War. Those Rebels had fired on fort Sumter in Charleston, South Carolina. Our state of Missouri was a divided state, mixed with slaves, slave owners, and quite a few abolitionists. The South had an army recruiting depot way outside of the main city near St. Louis, and the Union army placed theirs on the main street, distant a few blocks from my home. Strange, there was no bickering or fighting among the soldiers, for a man could enlist in either army he chose. Everyone seemed to have that understanding. Why, did you know that Mark Twain, up in Hannibal, Missouri, enlisted in the Confederate Army? But I don't think he stayed in very long at all. This was a shock to young Stu, for Mark Twain was an author hero to the boy. He had just completed the study of Tom Sawyer and Huck Finn in his reading classes (in last year's 8th grade reading in English classes.) Stu, the Kansan, didn't know how to answer that bit of information. So he wisely remained silent.

Sam moved closer to his grandson, sliding the rocker over to look at him close up. the old man said, "Stuart, did your dad ever tell ya what happened in St. Louis to my family in the Spring of '61? I guess it was later on, in the Summer of '61 it happened to us." Stu nodded in the negative, and he could tell from his dad, Will's expression that it was a mighty important happening in family history.

"Well, one day good old dad and two older brothers got into a very "patriotic fervor" and went down to that Union recruiting depot, and all three enlisted in the army that day. In several days, they were smartly clad in the blue of the Union privates, bade us all goodbye, telling us they were all going to help settle this rebellion and soon be back home. We soon got letters once in a while from Ft. Defiance, way down at the Southern tip of Illinois, where the Ohio dumps into the Mississippi River.

I never saw any of the three men again! Mother did take a steamer down to Cape Girardeau, Missouri, near Cairo, a few months later and saw them all. She came back with glowing accounts about how good they looked, how Army life seemed to agree with all, how suntanned they were getting out on the field of military drill. She told us at home in St. Louis that the whole camp was boasting that they would take care of the Confederates in one year's time." Samuel's face fell as he related the sad news that came to our family 76 years before this, Stu's first day of his visit to St. Louis.

"Well, ye've heard of the Battle of Shiloh, Stu?" Yes, the youngster had just completed an 8th grade history class that year. During their Civil War chapter, it had mentioned that bloody encounter in Tennessee. Stu nodded slowly to his grandfather that he knew of it. "Shiloh got all three of my family, son. All killed the same afternoon of April 6, 1862. We don't know if it was in the wheat fields, the peach orchard, or the Hornet's Nest, or really where. I've been down there a couple of times to see the site. It's in heavy woods. Killed the first day there! My daddy and brothers are all buried in an "ossuary," a common grave where they had to bury hundreds, thousands of blue clad dead that evening, for the battle went on the next day. There is a National Cemetery there now at the bend of the Tennessee River, almost down across the Mississippi border.

Yeah, I'll sure never forget the day that my Mother received the news from the Army. She had to break the news to the remainder of her family when we returned home that night. Well, the rest of us had to go out into the city and go to work, steady, to keep alive from then on. I got practically no schooling, worked all my life as a watchman at a tobacco warehouse down on the river." The old man's eyes were moist with the tears of recounting these events. Memories of long, long ago.

Stu's dad, Will, interrupted to tell his son, "There was no real baseball in the city of St. Louis until about the year 1876, then it folded for a year or so, then really picked up in about the year 1880. Your grandpa will tell you all kinds of old stories of early baseball in this city, after we've had something to eat." Will continues, "Your grandfather was over 30 in 1880, too old to play ball, of course, and he was hard at work making a living. When I was growing up in this part of the city, I had to work after school in an old German's grocery store and meat market. So I did not ever have time to play baseball, like some of my friends did, Stuart. Neither your pop or granddad ever played much at all, and never on a team. We'd play catch and hit the ball some with friends when we could find a place big enough to play. When weekends came, after a hard week of school and work, I'd go to the St. Louis games, with my dad or friends, to see the Cardinals or the Browns. They used the same ballpark, you know. The place is known as Sportsman's Park.

You can bet that, when we get you back to San Diego and its many playgrounds there, we'll see that you learn how to play ball. Maybe you can get on a sandlot team out there." Granddad and Stu looked very pleased at this suggestion by Will. All had just about talked themselves out on this exciting first visit to granddad, when Mae called the three generations in to savor her carefully prepared channel catfish dinner. A real old St. Louis, Missouri, treat. She had prepared green beans, fresh tossed salad, corn on the cob, and catfish rolled and cooked in cornmeal.

Scarcely had the four sat down to dinner when Stu, as is often the habit of youngsters, excused himself to go to the bathroom. Mae arose from the table to show Stuart the way to the toilet, located down the long dark hallway in those old houses. They came to the room lighted by a bulb hanging from a long electrical cord. This was the old traditional chain pull switch.

After the door to the hallway had closed and locked behind him, Stu looked over at the toilet itself, a strange looking contraption, surely unlike any toilet arrangement he had ever seen. It was a high water tank placed way up on the wall, connected to the toilet bowl by a single pipe, but with the pipe was a long pull chain. The chain was a fancy design and had an old worn but ornately designed pull handle. Stuart was used to antique toilets, so to speak, for his Washington Grade School, in Liberal, Kansas, built in 1909, where his Mother taught and he had gone for six years, certainly hadn't updated their lavatory facilities through the tenure of the time he was there. But this thing was even older. Positively Victorian. Exactly, he later found out that these were the very first inside toilets placed in the houses of St. Louis. Before that time, people used either chamber pots or an outdoor privy. St. Louis had seen these buildings go up around 1875. Stu cautiously approached this oddity and sat down on the worn old wooden seat, then did what he had come to do. When he pulled the chain to flush the device, he was just about lifted off the wooden toilet seat with a gush of water bathing his whole underside. He somehow found something in the room to dry off this portion of his anatomy and wondered if each person in the house got a semi-bath every time they flushed. When Stuart again found his place at the dinner table he commented on the new discovery, the bath he got, and the strange appearance of the entire mechanism. Mae, Sam, and Will laughed and laughed some more at Stu's wonderings. "Why, where have you been, son?" Will added. He told Stu that he had used those old high water closets since he was old enough to remember. Then it was a chuckling granddad Samuel who peered at the grandson, adding these bits of trivia, "Do ya know who invented the first funny looking toilets like we have? Do ya? It was a Victorian age Englishman named Sir Thomas Crapper." My, that caused a roar of laughter from the old man.

"Yes sir, old Thomas Crapper. Did you ever hear that name before?" An embarrassed young man looked around while the others giggled at him. He had recalled hearing the word used in other ways as he grew up in the city and on the farm Summers with his cousins. Stuart thought his good old grandpa would fall over backwards, his chair tilted back on two legs, the old fellow laughing so hard. He had decided the old man really had a great sense of humor. Stu joined in the laughter for a while until the conversation again turned to old St. Louis baseball. Will reminded Stu that his grandfather had seen the first baseball games ever played in the big city, in the late 1850's and early 1860's.

Will had opened the floodgates again to the dam of interesting tales. What a series of baseball accounts this old man burst forth to relate to all at the dinner table. We were all to be entertained as dinner was finished. Stories of the earliest recollections of the great game.

A "doggone" good way to break up a good
baseball contest.

BASEBALL STORY NUMBER 1 - 1861
THE NORTH VS. SOUTH BASEBALL GAME
OR
A "DOGGONE GOOD WAY" TO BREAK UP A
GOOD BASEBALL CONTEST

YES, STUART, I RECALL THE first time I ever saw the game of baseball here in St. Louis. Sure different than they play it today. An odd contest, that first one. In fact, it was just a few months after my dad and two brothers enlisted in the Army, in 1861. There were two kinds of armies in St. Louis then, or rather recruiting stations for those armies, so it was natural that there be some rivalry of Union versus Confederate. Not wanting to wage war right there, and shoot it out on a Missouri Street, they chose to challenge each other in a game they titled "Field Ball."

When the War broke out, and Fort Sumter was fired upon in April of 1861, old Missouri was a divided state, a lot of pro-slavery sentiment existed in this area. Slavery was practiced in some areas, but the general feeling around St. Louis was toward the Union and its preservation. Why, those Confederates had a recruiting station and a training camp not far out of St. Louis. They called it "Camp Jackson," and they were mustering and training a regular army of Rebels there. It only lasted about a month, because a Union officer by the name of Nathaniel Lyon led the Federal troops over there early in May and wiped them out. (But not before those rascals had scheduled and played the new game of baseball or "Field Ball" with their Union opponents down in St. Louis one day late in April.) It was the only game they got in, for Southern sympathizers were soon pushed way back into the hills west of St. Louis and spent the rest of the war in Southwest Missouri, or raiding and marauding in guerrilla tactics, all over the state.

It was to be played on a baseball field, and their rules agreed upon were quite different than the eventual game we know today as baseball.

These units were to compete on a fairly level pasture big enough to allow the outfielders to play back against the heaviest of hitters. An announcement came out in the local newspaper and posted bulletins around the city that this game would be held a certain hour of that afternoon, so I walked down to see it with some friends my age. Nothing to lose, we figured. Little did I know then that this game would be of great interest to me all my life.

They had a ball diamond laid out, all right, but the bases must not have been over

80 feet apart, certainly not the full 90 feet of today. The teams played eleven men on each side. Baseball rules were in their formative period, so they were kinda loose and varied by locale then. The army units decided that every man of the eleven would hit every inning. The inning was over after all had batted, then they switched from hitting to fielding. There were no three outs or nine innings. It was decided that the game ended when one team reached 35 runs scored. This arrangement may sound as though it was quick, easy to get those 35 runs, but the game lasted close to three hours, and the Northern boys beat the Rebels 35-18. Almost doubled the score. There were root-ers for both sides, and they let out a terrible volley of shouts and screams when a good play was made or the runs scored for their side. Pitching in that game was more under-handed or sidearm, and the pitcher tried to get the ball over in order that the batters could hit the ball and put it into play. It was a fielder's and runner's game, not a pitch-er's. Gee, the fielders sure got plenty of action out there. Their defense usually had one man playing behind each base with one between bases, thus a five man infield. With the pitcher, catcher, five infielders, and four outfielders, they covered a lot of ground for playing hit balls. Oh, that extra outfielder was called 'the rover.'"

Sam Southworth took another bite of catfish and greens when Stuart interrupted, saying, "Grandpa, we play a game something like that first one you saw. They play it in Liberal in softball. Eleven on each team, a roving outfielder, but we use three outs. The whole team doesn't hit each inning."

The old man then told will, Mae, and Stu all about the game equipment of 1861 baseball. It was as old as the game itself. "Their bats weren't all completely round. Some were fashioned out of tree limbs, barrel staves, and whatever they could find. I was afraid they would swing and hit the catcher with that assortment of sticks. But those catchers stayed back pretty far behind the swingers. And that darned ball— where they fashioned it, I didn't know. It did seem pretty hard, as I recall. Each team warmed up with whatever kinds they had. Soft little punkin ball types, I guess made of tight wound yarn and rags tied around into a ball. I think I saw some wooden balls, too, as they played catch. The game ball had some kind of cover sewed around it with leather. It was the only game ball they had, and it was hard enough, but larger than a baseball. Kind of brown in color, not white like today. Someone had done a real fine job of putting that cover on, for it stayed on during the whole game, and 53 runs scored, total.

Well, the crowd, a big one, stood along both foul lines, maybe back a little. After several line drives into the crowds, they moved back considerable. Those watching the first baseball experiment in St. Louis quickly got into the spirit of the thing, no doubt about it. They knew some of the Army boys playing, and of course, they were North or South sympathizers. Boy, did they get into the game when a Louisiana boy on the Reb team hit the ball a "country mile" for a four run homer. That was some blow! The poor outfielder had to go get the ball, for they only had one for game play.

Three of us lads were there together and gradually felt the chill of excitement of such a contest. Stu, I stood there and wondered how any grown man could drive a ball that far with a piece of wood. "Wowee!" The gray haired gentleman's eyes opened wide and flashed. "Why, we left that game, and we all fashioned balls and bats, for every last one of our crowd of kids wanted to try that ourselves. It looked easy to connect and knock that sphere out to eternity."

Then Sam got into the heart of the story, the game itself. "That big Blue versus Gray crowd was patrolled by their own men. Heck, they had no need for lawmen to keep order. Reb soldiers covered one foul line crowd, the Union guys stood on the other side and behind the batter and catcher. Some of the men of war had rifles at their sides, some had no arms with them. Some Reb fellows had rifles stacked in a tripod form, just leanin" on them. After an hour had gone by, the North led the South by three runs, I think the score was about 15-12. That first part of the game was close. Some lively betting took place among soldiers of the different camps. Wagers also were laid between spectators and some big businessmen, who were the true sporting crowd.

About that time up strolls another Union army patrol from down by the recruiter's headquarters, and one feller in that bunch had a big spotted dog. Some kind of mongrel, I reckon. No sooner had that soldier and his dog arrived on the scene, and no sooner had a ball been hit by a batter, than that canine, I guess never having seen a baseball before, lit out after that rolling brown object. Had it in his huge mouth before any outfielder could get close to it. Barking and standing, staring, the big bowser dared anyone there that day to catch him and take that ball out of his mouth. Suddenly the crowd yelled, the players cried out, and defensemen started after the dog. the long chase was on. From that point on, that was the craziest thing I had ever witnessed. Big dog heading up the streets and alleys of old St. Louis with both Blue and Gray in mad pursuit, the crowd waiting impatiently for those solder boys to retrieve that stolen ball. The game had to be halted until the dog was caught. But the wild crowd who had come to watch a ball game turned their hootin' and hollerin' toward the "dog versus soldier" game. In and out of open fields, near stores, up and down steps of house fronts, in several buildings and out again—that mongrel had learned how to elude a mob in a chase. The mutt led that body of men everywhere. In what seemed like an hour of elapsed time, the armies (combined) emerged from behind a grove of trees down by the river. The crowd saw one boy in gray hold the ball aloft, triumphantly, and give a little Reb cry. When the ball was returned to the playing field, and the dog brought to the sidelines, the game ball was slightly out of round and had not only the sewn stitches decorating its surface, but deep teeth marks as well. The crowd then noticed a deep red gash along the dog's right rear that was bleeding freely.

We learned later that the Rebel who had retrieved the prize had used a sharpened tree branch, jabbing that wicked spear into the dog's rump, whereupon the mongrel gave up the ball with a wild yelp. Pretty hard for a wounded dog to yelp and hold a ball tight in his mouth at the same time, eh? Rumors had it in the crowd the remainder of the game that this just about touched off the first Civil War battle in Missouri, for the Union dog owner took exception to the Confederate's "cheap shot" and the "Reb" was soon after treated roughly by him.

Oh that exciting game was on again, and the "lost ball incident" soon forgotten. This interim incident seemed to spark the crowd, the Blue and Gray players, the patrolling armies on either sideline. Scoring came hot and heavy from that point on for the stronger Union team.

No one in those days had ever heard of wearing a glove to catch the grounders, hot line drives, and popups and deep fly balls. Even the catcher's hands were unprotected. By the time the 35th run was scored, there were many sore, bruised, puffed up hands showing on the players, and jammed fingers were numerous.

The working umpires declared the game ended. It was getting late in the spring afternoon, and the enthusiastic throng were thirsty and very hungry from the long, exciting events of the day. The South made sure that the North promised to meet in two weeks for a revenge match, but this never occurred, for the Rebels were soon driven out of the St. Louis area. At this suggestion, all the crowd shouted their hearty approval and dispersed. No prize was agreed upon for the winner of that first ball game in St. Louis, but the Union blue set up drinks for their gray Rebs in one of the many saloons downtown after the game was ended. Yeah, Stu, this was the very beginning of my baseball career. From that day on, at age 12, I played catch with the boys and could hit that old ball farther and farther with each practice session.

That gloomy day Mother received the telegram from the War Department - telling us that dad and my two brothers would never be coming home—that ended my hopes of ever playing this new game I had fallen in love with, that first afternoon. I had to love that great national pastime from quite a distance.

Oh, Stu, did I tell you that Dad and brothers fell, side by side, as they were advancing toward the Rebel lines that afternoon at Shiloh? Many brothers, or father and brothers, fell side by side in the War between the States.

Young Stuart stared in silence at his grandfather when the old fellow had finished that good meal and his first early baseball tale simultaneously. Finally the grandson broke the silence, asking, "And you never did get to play any ball at all after that game you just told us about, granddad?" "Very little, son," the old gentleman sighed. "Mom put the whole family to work in the city here or closeby. We pooled our earnings and made it, somehow. There was no one to support our large family, so everyone worked hard until the last child left home on his own. Mother died a few years later."

The three generations excused themselves from Mae's table, complimenting the cook on her excellent catfish dinner. The evening was cooling off some, and up went the sliding windows in the old bay area of the living room. A slight breeze stirred up and down Shenandoah Avenue. Granddad was seated comfortably in his old well-worn rocking chair when he turned to Stu's dad and asked, "Will, recall me telling you about the game and brawl with Alton, Illinois, we had here in '63?" William Dallas Southworth nodded quickly to the question in the affirmative, followed by "Many times, Dad. Why don't you tell Stuart all about that weird game's end?"

Although Stuart had never been on a real baseball diamond or seen a game played, he was getting into the excitement toward this "old" (new to him) game being unveiled before him, in this old Victorian setting.

BASEBALL STORY NUMBER 2 - 1863
THE DAY ST. LOUIS SENT THE ILLINOIS COUSINS BACK UP THE RIVER AS WINNERS (THE GAME'S FIRST MAJOR "RHUBARB" IN ST. LOUIS)
OR
GEE, BUT THOSE BIG FARM BOYS COULD HIT THE LONG BALL

GRANDPA SAMUEL BEGAN AGAIN, "By 1863, two years into the Civil War, old St. Louis was mobilized and filled with military. Within the two years, though, the game of baseball had become contagious in this major river port. More teams formed, players from the armies moved about, and the baseball rules began to change. They became more standardized.

Up the Mississippi River, high on a bluff there and down by the water, sits the town of Alton, Illinois. The little town was fast becoming a river port, farming and manufacturing center, and a railroad terminus. That city and the farmers surrounding had formed an aggressive baseball club, the Alton "River Pirates." It had been known for many years that wicked river pirates lived on all the major waterways of the "West," up and down the Ohio and Mississippi Rivers, mainly, and its larger tributaries. Alton boasted up and down the river with pride that they would play (and soundly defeat) any club that cared to entertain them on any given day. This upstart town didn't even exclude big old St. Louis, down the "Big Muddy." So, the city fathers of St. Louis accepted the challenge, and this brash aggregation of Illinois river rats steamed down one day to take on the best team of the metropolis. This was not an All-Star group they were to play—the best team in town. Of course, the brand of baseball play had vastly improved in two years in St. Louis. Baseball, as it was now called, was experiencing exploding popularity in this city, Westernmost of America at that time. A great cause for this was the great Western migration..

Both teams prepared themselves with untold vigor when it was revealed to all that St. Louis firms (and their sporting owners, of course) had put up an added prize of $100.00 to the winning team of that big game. The hat was to be passed among the thousands expected for this first really "big game" in the city, to cover the prize money.

The Alton, Illinois, baseball "River Pirates" and rooters arrived the morning of the contest on their chartered river (sidewheeler) steamer. The group was obviously in a state of wild excitement when their boat docked near downtown, in anticipation of seeing the city and of "beating up" on the best team the city folks had to throw at them. This team was very smartly dressed, both on and off the field, for their image was at stake. By 1863 manufacturers were making some semblance of baseball "suits" for players, and both Alton and St. Louis were sporting the best money could buy. Colorful shirts, knicker pants were the only style accepted, caps to shield the eyes and face from the hot baseball weather, bats (now turned on a lathe) were of a larger selection for the player to use and of nearly standard length. The ball game was played with one dozen of the newest balls (now manufactured more easily than before) and had become more white and lighter colors than the old brown. The playing field was somewhat better, but still very primitive, compared to ours today. The diamond had an open outfield in left and center fields, and outfielders had to chase balls hit over them. But in right field, at a distance of 340 feet down the foul line, a new fence had been built the weeks before, separating the baseball playing area from a stinking, dirty, unsightly stockyard and slaughterhouse. The wall was eight feet high, so no spectator could see beyond. So, you see, good old St. Louis had improved their best baseball park considerably.

The crowd was on hand, it was to be a scorcher of a day, and the team warmups and rituals had been performed. From that day to this, the old glory flew from a flagpole at the park, whenever a game was played. The national anthem was sung by all. Rules were carefully agreed upon. The teams each had nine men, they could be placed anywhere on defense on the field that they wished. The winner would be the team scoring 25 runs first. Teams would change after four outs had been recorded, not the usual three outs. The game would last as many innings as required. Time limit was only the darkness setting in. There were two umpires from St. Louis and two umpires from Alton, to keep it as fair as possible. The umpires would change positions (rotate their positions on the field) every inning. The game lasted three hours, twenty minutes, ending in a near disastrous brawl. It was a very good thing that the Alton crew had a boat to escape to, as it turned out. The crowd was huge, for everyone in St. Louis, from baby to grandma, must have been anticipating this great rivalry. The order was kept by local law enforcement officers backed up, this time, by only Union army soldiers.

My boyhood pal, Johnnie Gooden, and I climbed up on the top of a storehouse nearby, with many others, of course. It was over 25 feet high, commanding a fine view of the entire diamond and looking toward that wall in right field. The game progressed with many fine fielding, hitting, and running plays. Scoring was fast and furious for both teams, in spite of all those good plays. Several balls were hit beyond the left and center field positions. Home runs were declared by the umpires on the long balls. The game was close, the rivalry was a hot one, several times the game was tied 8-8, 13-13, and finally, the last tie I recall was 20-20.

Certainly a feeling of the thrill of this new game of baseball was pervading this

Gee, but those big farm boys could hit the
long ball.

huge throng who had turned out, as the close game progressed. The Alton team was starting to crack from the crowd, the pressure, and the fine St. Louis play. St. Louis fans cheered their home team to a near win in a late inning as the afternoon wore on. St. Louis 24, Alton 22. One more run for the Missourians, and they could send those Illinois Pirates back up the river with their "big boasting." It was in the 16th inning that Alton came to bat. Two were out against this big team when two of their players beat out slow ground balls, ending up on first and second.

Who should step up to the plate for Alton but their "Casey at the Bat," their giant of a first baseman, a left handed hitter. As he stepped into the batter's area, this man's wide smile could be seen beneath the dark curled moustache extending to either side of that mouth. No mistaking this man as their power hitter. He had hit two balls sharply for outs the last two times up. On the second pitch delivered to this man by the St. Louis hurler, that hulk at the plate met the ball squarely on its nose. From where John and I were, way up high beyond the crowd, we could see the ball arc high and drop toward the top of that eight foot wall. At least a double was hit, scoring the two runners on base. The ball game would be over if that hit ball cleared the high wall. Suddenly a light breeze caught that baseball and kept it in the ball park. It struck the wall with a slight thud. (It should have sounded much louder than it did.) Alton's crowd was delirious with pride, for the score was tied and their hitter would be on second or third base. The outfielder in right went to the fence, turned his back on the crowd, held his arms up ready to receive the rebounding ball to relay it to the cutoff man. Everyone in the ball park waited for the ball to rebound - and WAITED, and WAITED, and WAITED. But the hitter didn't wait in circling the bases, for, by the time he had crossed home plate with the winning run and was surrounded by wild, screaming Alton fans, THE BALL STILL HAD NOT COME OFF THE WALL. IT WAS STUCK THERE. The game was over, or was it? Wait for the umpires to decide? Why was the ball up there? No one knew what to do or what to think. This was a strange phenomenon! How could a baseball stick to a point on the new fence? The four umpires, surrounded by both teams, ran out there to the ball. Finally, a ladder was produced from a nearby tool shed. Carefully, one umpire climbed up to the ball, lodged almost eight feet off the ground. He tugged and tugged at that darned ball. With a final tug, the ball came off, revealing a big nail (no, a huge spike) that some workman had left, in nailing from behind.

Well, by gum, those four umpires had to have a conference (away from the biased crowd). The two umps from Alton and one from St. Louis voted for the hit to be counted as a home run, for the runner did circle the bases before the ball was thrown home. "Sorry, St. Louis, about that big nail. But it is your park, and the nail should not have been there, eh?" They reasoned thusly. The one dissenting St. Louis umpire said it should have been ruled a double, since that is as far as the hitter would have gotten, had the ball rebounded quickly, as it should have. The waiting crowd learned of the final decisions of the umpires moments later. Dejected, the St. Louis team did not score in their final inning. FINAL SCORE - ALTON 25, ST. LOUIS 24. The country cousins won by one run. Oh well, there will be other days, eh?

The ceremonies at the conclusion of the game gave Alton the $100.00 prize, but St. Louis tempers were flaring. The visitors moved toward the boat landing without further delay, for they could see the nasty situation developing. Alton men motioned for the women and kids from Illinois to scamper for the landing. Fortunately, the Union army units and local constabulary moved in, to form a barrier between the two crowds, as they were bade a hasty farewell up the river. But fans and players were taking off their coats for some fisticuffs. Until it could be broken up, some men were thumping men, kids were thumping kids, and some of the girls and women were getting into it. Even two opposing umpires were going at it for a while. Order was restored, and the steamboat captain blew the whistle for the last time as the "last of the wounded" came aboard. The big vessel backed out into the water as shouts and curses were sent their way by the parties on shore. Some were shaking fists and yelling, "You just wait 'til the next game we have with you. We'll beat your pants off next time."

However, the real score for the day was ALTON - 25, ST. LOUIS - 24, and ALTON - three men unconscious, 8 wounded, ST. LOUIS - two men unconscious, four wounded.

Baseball in its truest form, and in the form for years to come, had arrived in old Civil War St. Louis. What a great tradition it has enjoyed since that day, here on the banks of the "Father of Waters."

Surely, if the Cardinals and Browns, of years to follow, could have been in the ball park that day, they would have burst with pride at St. Louis talent, hard play, determination to win, fair play, and never giving up without a fight."

The elderly Southworth continued into his next boyhood adventure with even better memory and enthusiasm than before.

BASEBALL STORY NUMBER 3 - 1865
ST. LOUIS SANDLOT'S CONTRIBUTION TO BASEBALL - THE INVENTION OF THE GAME, "OVER THE LINE," A HITTER'S GAME
OR -
THIS SKILL GAME CAN BE SO FRUSTRATING, IT WILL SURELY PUSH THE POOR BATTER'S MIND "OVER THE LINE," TRYING TO SCORE A RUN OR TWO

"**I** BELIEVE THAT I WAS** 15 years old, yes, it was in 1865, the last year of the Civil War. I recall I was running home one Saturday morning from doing an errand for my family there close by. By this time more boys than ever had taken up the new game of baseball, and some of the St. Louis lads were becoming very good hitters in their sandlot games. Others of them were developing the ability to hit the long ball. I knew that many were practicing a lot, but not until that day did I realize how and what they were practicing. I am reminded of that famous adage, "Practice makes perfect." That bit of wisdom should really be changed to read, "Practicing the right things in the right way, makes perfect."

That day I drew up short from my gallop home and watched a strange looking game that was going on at one of the playfields. THOSE INVENTIVE YOUNG-STERS HAD DEVISED A NEW HITTING GAME ON THEIR OWN. When I asked one boy what he called this new exercise, he replied, "Oh, 'OVER THE LINE.'"

I just stood and watched a while, learning the rules of this new creation as I could see the game progress. At the time I wasn't able to get time to play ball, but I sure wished that I might, and I found myself becoming deeply engrossed in all of this new activity.

The group had divided a regular 90 degree baseball diamond area by splitting it right down the middle. They had used a sharp stick to cut a trough, a thin line in the dirt and sand. The line started at the corner of home plate, went straight out to the far corner of second base, then it continued out to the far reaches of the outfield. One straight line dividing the whole playing field in half. The teams had decided to play

This skill game can be so frustrating, it will
surely push the poor batter's mind "over the
line," trying to score a run or two.

their game on the left half, leaving the right half as foul territory. No fielders were placed in the right half. Any number above eight, four on a side, could play. Probably four or five, but no more than five.

I discovered, at a later date, that this game could also be modified to be played on a full diamond, as a regular baseball game, from foul line to foul line. In that case, perhaps six versus six would make a good game. More than six would put the hitting team at a big disadvantage and prevent much scoring.

Apparently, as I could perceive this new game, "Over the Line" was to teach young players how to hit a baseball correctly, simulating a game type hit. I soon saw that runs were very hard to come by. Final scores were low. Teams could play either three or four outs an inning and play for hours at a time. Four out innings produced more runs, of course.

The major difference between "Over the Line" and baseball was this: In "Over the Line," the hitter's own team mate pitches to each hitter. He pitches the speed, type of pitch, and the location of the pitch that the batter wants to work on hitting. In an afternoon a young player might swing the bat 100 times or more, I reckon, until his arms were so tired that they felt like dropping off.

✪   ✪   ✪   ✪   ✪

THIS IS NOT A RUNNING GAME AT ALL. NO ONE EVER RUNS OUT THEIR HITS. CONCENTRATING ONLY ON HITTING PITCHES, AND JUST IMAGINING WHERE ALL THE RUNNERS WOULD BE ON BASES.

I later found that this new game, "Over the Line," teaches and demands from each batter these several things:

1. Home runs can be produced only if the ball is hit beyond the reach of the outfielder chasing it - or if it goes over the fence.
2. Discourages hitting grounders - any grounder hit anywhere, is an out.
3. All caught flies are outs. Do not hit any fly balls that can be caught. The only acceptable fly is the absolute home run.
4. Batter, look at the placement of all the defensive men. Try to learn to hit the ball to spots unoccupied and between the defense.
5. Pick out good pitches, but hit any and all strikes. Do not let strikes go by. The batter gets as many pitches as he wants until he gets the one he swings at. Each batter in this game gets just one swing each.
6. If using the full diamond, this is a good game to learn how to hit to the opposite field. It can teach good late hitting behind the runner.
7. BASICALLY THIS GAME TEACHES THE HITTER TO DRILL THE BALL OVER THE INFIELDERS AND IN FRONT OF THE OUTFIELDERS WITH LOW DRIVES THAT FALL IN FRONT OF THE OUTFIELDERS QUICKLY.
8. Over the Line teaches a team that they "must bunch their hits" to score. A hit here and there won't produce many runs. Work for five or six or more hits IN A ROW. The key to winning ball games is to "bunch hits."

9. A team cannot score, using singles only, until it gets four hits in a row. Of course, a home run hit anytime produces one run if no one is on base, or more, depending on the runners then on base.

SOME ADDITIONAL TIPS AND RULES - "OVER THE LINE"

1. You can use the same accurate throwing pitcher for both teams. If he pitches for both squads, then he does not bat.
2. A team can have their own team furnish the accurate pitchers, and the pitcher can then go and bat in rotation.
3. Groove the ball. Make every pitch good to hit. Do not waste the time by throwing balls, throw strikes where the batter requests them. The team wants so much hitting practice that their minds get into the "hitting groove."
4. Batter is out - if the ground ball is hit in front of the line.
5. Batter is out - on any popup fly, in front of the line.
6. Batter is out - on any foul ball or foul tip, hit anywhere.
7. Batter is out - if a fly ball is caught by defense, over the line.
8. If fly ball is dropped by the defense on a hit over the line, the ball is counted as a base hit. But only a single is credited.
9. Batter gets just one swing. He is out if he misses it, fouls it, or foul tips it.
10. Batter is out if the pitcher catches a line drive through the box. It is a base hit, single, if he misses it.
11. All base hits in the game are either singles or home runs.
12. All home runs score as many men on base at that moment.
13. Unless the hit is a home run, the batting team scores only after the fourth consecutive base hit. Each successive single after that fourth one will force in another run.
14. Each team gets to bat an equal number of innings. A game can be any number of innings. It can last all day, if teams agree. No time limit.
15. Since a bunt is a type of grounder, no bunting is allowed in this game.

And so, on a Spring day in 1865, perhaps a few days before or after our beloved President Abraham Lincoln was assassinated in Ford's Theater, a group of young innovators, trying to become great baseball hitters, conjured up this "dream game," a perfect "self-test for a hitter," and extremely demanding to perfect.

The young grandson, Stuart, listened with fascination as his elder finished his tale of discovery. He had no way of realizing that his days ahead would be spent learning and perfecting this skill game. Nor did he know that his young teacher of the game the next summer would be a good friend and team mate at Golden Hill Playground in San Diego, California. This young friend would then be 15 years old, just as granddad had been then.

That boy's name would be Solomon Hemus, nicknamed "Solly," who would be destined to advance in baseball to the major leagues, play second base for the St. Louis

Cardinals in the 1950's, then be selected to be the St. Louis Cardinal manager for four years.

Yogi Berra and Joe Garagiola, both men raised near the old sandlot of this "Over the Line" history, would be extremely proud to know the details of this day in 1865.

Finally, Stuart would develop in his baseball skills in San Diego (and grow up playing with at least nine boys, he can recall, who went on to play in the big leagues). Every one of the nine players got their hitting start on the playgrounds of San Diego playing the old hitting game called "OVER THE LINE."

That evening of Stuart and Will's visit to Sam Southworth wore on into quite a late hour. Before the two younger ones departed and bade granddad good night, he had to spin the yarn about his seeing his first professional baseball team, the Cincinnati Red Stockings, 1869 version. This master teller of baseball tales gave a full account of that big day in St. Louis Baseball history. But this story has a strange twist to it, in the form of a dream that the grandfather had.

BASEBALL STORY NUMBER 4 - 1869
THOSE CINCINNATI RED STOCKINGS ENTER OLD ST. LOUIS TRIUMPHANTLY - THE PARADE - THE GAME - THE GREAT FOUNDRY FIRE
OR -
YES, I'VE HEARD OF A "RAINCHECK" BEFORE AT A BALL GAME, BUT A "SMOKE CHECK?" REALLY, NOW.

THE CIVIL WAR HAD ENDED with a Union victory throughout the land. This game which General Abner Doubleday (a hero at Gettysburg) and Alexander Cartwright had co-invented, so to speak, in 1839 and in 1845 or 1846, respectively, had survived the great war. In fact, not only had it survived, but in some army camps, both North and South, the game had evolved with increased interest and popularity.

In 1869, just four years after Appomattox, the city of Cincinnati, Ohio, saw the first professionals entering into the first "barnstorming." With such professional stars as Harry Wright, George Wright, and Cal McVey, this upstart baseball club took on any-one and everyone. In fact, they went clear out West to San Francisco to demonstrate the game. Artists from that day to this have learned that one night stands, concerts, revivals, ball games, any form of appearance in front of growing numbers of fans and hero worshippers, are a sure way to promote the artist, the game, and the sales of tick-ets. The Cincinnati Red Stockings played 65 games in 1869, winning 65 and losing none. In later years such touring stars as Paul Whiteman, Billy Sunday, Glenn Miller, Billy Graham, and Michael Jackson followed the same "on the tour" routine. This life, it would be agreed by all the above-mentioned, is a "tough grind." No doubt about it.

Actually, we are told by St. Louis baseball historians, that the Cincy Red Stockings were not really the first professional baseball organization to visit St. Louis in those early years. There were a couple of baseball teams from the New York area who preceded the Red Stockings in 1869 or earlier. The important fact to mention is that the baseball fathers of the growing city of St. Louis had provided a better field for their best teams now. The visitors were then entertained on a new baseball field, located out near Grand Avenue, the location where the early Sportsman's Park was finally constructed.

Our fourth tale of baseball in old St. Louis brings us to that grand day during the heat of a dry summer month when the Cincy team came out West to St. Louis, Missouri. We must recall that it was this same year that the railroad was just completed coast to coast, so a ballclub could be transported to St. Louis and on into the West to play their games. But St. Louis was still the last city of any size until you got to California. The city on the banks of the mighty Mississippi River was still thought of as "out West" by easterners.

The old gentleman relating this interesting story to his grandson, Stu, suddenly changed the subject and asked him a strange question, "Son, have you ever had a strange dream, one which you dreamed over and over again for a few nights or weeks, and the dream was revealed to you in pieces? Oh, I mean that it was like a continuing story, or a serialized thing?" Stuart didn't know how to respond to this query, so his dad, Will, broke in chuckling, and said, "What grandpa is saying, Stu, is that this first professional ball game in St. Louis came to him, a few weeks before it really happened, in a strange kind of dream. Let him tell you what he had revealed to him during those few nights."

The elderly Samuel Stuart Southworth unveiled this strange "series of dreams" for Will and Stu, much as he had done for Will years before. The boy was so taken in by the odd parade of events that he was transfixed until its very end.

"Yes, it was agreed upon that the Red Stockings would meet (on the diamond) the best that St. Louis had to offer. A two game stand in the old ball park, the only big one that was large enough to hold such a momentous game with its thousands of expected viewers. Ticket sales would be brisk, for sure, in St. Louis. To protect the paid customers from the unpaid, a high eight foot wall was built all around the park. It would remain as a permanent part of the field after the Cincy series. Of course, that right field barrier, very high and solid (that barrier which created such a terrible "rhubarb" with the Alton visitors earlier) hid the sight of what was now a foundry and adjacent buildings. The unsightly sheds, smoke, and fumes were hidden from the paying customers.

Oh, but those grounds were prepared and manicured carefully, days in advance of the arrival of the first professional team. Ropes were then tightly strung, leaving some foul ball area on the first base and third base sides. You must remember that crowds stood in those days, looking over each other's shoulders. The little short fellow or gal was out of luck unless he or she nudged a way in front. This was some years before there was seating in solid bleachers. All your ticket assured you was entrance into the ball park, but not a seat. Some people nearby did perch on a few higher structures, if there were any. Yes, even then they had the "Knot hole gang," a group who would peer through the knot holes left in the poor grade lumber of the fence pieces, or they would make a hole with some device that they brought for that purpose. Few high structures then existed from which to ascend and peer over into the playing field.

Well, I found enough money somewhere to purchase my ticket to the first of two games. But let me now tell you about the "hoopla" and our big grand parade of the day. (Remember now, I'm dreaming this, weeks in advance!)

On the morning of game day the big steamboat carried America's first great professionals in baseball across the muddy river to St. Louis shores. Our famous Eads bridge was not constructed until 1874, so everything still had to come across by boat, you know.

The main street of St. Louis was lined with thousands of viewers. A parade was contrived in old St. Louis for any reason, a favorite of St. Louis folks. First, the manager and captains of the Cincinnati Red Stockings, George and Harry Wright were greeted at the main landing by our illustrious mayor and every city councilman present. Cincy's baggage and equipment was loaded on a wagon and taken to the ball park. There everything was safely stored away in an equipment shed until the teams assembled for their warmup periods. The Cincy players and the St. Louis fans were equally in awe of each other. Here was a bigger and much more bustling large city than the Easterners realized had grown up out West. Many large modern buildings comprised the downtown area, and the entire city looked as if it were built of red brick with some stone thrown in to cut the monotony of the scene. A beautiful setting on a great river, very much like their own Cincinnati on the beautiful Ohio River.

Soon the huge parade began, covering the entire length of Main Street with every conceivable type of unit, marching or riding up on horses, wagons, or buggies, the planning committee had brought in a few brass bands, wagon floats, the visiting team carriage, the new horse-drawn fire fighting units. Not to be outdone, our GAR had a big delegation of Union veterans of the recent conflict—some in old Union uniforms. The parade route led through crowds cheering loudly, past big stores and buildings, up to the city hall and its statues and fountain at St. Louis' main city square. Around 10:00 a.m. there was a series of welcoming speeches, the key to the city was then presented to the Cincy ball club, collectively accepting, and in general, very good feelings were felt and exchanged. Printed programs were given to all present for all to follow the order of events of the grand day. These would be kept as a remembrance of this event in St. Louis history.

After the official parade and ceremony disbanded, the several combined fraternal lodges of greater St. Louis invited the ravenously hungry Red Stockings and the St. Louis team to free lunch (and free beer) at a large convention hall just newly constructed. The team players "lightened up" on their consumption of food and beer, for the game was to begin in three hours. Team leaders thanked their hosts for the ball clubs, and both teams were driven to the big ball park, where ticket holders had lined up after the big parade, waiting for both teams to arrive.

Most had come to see the rituals of "pregame warmups for a baseball game." The hour was 12:30 by that time. I recall filing in with several friends, finding a strategic spot down the third base line. Spectators found that they had to be very alert, for the many baseballs being played with, thrown around and batted, could find their way into the crowds with a high velocity. In that era serious injuries were pretty common to people struck by thrown or batted balls. Also, it was a common practice to throw the ball back onto the field if it went into the crowd. Boy, that custom has sure changed over the years, hasn't it? People who kept the balls in the early days were scorned, sought out, and asked to give the ball back to the teams. Some were forced to do so—even roughed up a lot.

About 1:30 both teams were introduced, the batteries announced first. Each player gracefully trotted out to one side of the infield or the other, doffed his cap to the crowds, some took a slight bow, as actors do. Their uniforms were "not uniform," as they came from various of the St. Louis clubs, were "All-Stars." Cincinnati's uniforms were quite impressive and very uniform. Many of the visitors sported long moustaches.

Certainly the home crowd was pleased when the visitors were held to no runs scored in their first half of the first inning. The local aggregation managed to eke out one run on a scratch hit, an error on a bad hop of a grounder, then a resoundingly solid single by a star St. Louis batsman. Wild cheers certainly filled the air as the locals got that lead run. Oh, but the hopes of the St. Louis folks rose to great heights. Mighten they defeat this first pro team from Cincinnati?

But alas, Cincy's pitching took its toll, however, the superior hitting and defensive play of the more experienced club throughout the remainder of the game found the local club trailing 6-2 in the seventh inning. The clock reading 5:00 p.m. then.

St. Louis viewers were becoming thoroughly familiar with "good baseball" when it happened. "It" was so unexpected that no one there dreamed of its occurring to mar such a spectacle. Why couldn't it have happened any other time?

Earlier I mentioned that old foundry (seen by me only in these dreams) on the other side of the right field wall? (To be honest, this part of St. Louis had no industrial buildings there, as this dream revealed.) Well, rising above the fence level of view was a large brick and wooden structure, just added to the foundry and metal works there. Some kind of a metal working mill, I believe. No one in the city even gave a thought when fumes and smoke, smelly and caustic, continually rose from that area of the city. They spewed from brick stacks on the property.

At around 5:00 p.m. the ballpark crowds" teeth were collectively rattled by a gigantic explosion ripping the St. Louis air. Shock waves shook the flimsy fences, the flames shot out of the wooden structure and elsewhere over there at the foundry. Soon a big portion of the area was engulfed in flames and smoke. The crowd came alive, screamed as they saw high flames licking beyond the right field barrier. The game was immediately halted, the crowd had to be held off the field. Players and umpires ran to the fence to look over at the scene. They could see foundry workers running about and wildly yelling.

By the time that the St. Louis Fire Department's largest fire wagons were pulled by horses toward the scene (the same wagons that had graced the parade that morning with their spit and polish appearance), and the hook and ladder crews clanged their bells down the main street, followed by their spotted Dalmatian fire dogs, easily keeping up with the horses, the surging crowd could hear them draw near to the entrance to the ball park. Oh no, the Fire Captain saw that the only quick way to get to the conflagration, quickly spreading to other foundry units, was a route that would have to take the equipment right through the ball park, directly across the diamond. Wide open the swinging ball park gates were flung, the three fire wagons, volunteers hanging on

Yes, I've heard of a "raincheck" before at
a ballgame, but a "smoke check?"
Really, now.

to sides and rear step, sped past. Across home plate, the pitcher's mound, crossing second base, those fire wagons, rumbled toward the right centerfield area. At the fence the fire chief had several big fellows chop a big hole in the barrier quickly, to open wide enough for quick passage. Of course, crowds on both sides of that field cheered them on (me yelling the loudest, I'll bet). They made short work of knocking down the fire, but the smoke that resulted was so thick that it became blinding and unbearable. During all of this, the police at work there did a fine job of keeping that mob in place and in order. Smoke settled over the park until nothing could be seen by anyone. The crowd filed out of the only exit there, the front gate, to get away from this new nuisance. THE GAME WAS FINALLY CALLED UNTIL THE NEXT DAY, TO BE CONTINUED BEFORE THE NEXT REGULARLY SCHEDULED GAME.

All of downtown St. Louis sky was in a pall of heavy, thick, caustic smoke. Like a sudden curtain of darkness. Downtown pedestrians could see but a block or two down the street. People who were exposed to this layer of caustic material were hacking and coughing terribly. The fumes and the smoke were of a toxic nature. The population was advised by the fire and police departments to remain indoors for the remainder of what had begun as a fine day. Ball players were hustled home quickly, and the Cincy team taken in a large wagon to their hotel. (In my dreaming this, I would awaken hacking and coughing.)

The following day all smoke had disappeared, for that very night a light rain fell in the area around the river, dispelling the smoke, and giving the ball park ground crew moisture needed to manicure the ball field properly.

The crowd was let in free the day of the second game, and they were doubled in size from the day before, for the financial managers of the game had no time to issue "rain checks" for the smokeout." But Cincy won the abbreviated "smoked out" contest 11-3 and the regular game 17-5. Holy cow, but did they show St. Louis what baseball was all about in that brief series.

"Well," Sam said, when this wild tale was ended, "that is just what I saw in that "imaginary ball game" when Cincinnati's Red Stockings came to town." Stuart had never heard anything so wild and amusing - a grandpa's version of a "Field of Dreams." We must remember that Sam was barely 20 years of age when this occurred.

The hour was very late, the old grandfather was very weary, and Stuart and Will had to be leaving, after that long afternoon's visit.

Just as they got up to leave, old Sam reached into a desk drawer, a very old keyhole desk, taking out a yellowed news clipping he kept carefully hidden in a cellophane folder. He handed this to Will, his son, advising him with these parting words, "Will, read this to Stu in the morning after you are rested. It is the true account of the day the Cincinnati Red Stockings first came to St. Louis, taken out of our newspaper, the morning after." Will very carefully handled the priceless clipping, dated 1869, placing it between two pieces of notebook paper. The boy and father bade the old man goodnight and headed for Aunt Hazel McCane's home on Grandview Avenue for a good night's rest.

The following morning both Will and Stu read the 1869 account of that first Cincy ball game to Aunt Hazel and her daughter, Elizabeth, as they enjoyed their bacon and eggs.

The reader will now enjoy the true account of Cincinnati's first visit to St. Louis and it's new ball diamond:

Hazel, Will, Elizabeth, and young Stuart carefully unfolded the old news accounts of the Cincinnati visit to the diamonds of St. Louis, poring over the scores of the two games, the attendance, and the general comments by the reporters who obviously had never seen "such a slick aggregation of ball players assembled" on one team. It was a warm day, September 15, 1869, that those Cincy Red Stockings walloped the St. Louis "Unions" by a score of 70-9. And on the following day, equally as warm, they took on St. Louis' other good team, the "Empires," who did somewhat better on the diamond in front of the home town crowd, being soundly defeated by only a 31-9 score. There were certainly no accounts of unusual happenings (fire trucks and foundry fires, great "smokeouts") - as 20 year old Sam Southworth had conjured up in his brain while "dreaming" of the arrival of the professionals, weeks in advance of their appearance. The huge crowd at the new ball park cheered for both teams alike, but all St. Louis knew, right then and there, that they were seeing the real forerunners of good baseball teams - eventually their city would have more major league clubs than Cincinnati would - the "Cardinals" and the "Browns," for a span of many years to come.

More surprising to the four Southworths and McCanes sitting there on that hot summer morning over breakfast, reading all the clippings and papers that Granddad had given them before departing the evening before, was the collection of interesting news articles which Sam had saved, following the Cincinnati Red Stockings until they disbanded after the season of 1870. One sheet had every date, score, and opponent for the 1869 and 1870 seasons, another told of the western tour to San Francisco, which were the next four the Red Stockings played - after leaving St. Louis in 1869, taking the newly completed transcontinental railroad to California, linked May 10, 1869, at Promontory Point, Utah.

Read along with Hazel, Will, Elizabeth and Stuart, some excepts taken from this rare collection of pages:

"On September 14 the Cincinnati club made preparations for its western tour to California - the first barnstorming tour of a transcontinental nature in the history of the USA. Taking the train that evening, the players reached St. Louis the next day, when they played the Unions of that city, and the following day also defeated the Empire club. On September 26, they played the Eagle baseball club in San Francisco. They remained there over a week, playing and defeating the Pacifics, the Atlantics, and three hand picked nines. Just for the sake of variety and amusement, they even played a game of cricket with the California eleven, in which they showed that they could play cricket as well as baseball, for the Western eleven lost in a score of 18 to 39.

After a most hospitable reception given the club in California, they were escorted to the train in grand style. Upon arriving into California, the Cincy Red Stockings had been met in Sacramento by a Welcoming Committee, escorted to San Francisco on the Sacramento boat, met at the wharf by another committee, and taken in no less than six carriages - to the fine cosmopolitan Hotel.

Now, the San Francisco Eagles had been consistently the champions of the Pacific Coast since 1860, with the exception of the 1867 season, when the Pacifics, an off-shoot of the Eagles, were the top team. Organized teams that early, in the 1860's, Civil War period, were pretty much confined to the Bay Region and Sacramento. After playing the more prominent San Francisco teams, those Red Stockings, enroute home, played games in the Sacramento area, in and around the boom town of Virginia City, Nevada, and, when they reached the Missouri River near Omaha, they took on the Nebraska City team and on into the city of Omaha - returning unbeaten for the entire year, East and West.

In Omaha, which they reached on October 11, they defeated their best club by a score of 65-1."

At this game were the Vice President of the United States, Mr. Colfax, General Dix and General Auger, who were stationed at the Western forts.

Another of Granddad Sam's clippings, yellow with age and barely legible, was a tribute to those Red Stockings. "The Red Stockings were not beaten until one year, to the day, after they established themselves as a great team, beating the Mutuals of the Eastern seaboard. Finally, on June 14, 1870, Flag Day, after their opening of the season with 26 straight wins, they were upset 8-7 (in eleven innings) before a crowd of 20,000 in Brooklyn. (Note: 20,000 people for baseball in the early year of 1870). They lost five more that season, then they disbanded in September. Mr. Wright moved on to the city of Boston, taking the name "Red Stockings" with him - and the Boston Red Sox name has endured to this day. So, today, both the Cincinnati Reds and the Boston Red Sox continue tribute to what was both the first and surely the most nearly invincible professional baseball club ever assembled.

In 1871, the concept of outright professionalism was widely established enough that Wright and some others felt free to break away from the National Association of Baseball Players and founded the pointedly named National Association of Professional Baseball Players."

Finally, the four breakfast readers found a last article, carefully saved in a sheet of cellophane by Sam. This writer really paid a fine tribute to the 1869 professional pioneers. Here are his glowing words:

"The old Cincinnati Red Stockings of 1869 and 1870 have immortalized Cincinnati in a baseball sense, for the wonderful success of their first professional team made its lasting impress on professional baseball. While it naturally stood out prominently as the best baseball club of the period, and while no doubt this prominence was in a great measure due to the fact that it was the "only full-fledged professional team in existence" at that time, yet no one can gainsay but that the Cincinnati Red Stockings were a remarkable band of ball players.

The two Wright brothers, Harry and George, left their impress on the game; the former for his high skills and managerial ability, as well as being a very skillful player; and George, on account of his wonderful skill as a shortstop. George's skill as a batsman, base-runner, and his attractive figure on the field - all of these have never been excelled."

Calvin A. McVey, R. F.; Charles H. Gould, 1st B.; Harry Wright, Captain and C. F.; George Wright, S. S.; Fred Waterman, 3rd B.; Andy F. Leonard, L. F.; Douglas Allison, C.; Asa Brainard, P.; Charles Sweasy, 2nd B.

CINCINNATI BASEBALL TEAM OF 1869.

From an original photo taken by M. B. Brady in Washington at the time when they played the Nationals

FROM ORIGINAL PHOTOS TAKEN AT THE TIME IN CINCINNATI,
BY HOAG & CO.

SCORES MADE BY THE FAMOUS CINCINNATI REDS OF 1869.
NOT ONE DEFEAT.

			RED STOCKINGS.	OPPONENTS.
Apr.	17.	Picked Nine	24	15
	24.	Picked Nine	50	7
May	4.	Great Western, Cincinnati	45	9
	10.	Kekionga, Fort Wayne, Ind	86	8
	15.	Antioch, Yellow Springs,O	41	7
	22.	Kekionga, Fort Wayne, Ind	41	7
	29.	Great Western, Mansfield, O	35	(3 innings) 5
June	1.	Independents, Mansfield, O	48	14
	2.	Forest City, Cleveland, O	25	6
	3.	Niagara, Buffalo, N. Y	42	6
	4.	Alerts, Rochester, N. Y	18	9
	7.	Haymakers, Troy, N. Y	37	31
	8.	Nationals, Albany, N. Y	49	8
	9.	Mutuals, Springfield, Mass	80	5
	10.	Lowell, Boston, Mass	29	9
	11.	Tri-Mountain, Boston, Mass	40	12
	12.	Elarvards, Boston, Mass	30	11
	15.	Mutuals, New York	4	2
	16.	Atlantics, New York	32	10
	17.	Eckfords, Brooklyn, N. Y	24	5
	18.	Irvingtons, New Jersey	20	4
	19.	Olympics, Philadelphia, Pa	22	11
	21.	Athletics, Philadelphia, Pa	27	18
	22.	Keystones, Philadelphia, Pa	45	30
	24.	Marylands, Baltimore, Md	47	7
	25.	Nationals, Washington, D. C.	24	8
	28.	Olympics, Washington, D. C.	16	5
	30.	Baltics, Wheeling, W. Va	44	(3 Innings) 0
July	1.	Picked Nine	53	11
	3.	Olympics, Washington, D. C.	25	14
	5.	Olympics, Washington, D. C.	32	10
	10.	Forest City, Rockford, Ill	34	13
	13.	Olympics, Washington, D. C.	19	(7innings) 7
	22.	Buckeyes, Cincinnati	71	(6 innings) 15
	24.	Forest City, Rockford, Ill	15	(4innings) 14
	28.	Empires, St. Louis, Mo.	15	0
	30.	Cream City, Milwaukee, Wis	85	7
	31.	Forest City, Rockford, Ill.	53	32
Aug.	2.	Forest City, Rockford, Ill	28	7
	4.	Central City, Syracuse, N. Y	37	9
	5.	Central City, Syracuse, N. Y	36	(8 Innings) 22
	6.	Forest City, Cleveland, O.	43	27
	11.	Riversides, Portsmouth, O.	40	0
	16.	Eckfords, Brooklyn, N. Y.	45	18
	23.	Southern, New Orleans, La.	35	3
	27.	Haymakers, Troy, N. Y.	17	(5 innings) 17
	31.	Buckeyes, Cincinnati	103	8
Sept.	9.	Olympics, Pittsburg, Pa.	54	2
	10.	Alerts, Rochester, N. Y	32	19
		On their California trip they won as follows:		
Sept.	15.	Unions, St. Louis, Mo.	70	9
	16.	Empires, St. Louis, Mo.	31	9
	26.	Eagles, San Francisco, Cal.	35	4
	27.	Eagles, San Francisco, Cal.	58	4
	29.	Pacifics, San Francisco, Cal.	66	4
	30.	Pacifics, San Francisco, Cal.	54	5
Oct.	1.	Atlantics, San Francisco, Cal.	76	(5 innings) 5
	11.	Omahas, Omaha, Neb.	65	(7 innings) 1
	12.	Otoes, Omaha, Neb.	56	(5innings) 3
	13.	Occidentals, Quincy, Ill.	51	7
	15.	Marions, Marion, Ind.	63	4
	18.	Athletics, Philadelphia, Pa.	17	12
	22.	Louisville, Louisville, Ky.	59	8
	24.	Cedar Hill, Cedar Hill, O.	40	10
Nov.	4.	Eagles, Covington, Ky.	40	(6 innings) 10
	5.	Mutuals, New York, N. Y.	17	8

THE REDS OF SIXTY-NINE.

BY HARRY ELLARD

An old man sat in his easy-chair,
  Smoking his pipe of clay,
Thinking of years when he was young,
  Thus whiling his hours away.

Thinking when he was but a boy,
  So full of mirth and glee,
And we hear him say: "How things have changed:
  They are not as they used to be.

"When I was young, and played baseball
  With the Reds of Sixty-nine,
We then knew how to play the game:
  We all were right in line.

"We used no mattress on our hands,
  No cage upon our face;
We stood right up and caught the ball
  With courage and with grace.

"And when our bats would fan the air
  You bet we'd make a hit;
The ball would fly two hundred yards
  Before it ever lit.

"A homerun all could easily make,
  And sometimes six or eight;
Each player knew his business then
  As he stepped up to the plate.

"Let's see! There's Leonard and George Wright,
  And Sweasy and McVey,
With Brainard and Fred Waterman—
  These men knew how to play.

"'Doug' Allison, too, could bat in style,
  And so could Charlie Gould,
While Harry Wright oft said with pride,
  'My boys are never fooled.

"The game you see them play to-day
  Is tame as it can be;
You never hear of scores like ours—
  A hundred and nine to three.

"Well, well, my boy, those days are gone;
  No club will ever shine
Like the one which never knew defeat,
  The Reds of Sixty-nine."

✪   ✪   ✪   ✪   ✪

During their two week stay in St. Louis the early part of June, 1938, William and Stuart shared an upstairs bedroom at the home of Will's sister and her family. Stuart was soon calling her Aunt Hazel, and he first commented that his aunt had the same name as his Mother. Aunt Hazel's husband, Uncle Lynne McCane, was Head Librarian at the St. Louis Law Library, located in a high downtown building, an imposing structure done in the Greco-Roman style of architecture.

In the home adjacent and to the South of the McCane residence, on Grandview Avenue, near beautiful Forest park, lived Will and Hazel's brother, Stuart Southworth, with his wife Emma, and their only child, Mildred. Uncle Stuart was Stu's namesake, and was the advertising editor for the newspaper, the St. Louis Globe-Democrat.

When Stu and Will visited Granddad Sam the next day, they found him to be in exceptionally good spirits. He had read in the local paper that morning the fact that the Ringling Brothers Barnum and Bailey Circus was coming to town, to be appearing in St. Louis for a few days and evening performances. Sam had always enjoyed watching the clowns and the acrobats under "the big top." It wasn't but a few moments after their arrival that Sam was telling Will and Stu a fantastic account of an acrobat from a circus, who eventually made a major league ball club in the early days, a few years gone by. The two listeners laughed uncontrollably when Sam reminded them that in one game that acrobat was running to third, the third baseman held the ball out—to tag the man out, and that darned acrobat did a forward flip over the baseman, landing on the bag. Will's laughter at this acrobatic stunt brought tears to his eyes, for his Dad had a knack of telling the stories so vividly.

Sam Southworth continued, excitedly, by saying, "Did you know, Will, it was on my way over to see the circus unload off the train and set up on the old circus grounds (I told you about this, one day when you were younger) that I stopped to see an unusual kind of baseball game in progress over at one of the big baseball sandlots near downtown. Oh, sure, you recall me telling of seeing my first game of "workup," back on that day in 1872?"

BASEBALL STORY NUMBER 5 - 1872
GRANDDAD SAM SAW HIS FIRST GAME OF
"WORKUP" IN ST. LOUIS - AT AGE 23
OR
A GREAT WAY TO "WORKUP" A GOOD SWEAT
REAL FAST, IF YOU ARE
ONE OF THE HITTERS OR RUNNERS

SAM SOUTHWORTH RELATED TO HIS son, Will, and to grandson, Harold Stuart, his story of seeing a local sandlot team practice in 1872, engaged in "an unusual game," as Sam defined it. This young man was 23 and had seen plenty of baseball up to this date. It had been around in St. Louis for 11 years, but this contest interested him a lot.

Sam was driving a small buggy down the main street of the big city one May day in 1872 and turned the corner toward the big river, and there he observed that sandlot game in progress. He later learned that it was merely a practice. The first thing he noticed, and Sam always paused to gape at any ball game in progress, was the fact that there were five or six hitters in a row, standing well apart from each other, taking warmup swings, waiting their turns to bat. He knew that it was usual that only two batters were "on deck" and "in the hole."

Upon further inquiry from a spectator there, Sam learned that this sandlot club was practicing for a key game, coming up in three days, against an arch rival St. Louis sandlot club. To maximize their time and hitting practice, they had invented another game, similar to the "over the line" game, which Sam had witnessed one April day in 1865.

The best six hitters on the team began the game as batters. They would hit and run out the hit, as in a regular baseball game. There was a base umpire, perhaps two, but no plate umpire needed. The batter waited and swung only at the pitch he wanted. The pitcher tried to get a good pitch over the plate for the batter to hit. All other team members were in the field, in their regular defensive positions. If there was a gap at a defensive position, a stranger to that position filled in but only for a few minutes. He wouldn't be at that position long.

Sam saw that the key to this strange hitting game is "rotation." That is to say that, when an out is made on a ground ball or any other method, except a caught fly, all the

A great way to "workup" a good sweat
real fast, if you are one of the hitters or
runners.

men in the field rotate in this manner: Left field goes to center field goes to right field goes to third base goes to short stop goes to second base, etc., etc., goes up in the same order, swinging, ready to hit. Runners may not steal in this game. Runners take only a ten foot lead off their bases. The runner only advances when the ball is hit, if they wish to go, unless there was a force out.

Pitchers all got a workout on the mound, catchers split the game and pitchers and catchers batted for a while, but did not have to go out and "workup."

This new practice game also helped any baseball player more fully appreciate and learn the rudiments of playing another man's position. Mainly it was invented as a "hitter's game," and hitters liked to stay at bat for hours, if possible. Sure!

If the hitter hit a fly ball, whoever caught it traded places, then and there - with the hitter. the batter had to go to that position. (Pitchers and catchers were exceptions to this, of course. If pitcher or catcher caught a fly ball, it was a "rotation" out for all who were on the field.) The poor batter had to trot out to left field and "workup" his way to bat again - through seven different positions.

Sam Southworth just sat there in his little buggy, admired the game and its ingenuity (and its purposes). Finally, after sitting there for 45 minutes, he just shook his head, yelled, "Giddyup" to the horse.

Away he headed for the Southworth home, saying to himself, "What won't they think up next, for this new game - Baseball?"

Don't we all wonder what he would think if he could now see a 1990 major league contest? Or how about a big college team - in full practice session?

Stuart and his dad, Will, had to run some errands at the food store for the elderly Southworth and wife, Mae. This gave the father some time to guide his son through the neighborhood in which he had grown up, and it was fun and reminiscent to shop at the old grocery store building near the granddad's residence, the one where Will worked for so many years, as a grocery clerk and stocker. Will had earned his money after school and on weekends to buy his tickets to the Cardinal and Browns games.

The two Southworths slowly walked up Shenandoah Avenue after their purchases at the old market, and when they returned to the old house Sam was chuckling about something that he had recalled from last night's "four fabulous baseball accounts" he had unfolded to the son and grandson.

Sam Southworth called young Stu over and said, "Ya remember that story of the near riot at the Alton game in '63?" Sam added, "Well, I should have followed that wild one with a game I saw around the 1870's when I was barely 25 years old. Funniest thing I ever saw, though. I'll let you and Will judge for yourselves, Stuart. This tale is about a home run hit out of a ball park that turned into an outfield out and eventual double play. My cousin Mark, and I couldn't believe our eyes. Neither could that big home run hitter that day.

BASEBALL STORY NUMBER 6 - 1874
THE WINDBLOWN HOME RUN THAT TURNED
INTO A DOUBLE PLAY
OR
WEREN'T THOSE BASERUNNERS TOLD NOT TO
ADVANCE UNTIL THEY OBSERVED THE
LONGBALL DISAPPEARING BEYOND THE FENCE?

SAM SOUTHWORTH WAS VISITING A cousin one day in 1874, up north of St. Louis, a considerable distance away from home, and not but a few miles from Hannibal, Missouri, boyhood home of Mark Twain. Sam and his cousin, Mark, were soon attending all of the ball games at the local park that hot Summer.

Now Sam recollects a tremendous home run he saw hit into the teeth of a howling gale on a humid, rainy Summer day. All in the ball park just knew it was a sure home run - sure to carry at least 400 feet from the plate.

This small Missouri rural town and its opponent (from across the Mississippi River, in Pike County, Illinois), were scoring hot and heavy in the middle of that terribly hot, muggy weather - with winds that would whip up out of nowhere and approach gale force, then just subside to almost zero, between sprinkles, with intermittent light hail.

The score stood 12-12 in the 6th inning. The home club from Missouri came to bat, had men on second and third bases, with just one out. To the plate strode the burly cleanup hitter, a mighty muscular man. He then carefully picked his pitch to hit. It was on the third pitch that this chunky home run slugger parked the ball, one which made the crowd rise to their feet in awe. The wind had been blowing from dead centerfield some, prior to that fateful swing. When the ball left the bat, it was headed for the deep centerfield notch, and the fences came together at the 380' point. Surely the ball would be rising as it cleared that centerfield fence. Of course, a sure homer?? Unfortunately, nothing can be assumed, or is certain, in this world of ours.

What could the poor centerfielder for the opponent do, other than streak hard for the centerfield notch and watch the ball disappear? JUST THEN, PRAYERS WERE ANSWERED (THOSE SAID BY THE PITCHER) AND NATURE INTERVENED. Just as the ball was getting to the centerfielder's position, a full gale force wind blew up, instantly, hanging the ball up, keeping it from going any further. It seemed to stop

Weren't those baserunners told not to
advance until they observed the longball
disappearing beyond the fence?

dead, directly over the centerfielder. The fielder looked up, from his deepest possible position at the notch where the fences met, and he saw the white ball sitting almost motionless, exactly above him. The two forces, the wind and the velocity of the hit ball, were resulting in zero resultant of forces at that second in time.

The erratic gale wind ceased as quickly as it had come up. The ball, now left hanging in midair, 380 feet from the plate, was at the mercy of nothing but gravity.

Sam Southworth and cousin Mark unbelievably saw that little sphere drop straight down, straight as a shot, plunk, into the two hands of the surprised fielder. He could not have chosen a better spot to be to field that hard hit fly ball. That catch was the second out of that sixth inning.

Both the second and third base runners, seeing the ball hit so hard, had come home, crossed home plate, and were waiting to congratulate the team mate who had driven them home so many times before. The home run hitter, chest out in pride, was doing his slow "home run circuit."

After the strange fly ball caught for the second out, that centerfielder instinctively fired the ball to the cutoff man, the shortstop, who then relayed it to the third baseman, who stepped on the bag, for the third out.

No runs scored, the game still tied after six innings, 12-12.

We will not record on these pages the surprise (nor the expletives uttered) by the three base runners and their manager and team, as well. They prepared to take the field in the top of the seventh inning, certain that someone in the village had put a "hex" on that ball club. Little did they understand the forces or quirks of old Mother Nature.

Sam, with the small baseball audience of his son, Will and grandson, Stu, by this time, chuckling loudly at the turn of events of that last baseball adventure, came booming back with a story of 1877, told to him by his cousin, Mark, some years later. Mark and Sam, cousins about the same age, visited each often, in each of the men's home towns.

Sam prefaced his wild tale by stating that the cities, towns (even the rural cross-road villages of America) by 1877, were taking to baseball like a "duck to water." By 1877, every kind of habitation, even rural districts where there were really no towns, were gathering men and boys to start the "sandlot level" of baseball history. Mining camps, logging camps, industries in towns, fishing villages - settlements way out West all were forming their teams. Eventually, a few of their star players would be told of (and scouted, to discover the talent there, by major league scouts). Walter Johnson, pitcher for far off Weiser, Idaho, is a very good example of a Western sandlot standout, whose fame quickly spread to the East.

Baseball was truly becoming America's pastime.

When the major league scout, early in the century, wired a telegram to his major league club back East, all about Walter Johnson's speed of his fast ball, the club president wired back these words, "We hear he is very fast, but can he get the ball over the plate consistently?"

In reply, that major league scout wired back these words, "If Walter Johnson didn't have great control, there would be dead men lying all over Idaho ball parks."

BASEBALL STORY NUMBER 7 - 1877
YOUNG MARK CUNNINGHAM REALLY "BALED" HIS TEAM OUT – THAT HISTORIC DASH
OR
SHOULD WE WONDER IF THIS OBSTACLE COURSE RUN WASN'T REHEARSED EVERYDAY IN PRACTICE?

ALBEMARLE WAS IN THE LAST innings of a well played contest with Rock Hill on a hot August day in 1877. This was only eight years after Cincinnati fielded their first really professional team, those fabled RED STOCKINGS. Town team baseball was becoming very popular in America.

We must remember that baseball in the USA was spreading slowly, still in its infancy. Also, baseball diamonds and the layout of playing fields saw many variations. For instance, in Albemarle, where the game was being hotly contested (the score standing 6-5 for Albemarle), there had been erected a right field fence, but the left field boundary, a line from dead centerfield to the left field foul line, was wide open. In fact, at that time most baseball diamonds had no fences at all. If a ground ball got by the left fielder very far, it was a "home run all the way." But, of course, some very very deep flies were caught, too.

Now what stood behind the left fielder in this ball park? In a direct line, right behind that left fielder were some obstacles, beyond an imaginary 320' line across the diamond.

First there was an archery range, with bales of fresh hay stacked up against posts, to hold the targets upright. Quite a few feet beyond the hay bales had been parked a hay wagon, with its long tongue jutting out toward centerfield area. Last of these obstacles, way back beyond the hay wagon, was a low line of cut shrubs, squared and trimmed about four feet off the ground. Some kind of heavy shrubbery. The shrub lined a fence way out beyond the diamond. Remember that these objects were far far in back of our fleet footed left fielder for Albemarle that day. The shrubs were at least 450 feet from home plate.

Well, as luck would have it on a scorcher of a day, Albemarle pitching weakened decidedly, and Rock Hill loaded the bases in that late inning. Two were out, but, down 6-5, Rock Hill needed but two runs to win the contest from the home towners.

Should we wonder if this obstacle
course run wasn't rehearsed
everyday in practice?

Steven Munsing was the hitter for Rock Hill. Steve's bat squarely met the second pitch thrown to him, and the sudden gasps then emitted from the collective throats of all present that day in the grandstand told the story to any passerby. GOOD GOD!! No person present at that game had ever seen a baseball rocked with such force! It was on its way completely out of sight! No chance of fielding it, everyone was certain of that fact. Four runs would score on this blow, the game would be won on the one blow, and this tape measure hit would go down in the annals of Albemarle-Rock Hill history. All this was concluded true by everyone - everyone except one brave soul, a Mark Cunningham, who just happened to be the Albemarle left fielder at that time. He must have been born on and camped out every day on that field - that obstacle course mentioned - for he was off and running in a flash when he saw and heard the bat meet the ball. Mark seemed to know exactly where the ball was heading and where it would land (wouldn't we all love to have three outfielders like that?) He turned on his heels, he made straight for the archery stack of baled hay, kept looking up at the arcing ball, went around to the left of the stack of bales, then headed for the hay wagon and jumped the wagon tongue, to the right of the wagon, Mark saw the white sphere coming down, dropping, dropping. . . . . and the fast runner was still sprinting when he reached up with his bare right hand (Mark was a right handed thrower) and caught the ball. There were very few gloves used by outfielders as early as 1877, so men playing those distant positions practiced grabbing fly balls out of the air with left hand, right hand, or both hands, preferably.

As Mark's grip tightened on the baseball, and he knew he had it securely, his body ran into that dense four foot shrub thicket lining a fence out there. Mark's body landed on top of it, his body lying on it face up, with the ball held way up in the air in triumph, for all in the grandstand to see. MARK HAD SAVED THE GAME AND FOUR RUNS. WHAT AN INSPIRING EFFORT AND CATCH!

As the inning was closed with that catch, it is reported that Mark Cunningham was raised on shoulders of coaches, team players alike in the next few minutes and paraded around the base paths a couple of times (amid wild, delirious shrieks and comments by all who saw the play he had made). So, for a few brief moments of their lives - both Mark Cunningham and Albemarle had their own "ticker tape parade - 1877 style."

Now the old man was really ready to go back and pull out all of his choicest diamond tales from the past, for Will and Stuart that morning.

Sam Southworth looked wildly at son, Will, and almost doubled over in laughter, reminding the man of a German woman, Helga Schwann, who lived just down Shenandoah Avenue from their residence, when Sam and his first wife, Emma, were raising their kids.

Helga Schwann was the only "lady" (woman) in all St. Louis who had been kicked out of a major league ball park there twice, for tanking up on beer before arriving at the grounds, then standing behind home plate, constantly berating the home plate umpire, as well as players from either team playing that day.

Old Samuel winked at Will and continued, "Yes, didn't we get a lot of laughs, and a few real embarrassments at the early games, from dear old Helga? That woman really was a lady when sober, but, with beer in her, just look out."

"But you know," said grandpa, "I heard a similar story, years ago, about an Irish woman who berated the umpire behind home plate. She was a ball fan in a big Eastern town. Danged if the two people (Irish lady and an Irish plate umpire she yelled at unmercifully) didn't end up falling in love and getting married. A most unusual last scene to this crazy baseball story. Do ya wanna hear about it?"

Who could deny the grandfather with the long white hair, at this point?

BASEBALL STORY NUMBER 8 - 1878
THE UMPIRE FINALLY MEETS HIS MATCH,
IN THE PERSON OF
MOLLY COLEEN O'FLAHERTY
OR
YOU CAN MEET THE MOST INTERESTING
PEOPLE AT A BASEBALL GAME

THIS PARTICULAR TALE DOESN'T HAVE a very happy beginning, the first scene being one in which any one present would have predicted a gloomy finale.

Somewhere in a large Eastern city in the year 1878 resided two Irish persons (actually we are sure the place was loaded with Irishmen) who become the main characters in this battle of the sexes. One Irish lady was a red-haired beauty, of real Irish tongue and temper, Molly Coleen O'Flaherty. The other Irish person mentioned was a man, shorter than Molly, a recent immigrant, named Richard E. Mulligan. Migrating at early ages to this beloved land, these two fiery Irish people soon learned to love us, our Nation - but especially our national pastime. Oh, Molly Coleen would never miss a ball game. The gentleman, Richard, soon learned his baseball on sandlots in that Eastern city, but he found the pay for umpires was far more lucrative than just the fun of the game. Very soon our good Richard became so adept at his new found profession that he was sought after by the better leagues, as their first choice of umpire. Richard knew the baseball rules well, but he could also become loud and unpleasant when a call was questioned. And his Irish temper showed.

Richard and Molly had their first meeting in the second game of that 1878 season. Behind the plate that day, Mulligan called not only some questionable pitches against the batters, but also he missed a call on a runner sliding in on a very close play. The verbal onslaught thus began from the high pitched voice of Molly O'Flaherty. Several times Richard looked into the crowd behind home plate to see who could ever possess such a terribly nagging voice. To Richard's utter surprise, this Irish man couldn't believe her beauty. He fell in love right there while she was berating his hard work behind home plate. After continued vocal harassment, umpire Mulligan walked to the screen behind home plate and conversed with Molly, suggesting she cease her loud, raucous remarks at his umpiring work. It was then that he saw those soft powder blue

You can meet the most interesting people
at a baseball game.

eyes. How could he ever approach her for an introduction (and a dinner invitation) after the game?

Several weeks later into the season, their second confrontation was christened with both beer and water - what a beginning to a romance? It was another close game, Molly was in good voice behind the plate, and Richard was working behind the plate again. Molly was full of beer that day, louder and fiercer than ever. After a called third strike, all hell broke loose from the crowd in the grandstands. Since it was the final out of the inning (with bases loaded. UGH!) Richard strode over to the water bucket for his tin cup of water, for he was really dry after that long, trying inning. Richard was a tea totaller. But not Molly. She was holding a cup of beer, a tin cup identical to the umpire's. This is where the exchange began. Behind home plate. As the young man approached her again to warn Molly that her conduct could get her removed from the ballpark, she laughed and threw the cup of beer all over his umpire's outfit. Through the screen, of course. He instantly countered with the cupful of water down her "cleav-age" and all over her neck and face. Irish words of wrath emerged from that lovely red head's throat. Richard was stunned, thinking how pretty she was, more so when she was really angry. That settled it. He knew he must have her now. She then retorted, "I'll meet ye by the clubhouse door, after the game, and me big boyfriend, Willie, will be there to take care of ye." She intimated that Richard was to be beaten to a pulp. Sure as her word, she was there, slightly tipsy from the day's imbibing. There was no big Irish boyfriend, though. Richard jokingly asked where her support, her man, was. She then declared, "Mister, a don't need 'nary a man to help me do what I'm a goin" to do to ye now. Ya ain't no gentleman throwing water on me in front of me friends." He had no sooner said, "Well, how about me? I smelled like your cheap beer the rest of the game. The catcher and all the batters asked me if I was drunk - like you." Just at that moment Molly let out an awful outburst. "Oh yeah," she yelled, and she started to raise her slightly freckled left arm to punch, hook, or slap him.

Richard Mulligan, we forgot to mention, was as handsome a man as any man could be. As she raised her arm to strike, he slipped inside it and embraced her, kissing her a firm kiss fully on her lovely Irish lips. A very long kiss, one which completely stunned (and sobered) Molly. She giggled and sighed. She said softly, "Oh, I ne'er been kissed like that before, man."

If must have been the meeting of the Irish minds (or lips, perhaps) for, after that sumptuous kiss, they just stood there, staring fully into big blue Irish eyes. Neither said a word for a few moments. It is reported that, when last seen that day in back of the clubhouse, they were strolling slowly, arm in arm, headed for the local "hash house" for dinner.

The home game several weeks later was preceded, as usually, by none other than home plate umpire Richard Mulligan's walking to the screen and facing the crowd. He announced the starting batteries for both teams, as was the custom in those days, before microphones were invented. The large crowd in that Eastern city, an overflow-ing crowd, was then treated to another following announcement by Richard, as follows:

"Ladies and Gentlemen, now hear this. At this very home plate next Saturday, I have the pleasure to announce the marriage of myself to none other than the strawberry blonde, whom you all know only too well, Miss Molly Coleen O'Flaherty. We have had a recent meeting of the minds. This lovely Irish gal has consented to be my wife, and I assure you that this is the only possible way I can continue to umpire for you here on this diamond. Miss O'Flaherty has promised that she will be most supportive of my calls, after we are man and wife. Molly Coleen came onto the field in back of the plate, and she gave Richard a huge Irish hug. The crowd roared approval at this unexpected turn of events - a bonus for all who came. And the game began. And not a word of derision was heard that day from Molly.

The following Saturday, as previously announced by Richard, there wasn't a seat left in the house. The spectators were even up on top of the roof and "hanging from the rafters," so to speak, just to see two such fine immigrants to the USA in wedded bliss.

After the local minister blessed them, and the vows were said, the two of them walked together slowly around the bases, the two batboys holding Molly Coleen (O'Flaherty) Mulligan's white wedding train off the infield dirt. During the game, the new bride sat in the seat that she usually occupied at most games, behind home plate, and the game began. The moral of this unusual tale is this: "ONE WAY TO KEEP A GOOD LOOKING IRISH BEAUTY FROM TALKING SO MUCH IS TO KISS HER."

During the boy's visit with his grandpa for their first meeting, they talked of many things, of life in St. Louis, Missouri, and in Liberal, Kansas, their two home towns. They discussed the many similarities and differences of the two locations.

This second day of visit was pleasantly cooler outside, brought on by overcast morning skies, and the breeze felt good coming through the house through the high, narrow victorian windows in the living room bay.

Stuart told granddad Sam of the many fun activities the kids of Liberal conjured up each season of the year. His friends, school life, and the people who, in reality, were all helping to raise the boy - he gave the old man a good picture of his childhood. Especially did they get off onto the subject of Winter in both towns. It was a favorite season of the boy and his grandfather, and they compared the games and fun they enjoyed when the snow flew. The friends Stu went to school with loved to sled down the only two small hills in that flat Western Kansas town. But oh, how they loved to ice skate on the ponds, if there were any, and on the flooded tennis courts. Grandpa Southworth chuckled, listened well to each account, then he remarked, "Yeah, Winter used to be fun to a young guy, but it is so long to an old fellow like me, and it is usually pretty darned long in St. Louis. Besides that, I hate it anymore, because there isn't any baseball going on then."

After an hour or so, Sam Southworth's memories turned again to some of his boyhood friends, all growing up with him in St. Louis, from the Civil War days to the 1870's. The old man enumerated some by name, but one, in particular, a young man named Mike, sure caught the attention of Stuart and Will. (None of the three sitting in the old Victorian living room that day would have ever guessed that old Granddad Sam would someday have a great grandson named Mike - in fact, his descendants presented him with two fine boys - each of them named Michael Stuart. One would die during a college weekend kayaking vacation way up on the headwaters of the James River, in the mountains of Virginia (when in his twenties) and the other would live to coach both the sports of baseball and basketball, and pass his forty-first birthday.)

BASEBALL STORY NUMBER 9 -1880
"JACK THE RIPPER" WILL TAKE OFF YOUR GLOVE WITH HIS BASE HIT - THAT'S A PROMISE
OR
OUTFIELDERS HANDLED THIS SLUGGER "WITH KID GLOVES," YOU CAN BET

IT APPEARS THAT MIKE WAS a bosom buddy of Sam's from 1860 - 1870, but, about the time the two boys grew up, Mike fell in with bad company. After two robberies of East St. Louis, Illinois, stores, pal Mike was sent up to the Illinois State Penitentiary.

Now Mike had played some pretty good baseball in his earlier days, so he joined the ballclub at that institution. Still corresponding with his old buddy, Mike, on invitation, Sam was making trips across the river into Illinois to see Mike perform as an "incarcerated pitcher."

On a particular afternoon in the 1880's, Mike's team prevailed 10-3, and during later visitor's hour, after the game had ended, the friend passed on a wild tale to Sam. This was the type of story that finds its way "along the grapevine" inside prisons of the Nation - all about a big convict fellow in a Georgia prison, a talented baseball performer. He became known through the penal grapevine, as "Jack the Ripper." Sam didn't miss one important detail, in recounting to Will and his son, Mike's story of baseball in a Georgia "pen."

Early baseball gloves were not much protection to the hands. They were loose fitting, odd looking, but they did assist in stopping a hard ball hit and to make a catch of a fly or a thrown ball. By 1880 some gloves were appearing, but some hard-handed players could handle their positions without one. Imagine being a catcher in those days and no hand protection? Of course, there were no Bob Fellers or Nolan Ryans who threw pitches to a catcher at almost 100 miles per hour. Ouch!!!

It was customary, in the 1880's, for prison teams to invite, into their confined world, neighboring ball clubs. Particularly did they like to challenge local school, academy, and college teams. Even some military academies nearby.

Our story of "Jack the Ripper" takes place in a prison compound in Georgia, where there was actually a marshy stream flowing at one of the ends of the prison compound, and the north end of the high surrounding prison walls had been built to enclose this flow. Rather unhealthy. At the other end of the prison yard was a baseball diamond laid out. They had placed the left field wall, about seven feet high, in front of the watery marsh. Besides the outfield fence for baseball, it made another barrier for prisoners to scale, if an escape was planned at that end.

A nearby military academy, reported to have a fine baseball squad, was escorted through the many sliding and swinging prison gates one day for a game. The coach and players found themselves in a large yard, surrounded by high walls over 20' high. Trapped, they thought, for a few hours. They were to play a doubleheader. This young team felt real strange as they warmed up, but even more unwelcome when they saw the size and strength of some of their prisoner opponents.

This prison in Georgia boasted of having an ex-professional ball player who had been incarcerated for murder - his wife was done in during a mad rage. The inmates had nicknamed this big guy "Jack the Ripper," not for the manner in which he had extinguished his wife's life, but rather for the way he hit baseballs to all parts of that prison compound - even out and over the prison walls. He actually flattened the baseballs against the high brick walls. Read on.

We shall now unveil two of his exploits performed that afternoon in 1880. With his cap tilted slightly to the left on his immense head, this muscular brute swung on a pitch in the third inning of that game. The pitcher had delivered a fastball-inside. The young chucker had not been told that this batter was a notorious pull hitter.

Jack the Ripper hit the ball so hard that it whizzed by the head of the collegiate third baseman without the infielder even having time to duck or raise his glove in defense. That blow travelled about seven feet off the ground to the left field corner.

The academy's young left fielder did have a sort of a primitive glove on his hand - but not for long. As he raced to that corner of the field, he raised his loose fitting glove to grab the hard smash, travelling at an amazing velocity. Before the hit rocketed over the seven foot fence, barely, our academy left fielder got the web of his loose fitting glove in the line of the ball. It turned out to be a gross mistake, for all the prison spectators and players alike saw the ball fly up in the air in one direction, the glove flying in the same direction. Both were hit over that low fence for a home run.

The nearest umpire directed the outfielder (who was stunned, standing there, looking at his empty glove hand) to "shinny" over the fence, pad around in the oozy marsh, retrieve his glove, then find the floating baseball and throw it back over the fence). (Prison athletic budgets were thin, then).

The embarrassed outfielder could do nothing but comply with the order of the umpire. Jack the Ripper had made his home run circuit and was seated in the dugout, chuckling as he first saw the glove fly back over the fence, then the wet ball, followed by the outfielder climbing backover the wall to resume play. The big hitter just smiled beneath his big handlebar moustache to see that young kid beholding to him.

In his last time at bat that day, and there were many, you can bet, big Jack the Ripper mashed a hit to the right field wall, on a direct line. The wall probably wasn't more than 280' from the plate, made of solid brick. The ball, a home run in any park,

Outfielders handled this slugger "with kid
gloves," you can bet.

bounced so hard off the brick wall, Jack was held to a single. Yes, a single. It rebounded back to the cutoff man instantly! It was actually hit too hard for that prison field.

The umpire examined the ball after the hit. He laughed and just shook his head, throwing the ball out of the game. That baseball had been literally flattened on one side, resembling a sphere with a wedge sliced out of it with a knife. Or a cannon ball that had been flattened by striking a solid object.

✪   ✪   ✪   ✪   ✪

The last part of the first week in St. Louis that Summer, Will took Stuart out into the woodlands around the city, through the immense Forest Park and its zoo, to the beautiful setting on a very wide river in a heavily wooded section of the Eastern Missouri hills. Stu's dad had two German friends (who had driven out with them to visit in St. Louis) - Fred and Frank. They both had migrated from Germany, spoke with a very broken accent, and consumed beer by the gallon. The four of this party rented a cabin in a heavy grove of big trees, fished in the river part of a day, and Stu and his Dad drove over to visit the Merrimac Caverns. When they returned to Fred and Frank, those two were with beer bottle in hand, in their usual glassy-eyed state, and arguing loudly. Young Stu had a memorable time exploring the woodlands along the river bank and viewing the panorama of the Merrimac River as it flowed to join a larger river nearby. Stu loved trains and sat by the hour watching the number of them winding along the water grade.

The last day near the river was misty in the morning with a low fog hanging over the entire valley after a hard Summer rain the night before. It hung a few feet off the ground and river. Boating was no fun in that weather, so Stu and Will took a long walk through the thick green Missouri woods, talked about many things and enjoyed each other.

Upon their return Monday morning, their visit to Sam and Mae found the grand-father ready to unload a choice tidbit of baseball lore he had forgotten to divulge on earlier visits. Grandpa Samuel S. Southworth had recalled (during Will and Stu's enjoyable trip to the Merrimac River setting), a tale of midwestern baseball - and an old clipping he had saved (among dozens of them, in a large drawer of his keyhole desk) was pulled out to show them upon their arrival - for they had been gone from the old man for almost a week's time. Time for Sam to recall many new baseball adventures from his memoirs.

The news article, dated 1885, from a paper in a town called Albion. No clue on the clipping told what state it was from. Just Albion, and apparently a small town. The early sports editor had made light of the local town team baseball star (a home run slugger from their proud championship squad) who had actually run the bases backwards, after he had belted a monstrous hit out of the local ballpark.

What made Sam and Will chuckle the most from this news clipping was the name of Albion's home run slugger - the "reverse home run trot innovator" - a guy named NED WALK. What an odd name for a long ball stroker, they thought.

BASEBALL STORY NUMBER 10 - 1885
WE DIDN'T REALIZE THAT HOME RUN HITTERS ALL HAD A "REVERSE GEAR" IN THEIR RUNNING MECHANISM
OR
MAYBE HE WAS THINKING IT WAS SHORTER AROUND THE BASES THAT OTHER DIRECTION?

ALBION WAS A TEAM OF heavy hitters in 1885, but the heaviest of them all was a guy named Ned Walk. What a moniker for a home run slugger, eh? Walk. Ned Walk. The Albion "Hawks" were playing the Titusville "Colts" that cool Summer day when Ned Walk came up to bat for his second time in the game. Ned had hit five home runs already that early in the long season, and, in his first time up that day, had chased the center-fielder back to the wall with a long deep fly ball. But his fly ball was caught for the third out.

Now we should take time out here to inform the reader that Ned was an imaginative and creative thinker. He had long ago decided that, since he would probably hit many home runs that season, and run the "home run trot" in the correct order of bases, why not run one of the home runs in reverse, just to see what would happen? Shake people up a little, and maybe get some free "ink" at the local newspapers. It seemed like an original trick (actually, we find out later in our careers, that nothing is entirely original in this great game of ours). If you hit a home run out of the park, and no throw is coming in to get you, isn't it the same distance either way around those bases." Chuckle, chuckle, by God, he would do it on the next home run hit.

Later that day in 1885, Ned Walk, his team leading 13-2, really got a hold of an outside ball, drilling it over the right field wall. He knew it was gone the second he hit it, and he instinctively started one step toward first base, as he had always done. My Lord, aren't we awful creatures of habit? He then corrected his instincts and thoughts trotting down to third base slowly while his manager, team, the crowd, all opponents stared at his intended moves. As he rounded third base, he took off his cap, doffed it to the crowd, and proceeded to second base. Just then the crowd came to, realizing his intentions, and they stood, giving Ned a thunderous roar. All the place came apart at this "reverse run." By the time Ned was touching second and coming down the line, in reverse, toward first base, his girl friend was waving her hanky at him, screaming

Maybe he was thinking it was shorter
around the bases that other direction?

approval of this novel idea he had cooked up. Ned's parents were sitting together near the outside aisle at the game. They started laughing so hard that they embraced each other actually leaning on each other as they hugged, and finally toppled over onto the aisle area, still embraced, laughing, crying, and thus caused their neighbors sitting nearby to go into hysterics. The Albion home crowd's noise became such a tremendous din that you could have surely heard it in downtown Titusville, a good twelve miles away.

Ned Walk completed the slow paced home trot as he stepped on home plate, then stopped, taking another bow to the right, the left, and to the middle. During his bowing, he held his baseball cap over his heart. This last move was too much for the Titusville team, who were registering more and more disgust at Ned's actions - rubbing it in.

The Titiusville catcher made unkind remarks to the effect that Ned was a big "Ham" and "conceited beyond words," etc, etc. Ned replied that "The catcher would never hit a home run in his life. How would he know." Words to that effect, avoiding a fist fight on the spot.

As Ned headed for the dugout, the plate umpire changed the mood of the crowd and teams instantly - with these words, "The batter is out, and his run doesn't count. Runner ran the bases in the wrong order."

Now, that crowd was ready to lynch Umpire Tibbetts. But his instant decision stuck, after some wild arguing and pleading, for the ump was a man of 6'5" height, weight 253 pounds, and was not one to be swayed.

Years later now, we can divulge the fact that it was a bad call. You see, prior to Germany Schaefer's (Detroit Tigers) doing this same trick, twice in succession on two pitches in major league ball, in a game with Cleveland's Indians in 1908, there had never been a rule in the rule book prohibiting a ball player from running the bases in the reverse order. Nor was there a rule for running a home run in reverse order. Rules makers figures, "If a team is dumb enough to get a man on an advanced base, and they want to go backwards and give the base up again, let the dummies do it." So, after the rules committee ruled, the day after Germany Schaefer's bold reverse runs, that it was an attempt to "make a farce and a travesty" of the game of baseball, from that day to this, a runner is out if he tries it. Also, his home run does not count. Also, all other base runners return to their original bases, where they were standing when the errant runner tried this "reverse trick."

We'll never know, will we, whether the Umpire Tibbetts called Ned Walk out because he was such a "ham actor" or because he did not really know the base running rules of that year.

Years later, in 1963, on the New York Mets club, Jimmy Piersall did this identical trick, and he was immediately called out, his run taken from him.

About a week later Aunt Hazel and Aunt Emma invited the family over for a big picnic in the backyard of their homes, which, as was mentioned earlier, were adjacent on Grand Avenue. Everyone was present that warm day, and it was rather held to honor the two guests from the West - Will and Stuart. In fact, at the picnic were the two Stuarts, the father of Mildred, and the younger, Harold Stuart, from Liberal, Kansas.

Someone went over to get granddad Sam and Mae, and the entire St. Louis entourage was gathered, with their visitors, for a great visit and wonderful German cooking of Emma and Hazel. Sam and Mae thoroughly enjoyed the whole affair. Uncle Lynne McCane came home from work at the Law Library, and he was ready for his favorite drink, good Scotch whiskey with water or soda. As he was preparing drinks for the men he asked granddad, "Sam, how about a scotch and soda?" And Samuel Southworth replied, as his grandkids will remember him doing so often, "Yes, I believe I will, I believe I will."

The sun was going down when all had finished he fine picnic food and barbecue meat (for Hazel and Emma were renowned for their fabulous cooking). Somehow the conversation among all of the men got around to baseball again. Those St. Louis Cardinals and Browns seemed to be the main topic of discussion. About that time granddad asked Will to get his jacket for him from the living room, for the evening air was cooling off.

Sam reached down into one pocket of that old worn jacket and produced a letter, an envelope brown with age and nearly falling into pieces. He handed it to the men of the group, Stu sitting among them, and he asked Uncle Stuart to read it slowly to everyone present. It was an envelope postmarked Bodie, California, dated 1886. Sam Southworth asked the men if they recalled him telling them, quite a few years ago, about one of Sam's boyhood friends, Clay Washburn, a big strong fellow who played professional baseball for the St. Louis Browns in the 1880's? Most of the male group did recall the name. Clay Washburn wrote these words in that letter of 1886:

BASEBALL STORY NUMBER 11 - 1886
A BASEBALL LETTER FROM THE GRAVE
(BODIE CALIFORNIA'S
FIRST TOWN TEAM BASEBALL OF THE
1886 SEASON)
OR
A PASTIME IN THAT "BAWDY" MINING CAMP

JULY 21, 1886
Bodie, California
8800' elevation
White Mt. Range
California

Dear Sam Southworth and the old St. Louis gang:

It is certainly not like me to fail to correspond with such fine old friends for so long a period of time. So please, Sam, pass this on to all the friends. This letter and the accounts within will probably explain my delay in keeping you up to date on my many activities. The last that you heard of me I had been working in the lead and zinc mines of Missouri and Oklahoma for a couple of years. On my last visit to you and the rest of our gang I was considering the move out West where the miners are the highest paid workers in the entire World at present. Western miners really are living high on the hog in comparison to other laborers of this country. I was lured by this claim of high wages, which has turned out to be more than true. I found myself last Fall in Bodie, California, a mining city which is taking a lot of "pay dirt" out of the bleak sides of the White Mountains. Rich in gold and silver. A couple of engineer brothers named Hoover (one is named Herbert, I believe) own the mine I work in. The location of Bbodie is very high in elevation, above any kind of vegetation at all, except a gray scrubby sagebrush type, and is set across a broad valley from the main Sierra Nevada Range.

I was in deep shaft mining all winter, and the temperature was quite warm down at that depth. I watched many men die of pneumonia as they would climb out of those warm pits suddenly into air above (which registers down around 20 to 30 below zero, daytime readings). Snowdrifts reached over 20 feet in height last Winter, and tunnels were dug at the bottom of the drifts to cross from one side of the main street to the boardwalk on the other side. God, I never realized there was this much snow in all the world. With so many deaths in a town of this kind, they held the funeral for each of the deceased in churches, then they bound each corpse with a white canvas cover and stacked them in a large cold room, in the rear of the saloon. The room was unheated, with windows left open all Winter. The undertakers of Bodie also had their quarters in the rear of each saloon building. The graves for the dead could not be dug until all snow melted and the ground thawed, which, at this elevation, is very late in Spring.

Several weeks ago, all the graves for the Winter dead had been dug, the corpses deposited in proper order, headstones placed on some of them; but the grave diggers dug three new graves, also for the townspeople who had died within the last week or so. The cemetery was sitting there this week with three open graves when a slight snow fell, a very late one, even for this location and elevation.

I have to tell you, of course, that a rich town such as Bodie has lots of money, town pride, and a well-equipped and manned baseball team. This famous "bad town of the West" is not going to be outdone by anyone in sporting a competitive ball team. Bodie holds their own very well with other mining, logging, and trade center towns of this area. Of course, the terrain and roads restrict the distances traveled for games.

Well, yours truly, old pro Clayton Washburn joined the "BODIE MINERS" ball club, and let me tell you right now that it isn't good old St. Louis. But we still use a ball and a bat and cleat anyone who gets in our way, by God. I'm now sporting a dark blue uniform with a white "BODIE" emblazoned across the front of the jersey and a number 45 on the back of it. It was my old number with the St. Louis Browns, you recall? Two years professional experience at Cincinnati and in St. Louis sure established me as the team slugger and now I am captain of the squad.

I can't make this letter much longer, for the mail goes out on the stage soon. No railroad trains to put it on up here. Mail doesn't go each day, either. So I'll hurry and get the rest of this written down. I've got the craziest baseball story for you that can be imagined. I saved this one for you, Sam, for you were the one who collected these strange happenings on the diamond. You can keep this one to show your grandchildren, who may some day, a good many years up the road, visit old Bodie and see where this odd game took place.

So, Sam, here are the bizarre events of the finish of our first ball game of the season up here. We are in Mono County, and the county seat is a little burg named Bridgeport, sitting in the most beautiful valley you ever could imagine. Cattle feeding in grass in pastures criss-crossed with bubbling Sierra streams and grass up to the cow's neck. This valley is about ten miles by ten miles. That's where they grow the beef that supplies Bodie. They have a good baseball team and a better diamond than ours, by far. Well, their team and followers came up by wagon on that rough 28 mile road on Saturday, with revenge on their minds (for their two losses to Bodie in 1885). It was a rough trip up, and we fed them, and they bedded down early Saturday evening, for not too many wanted to visit our rough saloons in town.

Sunday morning dawned clear and fairly warm. Those smartly garbed guys from Bridgeport, dressed in their latest style baseball uniforms, cut quite a figure during warmups sunday morning and pregame in the early afternoon. Our diamond at Bodie is the only level place you could find in that big in area in the town, and the infield was cleaned away by horse drawn drags and scrapers. The outfield is sagebrush, really the only vegetation that grows at this elevation. However, let me tell you that the southeast corner of our Bodie graveyard sticks its square corner out into right center field quite a few feet.

The curious crowd that gathered to watch these two Mono County rivals go at it was a big one that Sunday. No seats here, unless you bring your own chair, and few did. Men and women alike, stood. Of course, the kids didn't mind at all. Lively betting was being carried on, even before the game began, and the wagers were of considerable size in some cases. I felt like I was back in St. Louis, in that respect.

I beat out a long blow for a home run in the second inning. We scored four more runs later in the game, but the contest was no pitcher's battle, for sure. Going into the final inning our bodie Miners trailed the Bridgeport visitors 7-5. Our big hitters came up, and the opposing pitcher could be seen to weaken considerably. Sure enough, we got two men on base after one was out. Both reached base on walks. I stepped up to the plate and gave that tiring pitcher my old "St. Louis rip" on his third pitch. I hit it late, and that ball sailed over the head of the right fielder. That Bodie soil is so hard, the ball took a high bounce and jumped the low ornamental wire fence - into that cemetery, bounding around among the dead.

I forgot to tell you the ground rules on the Bodie diamond. If the ball is hit and bounces in to the graveyard, the fence is so low that the rules have it that the outfielder has to go and retrieve that hit ball, firing it back to the relay man. Now the crowd saw that the two previously walked runners came around to score and tie the game at that point, but their screaming, waving, yelling indicated to me that I had a chance to make it, also, and register a second home run for me in the game. I was the winning run, to make it even sweeter. Oh, how I turned on the steam, Sam. I ran slower than that in pro ball in St. Louis, and dug up the ground as I slid into home plate, safely. All of the crowd expected the ball to be thrown back over the fence long before I got home. I got up and with the crowd, umpires, the Bridgeport defense - we all gazed way out toward the right field area where the second baseman stood with arms up to give the right fielder a target to relay the ball to. There not only was no throw home, but there was also no outfielder to be seen anywhere in that maze of gravestones in the cemetery. Where was that retriever? The people in the crowd said that they had first seen the ball on top of old George Bodie's (Bodey was the real spelling of the name) grave marker. The stone was a fake, placed there to honor the founder of Bodie and the finder of pay dirt in the 1850's. He really perished in a bad winter blizzard, the animals getting his remains. Members of the crowd then yelled out that they had seen the ball bounce the second time, grazing the white obelisk monument dedicated in 1882 to the slain President James A. Garfield (actually the stone was ordered made in San Francisco by the widow of a wealthy mining engineer for his grave. When it was cut and arrived, prior to carving the inscription on it, the town folk caused her to relent, coaxing her to have it carved and dedicated to the recently departed President of the USA).

A pastime in that "bawdy" mining camp.

Beyond these two bounces mentioned, the ball and the outfielder had just disappeared! No sight or sound of him from that area.

Oh, Sam, you'll never believe what we found! Only too soon were we to learn. The whole crowd surged forward, spread out searching for the ball and the man, for the game was over, and people were starting to head for their homes. We all took part in the search, spurred on by faint cries of "Help" and "Someone help me get out of here." We pinpointed the noise we heard, and the crowd gathered, circling around a freshly dug grave. Looking down into the pit, we all saw the "lost outfielder," holding the ball up in the air with his throwing hand, at about the same time. Some laughter came from the members of the crowd, but it was soon silenced when everyone realized the plight of the fellow in the grave pit. In fact, the grave diggers had done a specially good job of digging that hole. It was seven or eight feet deep, not the usual six feet. The Bridgeport right fielder told us that the ball had rolled into the pit on the third or fourth bounce, he climbed in after it, sure that he could get out by himself. After all, the winning run was coming around the bases. "Yes, wasn't it," I thought to myself, with a wide grin.

Sam, as soon as several strong men reached down and helped that poor soul out of "an early grave," you know the first thing he yelled at the umpires, who were standing next to him? He said, "Umps, that ball should be declared "dead" the minute it rolls into an open grave." "Dead," Sam, should be "dead." Everyone there just about doubled up and roared with laughter at the poor fool's "inference to the deceased." When the plate umpire had composed himself, wiped the tears from his eyes from all the laughing he'd done, he finally took charge, stating to the entire crowd, "This baseball game is officially ended. the home run does count, and the score ends up 8-7. When the game began we agreed that the cemetery was in play if a ball did bounce in it. ALL OF IT IS IN PLAY - WHETHER ABOVE GROUND OR BELOW GROUND.

Then there began the fiercest argument you ever witnessed, Sam. I really was afraid that some of those miners and the like were going to settle it with guns right there in that graveyard. Well, come to think of it, I guess a cemetery would be as good a place as any to settle a dispute "to the death." Boy, the mood changed real quick. Several people scattered and scampered to safer areas. A lot of pushing and scuffling ensued, a few blows were then struck, and the foulest language ever heard, even for mining camps.

Fortunately, the Marshal of bodie and his deputies were died-in-the-wool ball fans, and that Marshal drew his gun and gave it a squeeze up in the air. People who were falling over grave markers rassling over the graves ceased what they were up to - real sudden-like. The altercation was soon dispelled. Some thinking person on the Bodie team yelled, "The Bodie team sets up drinks for everyone at the Old Miner's saloon."

It is amazing how a foot up on the footrail and an elbow on the bar can sooth one's nerves after such a game and game-ending extravaganza, eh? Differences soon forgotten, all stepped up to the bar, courtesy of the wealthy winning team and its sponsors, and with each drink less hostility existed and old baseball tales got wilder.

Kinda reminded me of you and me down at Silky O'Malley's dive in St. Louis. We could swig and make up some tales that couldn't possibly have happened in a real game, couldn't we?

Boy, this sure ain't St. Louis, Missouri, Sam. Mail me the news and let me know who's winning the ball games.

Respectfully from California,

Clayton Washburn

That day had to arrive, too soon, for Will and Stu, to take their leave from the Southworth and the McCane clans, and to head West for Denver. Will, Stu, Fred and Frank were to drive the man and son to the mile high city and there meet Hazel, Stu's mother and Will's former wife. William Dallas Southworth and Nora Hazel (Bolinger) Southworth had divorced in Dallas, Texas, when Stuart was six months old. Here, thirteen years later, the former man and wife had decided to remarry in San Diego, California, upon their arrival there some three weeks later. After a memorable bit of nostalgic reminisces in Denver and suburbs, the three climbed aboard a bus and headed for California again.

But on the morning of parting from the old gentleman, Sam, it was always a difficult breaking away after a good visit for Will, and so it would be for Stuart, for he had finally gotten to see and know his other grandfather. How he enjoyed visiting with the old man, listening to his accounts of the family in the past, and Stuart had learned so much about baseball, a game he had never played or even seen played. With grandpa Sam being 90 the following October 12, it was not always certain that he might be alive when the next trip to St. Louis occurred. No one ever knows those things. They finally parted, tears in Will's eyes and Stuart having given his granddad Sam a kiss and some big hugs. Stuart would see Samuel Southworth one more time, November, 1945, a few days after the young man was commissioned, as an Ensign in the U.S. Navy from Columbia University, New York City, Midshipman School.

Just before they left, though, Samuel had saved for the boy and Will one of his craziest and best ballpark adventures. He related this tale shortly after they had finished breakfast. Old Sam had dug this one from the 1889 season, the year he turned 40.

BASEBALL STORY NUMBER 12 - 1889
ACTUALLY, THAT DIVING BASERUNNER "LIED ABOUT" WHERE THE BASEBALL WAS
OR
A MIDWESTERN NIGHTMARE FOR THE DEFENSE DURING ANOTHER OFFENSIVE "HIDDEN BALL TRICK" BY THE RUNNER.

IN 1889 TWO MIDWESTERN SEMI-PRO teams, Carleton and Milford, met one fine Saturday afternoon. They played on a diamond which had suffered the bad results of a heavy rain the night before. They really should have had the game cancelled, but it was a red hot rivalry between two small towns. The ground crew had done its best to make the dirt infield playable, but the areas around the bases, being somewhat lower than the rest of the ball diamond, showed some slick spots under the drying summer sun.

Of course, much base running was out of the question on that diamond that afternoon. So both clubs relied completely upon its hitting. Few hitters found their way on base for the first 8 innings, and the score stood scoreless going into Milford's lower half of the 8th. The second Milford hitter reached second base on a hard stand up double. With one out, Spud Mc Ginnis walked. Spud was the "town character," the team clown, and if ever there was one who might pull a trick or two, it would be Spud. And a real "ham" in every respect. The Carleton pitcher had such a quick right hander's pickoff move to first, Spud usually took no liberties with this thrower. But with a scoreless tie game, things could be different.

The clown runner tempted the pitcher by daring more than he should have. The quick-moved pitcher whirled and fired a bullet to the covering first baseman. Dust and sand flew in all directions as Spud slid back to first base on his belly. Just before each inning of that particular game, the ground crew had brought a load of dirt and sand mixture out in front of each base, depositing the same, raking it down smoothly, leveling it and packing it down some.

In the cloud of dust created by Spud's slid, the thrown ball had been lodged beneath the body of Spud Mc Ginnis, squarely beneath his navel, so that not a soul in the ball park could see it. Not even Spud. But the runner lying on his belly could feel it down

A midwestern nightmare for the defense
during another offensive "hidden ball
trick" by the runner.

there, like lying on a small cannon ball. The team mate of Spud, the runner on second base, couldn't see through the cloud of dirt, and he thought the ball had been over-thrown. So did the first baseman (and most of the defense on the field), for that poor guy was still trying to wipe the sand from his eyes at the same time he searched for the elusive baseball. Suddenly the pitcher and second baseman joined the first base-man in searching for the ball behind the base, all the way to the fence. Spud laid there, then suddenly let out a yell, grimacing, "Oh my wrist. I've jammed it. Owee. Ow." He gave a fine act of being injured on that last slide. By this time, the runner from second base had rounded third and made a beeline for the plate, seeing that he was not to be threatened by any "visible ball in play." He streaked home with the only run of that game. (Milford held the opponents the next inning and eventually won the game 1-0 that afternoon.)

Now the umpires entered the search for the ball, along with the two team managers, When Spud Mc Ginnis thought that everyone involved had been put through enough suspense, he lifted his body off the ground slowly, as if nursing his sore wrist. Just as he rose to a kneeling position, he yelled out, perfectly innocently, "Hey, the ball was underneath me." "Well, I'll be danged, I never knew it was there at all."

The Carleton manager was furious at Spud Mc Ginnis and wanted to stomp his face into that wet field, accusing Spud of "skulduggery and gross chicanery" and even making reference to some of Spud's family lineage. Spud's innocent look won the right folks over, though. The umpires declared that the run scored would count. They stated that it was the defensive team's responsibility to know at all times where the baseball was, in any game. The offensive club might occasionally lose the baseball in a game, but the defensive team could not. Case closed.

And thus was born baseball's very first "offensive hidden ball trick".

THE SECOND MEETING OF THE BASEBALL NARRATORS NOVEMBER, 1945

A BOY CAN CHANGE A lot in seven years, from ages 13 to 20. Samuel and his grandson, Stuart, didn't see each other again from the Summer of 1938 to late November of 1945, Sam's 96th year.

Upon leaving Sam Southworth after the first visit, Stu did go to San Diego and learn the grand game of baseball, with his Mom and Dad's support and attendance at the games. Harold Stuart Southworth grew in height, weight, and every way a kid can grow. His baseball ability increased by leaps and bounds, and his deep love of the game grew and grew. From the American Legion teams, to high school, and on to college baseball as a pitcher for the University of Denver, the Spring of 1943.

World War II interrupted many lives from 1941 - 45. After entering boot camp at Farragut, Idaho, Stuart was soon training to be an officer, to be assigned as ship's Navigator. While being stationed at the USN units at Whitman College and the University of Washington in Seattle, the tall right hander was varsity pitcher for both colleges in 1944 and 1945 respectively. He was a member of World War II's US Navy "V-12" units.

Granddad Sam was delighted to learn from Mae one day that his grandson would be in St. Louis for a visit a couple of days on his way to the first duty station as a Naval officer. He had just been commissioned as Ensign (USNR) at Columbia University Midshipman's School, New York City. Seven years it had been since grandson had listened to Sam's super baseball tales.

The evening of his arrival found Ensign Stu dressed in Navy dress blues, for the weather was very cold in the Midwest that week. Stu took off his bill cap and greeted Sam with a hearty, "Hi, granddad," and he gave him a big hug and a kiss on that same cheek as before. Grandpa Sam then said, "Stuart, stand back a little farther. Let me take a long look at you now.

Sam said something that Stu told his dad, Will, later, and which he would remember the rest of his life. The old man giggled at seeing the new dress blue officer's coat, gold buttons, the Ensign's stripe and the star above it (indicating that Stu was an "officer of the line"), reacted to what he saw by suddenly blurting out these words, "Boy, they sure dress you guys fancy nowadays." Stu stood there in front of his grandpa and couldn't help but laugh heartily with him, and he agreed that military uniforms had come a long way since Sam had seen his dad and two brothers, for the last time, take off in probably ill-fitting blue jackets and pants of the 1861 Union army. Stu knew Sam was thinking back almost 80 years to his childhood impressions.

Sam, you can bet, had not forgotten the love for baseball stories which Stu showed when he was 13, so he had one all ready for the young Ensign. This is an incident he had forgotten to mention seven years ago.

Baseball Story Number 13 - 1890's
Those Innovative Tricks Were The Orioles' Trademark (Wee Willie Keeler, "Muggsy" McGraw, Hughie Jennings and Ned Hanlon)
OR
(Thereafter, Muggsy McGraw Taught His New york Giants How To "Mug" The Opponent In The Old Oriole's Fashion)

THERE ARE, IN BASEBALL OFFENSE, exactly 28 plays that can be set up with a signal for proper execution. Several of these - the fake steal, the hit and run, the run and hit, fake bunt, the fake bunt and slash, etc. - are credited to those "sitting up at night, thinking up cute new plays and tricks" Baltimore Orioles of the 1890 era. Ned Hanlon was manager, and he and his innovators would dream up plays on paper, wake up at night and write down inspirations which came to them in sleep, then go practice them over and over. This was baseball's first ever real "team concept" - between dugout, base coaches, runners, and batters.

Manager Ned Hanlon, Baltimore Orioles of the entire 1890's era, was not honored for the great genius he was for over 100 years. He and his Orioles changed baseball completely. They gave us the plays and strategy 100 years ago which we now use as our "standard baseball repertoire."

Manager Ned Hanlon was inducted into Baseball's Hall of Fame at Cooperstown, N.Y. several years ago – enshrined – as he deserves to be. Of his starting Oriole nine in those years, seven have also made it to the Hall of Fame with their Manager, Ned Hanlon. What a record."

Several sources mention specific plays, and one example would be a cute play in which John McGraw, leadoff hitter, and Wee Willie Keeler, the next batter, worked on, religiously, in that 1890 period. If McGraw got on, he would use the fake steal to second. Just dart off on a fake quick dash of a couple of steps on the pitch. All the defense would yell, as the pitch was released, "There he goes." This would tell McGraw and Keeler who was covering second base on the steal attempt, the shortstop or second baseman.

Thereafter, Muggsy McGraw taught his
New York Giants how to "mug" the
opponent in the old Oriole's fashion.

On the pitch which McGraw did choose or was signalled to steal on, Keeler would shorten up on the bat and punch the ball right where the second baseman or shortstop had been, but vacated to cover the steal throw. On that hit, the Oriole runners often ended up on third base and second base, if the outfielder threw to third base and had no cutoff, or relay was late. This was a dandy play to perfect, for the Orioles would then have two men on, no force outs possible, and no outs.

Another Oriole innovation and experiment of the 1890's was the fake bunt and steal or the fake bunt and slash.

In the first case, the batter faking a bunt while the runner steals successfully gives the play complete success, without sacrificing an out to bunt the runner over. The batter simply gives up a strike.

The "fake bunt and slash" is merely a maneuver to get certain infielders to creep up and in, on a suspected bunt. When an infielder does come in too far, the batter (with good practiced bat control) merely pops the ball, with a short "pop stroke," over the head of and behind the creeping infielder. The base hit drops out in short outfield area, and it dies quickly. The batter gets a base hit, and all the runners move up one base each.

In conclusion, those innovative Baltimore Orioles surely gave to baseball many of the plays which were eventually accepted by all in the game, have been used now for 100 years to advance runners, put men on base, and score runs.

✪   ✪   ✪   ✪   ✪

There they were gathered about the dinner table, that first evening of Stuart's second visit to Grandpa Sam's home in St. Louis, Missouri.

Unlike the first visit in 1938, a very warm period in June, this was during a very cold early November, 1945. Seven years had flown by so quickly. Stu was cold, so he kept his Navy blue Ensign's coat on at the dinner table. The old post-Civil War red brick home did not retain the heat very efficiently.

Sam Southworth and grandson, Stu Southworth, could now discuss the game of baseball on the same level, for Stu had played the game almost continually each season since their first meeting in 1938. Seven years ago the young Ensign hadn't even appeared in the first ball game of his life.

The two men, two generations apart, began talking some of the finer points of the grand old game, the conversation drifting to Stu telling his white-haired elder of some of the great pitcher pickoff plays he had learned as a college pitcher.

Soon Sam began mulling over in his 96 year old mind (of which 85 of those years were in seeing, reading, and hearing and talking of baseball incidents), and he soon was into the "craziest pickoffs he had ever seen."

There was no doubt in the minds of either person that Sam's tale next related had to be "the most bizarre of pickoffs" tried on the ball diamond - and certainly the most complicated. The reader will think it was devised to get every team member handling the baseball, in some way.

BASEBALL STORY NUMBER 14 - 1893
HOW TO PICK UP AN OUT QUICKLY
AS A BASERUNNER
BY NOT "PICKING UP" THE LOCATION
OF THE BASEBALL
OR
DIDN'T HIS MANAGER WARN HIM -
"NEVER MOVE OFF A
BASE UNTIL YOU HAVE LOCATED WHO
HOLDS THE BASEBALL?")

THIS STRANGE TALE COULD OCCUR AT any level of baseball, but, to our knowledge hasn't been pulled off at the major league level. The key to making this play work is to remember that the second base runner's back is to the centerfielder.

One afternoon in the 1893 season a weird play was actually rehearsed and sprung on an opponent in time to prevent a key run from scoring. There was a man on second base, the tying run sitting there in scoring position. Suddenly, the opposing pitcher whirled and let loose a low throw into the dirt, intentionally low. The second base runner dived back hurriedly, of course, the ball rolling out to the centerfielder, who had made a very nice play in backing up the throw, and he had the ball in his glove after picking it up. The second base runner did not dare advance on the good backup play. Then the second baseman turned his back to the infield and walked out to the nearby centerfielder. They went through the simple motions of the fielder giving the ball to the second baseman - only it was a fake. The centerfielder kept the ball hidden, squeezed inside his mitt. Everyone was fooled by this fake exchange, and the outfielder moved to his normal position, then came back slowly to shallow centerfield position. Now the second baseman did another sudden move. He ran over to the pitcher to give him a few words of advice while he was faking giving the ball to him. Pitcher now acted as if he had the ball, as he moved toward the mound, staring at the catcher, off the mound.

The centerfielder just stood out there, shortened up in his shallow position, hands on knees, with squeezed ball in his mitt, deeply hidden. He yelled encouragement to the pitcher as the hurler started to go to the mound area.

Didn't his manager warn him? "Never
move off a base until you have located
who holds the baseball?"

We failed to mention that this play was rehearsed for the benefit of those daring baserunners who take chances, get off the base before the pitcher is actually in his stretch, and, in general, a "hot dog" of a runner. As the pitcher started to ascend the mound, this daring runner shouted words at the pitcher, darted off the base too far, daring him to try to pick him off again.

The shortstop shaded over toward second base, to chase the runner back. When the shortstop returned to his normal position again, the runner came off base again - this time, too far. As the shortstop moved back to his position this trick play began.

On cue, the second baseman broke for second base, but the pitcher didn't make any move to pickoff. The short throw from the centerfielder came booming in to the second baseman covering. The surprised runner was out by one long step. There the ball was, waiting for him. He then stared in the direction the ball came from - center-field. What a shocked look on the base runner's face as the base umpire raised his right arm in a jerking motion, saying "Yer out."

Let's see now. That defensive pickoff play involved the following positions in this order: Pitcher, second base, centerfielder, second base, pitcher, short stop, second base, centerfielder. Complicated?? Yes, but well rehearsed by master actors. So - one day in 1893 this strange pickoff play was engineered and made to work, knowing that the fast base runner would lose track of where the ball was.

Stu told Granddad Samuel Southworth that, if he ever was a baseball coach, he'd be sure to try that "intentional overthrow pickoff play" - pitcher to second base. In fact, many years later, following this not forgotten promise, Stu's team rehearsed this odd play religiously, and actually made it work successfully twice in three seasons. Each time it worked, Stu could but smile - a great big one - recalling his old grandfather teaching a little very tricky baseball defense - that night in St. Louis.

On this last visit the recently commissioned Ensign (USNR) would ever have with Sam (the last time the man born in 1849 would see his grandson, born in 1925), the two men had retired to the big barn of a living room, and they enjoyed their baseball and Navy talk, far into the evening.

Stu found that some of Samuel Southworth's baseball memorabilia were centered around "famous boners made by big league ball players which have lived on to haunt them, making them notorious." Sam must have enumerated ten or more of these "goofs" made by the "goats" of the game, to his young grandson.

Throughout the years the following incidents stick out in the mind of the baseball listener (and future coach of the game, now over 60 years of age) more memorably than others. Listen and sympathize with the men of the diamond who pulled these "mental errors," unwittingly.

BASEBALL STORY NUMBER 15 - 1896 MARKLE JOINED THE 1908 NATIONAL LEAGUE PENNANT CELEBRATION RATHER PREMATURELY. HOW "DE-BASING"

OR

WE WONDER IF MR. MERKLE ATTENDED THE 1908 CHICAGO CUBS-DETROIT TIGERS WORLD SERIES?

BASEBALL HISTORY, THROUGH ITS THIRTEEN decades of professional play, is filled with players' names made famous by a particular "unusual boner" stunt, gesture, or misreading of the official rules of the game.

Fred Merkle's 1908 boner in not running to second base to finish the inning, or Mickey Owen's dropped third strike in 1941, are two of the most mentioned incidents through the years. But there are many others.

Merkle was guilty, while running first base to second base as the winning run was scoring for his New York Giants, of not completing his run to second base, opting to veer toward the celebration and the club-house instead. If he had done his job correctly as base runner, his Giants would have won the pennant and been in the World Series of 1908. As it turned out, that game ended a tie, was continued next day, and the Giants lost. The Giants then lost their last five games, allowing the Chicago Cubs to win the National League Pennant. What a costly mental error was made on that one play!

Although this famous "goof" was practically unheard of until 1908, we are reminded that it occurred several times in earlier years - one in 1896 - we will relate from a Louisiana ballpark.

The situation was the same. Men were on first and second bases, the winning run being the second base runner. The home club, in their final at bats, singled in the winning run, but as the hitter reached and touched first base, after his base hit, that first base runner became so excited over the win that he veered from his running path to second base. Instead, the unfortunate fellow headed for the clubhouse or the celebration on the field, wherever the team was assembled. He never did touch second base. When the outfielder who had fielded the base hit picked the winning hit up in his

We wonder if Mr. Merkle attended
the 1908 Chicago Cubs-Detroit Tigers
World Series?"

glove, he instinctively threw to his cutoff or relay man, the shortstop. The shortstop then went over and touched second base. That created the third out of the inning.

In the official rule book of baseball it clearly says that all runners must touch their next base before a final base hit can score a winning run. NO RUN CAN SCORE WHILE A FORCE OUT IS BEING MADE FOR THE THIRD OUT.

So, we don't know who won the Louisiana game after that boner, but we do know the game went into extra innings. But the whole darned world sure remembers who won that Giant game in 1908.

✪   ✪   ✪   ✪   ✪

The next morning Stuart took a cab to the old Shenandoah Avenue building. He didn't know then that this would be the last time he would see his grandpa Sam. Stu was 20, barely, still just a youngster, and his grandfather had 76 years on him. Although the hour was very early, Sam was sitting in his rocker in the bay window anticipating Stu's last goodby.

The three Southworths, Stuart, Mae and Sam, had something warm to drink, for it was a bitterly cold morning in late November, but they did not breakfast together that day. While drinking his coffee slowly, Samuel told his young Ensign grandson how proud of him he was, but, more than this, the old man was perceptive enough to see that, in his grandson's only two visiting periods to him and St. Louis, Stu had become fascinated in every detail of the many baseball bits of history of that game shared with him by the old man.

Then Sam said something which deeply affected Stuart for the remainder of his life, in these words, "Stuart, we've shared lots of great and funny moments of the past in this grand old game. I hope you'll remember them all and pass them on to your children and others who will enjoy them." Old Sam had no way of knowing the number of athletes that Stu Southworth would coach in baseball through the years to come. Over 1000 young men, he passed on many of Sam's stories among.

Sam took out from his desk drawer a packet, a sheaf of papers that he had been saving. He wanted to give them to Stu to keep. Stu could tell from the manner in which he handed them to him, they must be most special to Sam. They looked pretty old, for the edge of the notebook paper written on was brown with age. Stu sipped his cocoa and wondered what could be so important to be kept this long in that top drawer of the old keyhole desk.

When Stuart opened the papers and read the title of the front sheet, he could see that Sam had saved one last great baseball story for Stu. It was entitled "THE GEM OF HIS CAREER - DAN O'ROURKE'S LAST BASEBALL PLAY." Sam then explained to the young Naval officer that it was an account that he had heard of years ago, just after the turn of the century, and it involved a town team coach (actually the ADAMS MILL COMPANY team) in a little burg in New York state who discovered "how to steal second base with the bases loaded" in baseball. Stu's brow showed a questioning frown when he heard that last statement from his grandpa. He didn't really understand how this trick could be performed in the game of baseball, and Sam just howled, really chuckled when he could see the look of puzzlement on Stu's countenance. "Read this story, and you'll see how, son. It's possible. I really don't know why the big leaguers don't use this play." He wanted to tell Stu all about oldtime coach Dan O'Rourke, but he told him to read it slowly before he left. How could grandpa have known that Stu would even be a baseball coach in less than five years time from that date, or that he would be using this very play described in the 1898 story handed to the young man to read? A full account of granddad's last baseball adventure in story form is here revealed.

His last play (stealing second base with
the bases loaded.)

BASEBALL STORY NUMBER 16 - 1898
THE "GEM" OF MANAGER DAN O'ROURKE'S COACHING CAREER
OR
HIS LAST PLAY (STEALING SECOND BASE WITH THE BASES LOADED)

THE EVOLUTION OF THE OFFENSIVE PLAYS OF BASEBALL IN THE COACHING CAREER OF DAN O'ROURKE, BASEBALL COACH, (FROM 1895 TO 1898) "THE GEM OF HIS CAREER - DAN O'ROURKE'S LAST PLAY"

In 1895, there lived a big Irishman named Dan O'Rourke. This man of 6' 4" height and 210 pounds weight had played some baseball as a boy. But now we see him as an adult mill worker, tough as nails, married, a solid employee who played Saturday and Sunday baseball. Dan O'Rourke was the coach of the ADAMS COMPANY MILL baseball team. We begin this trip through four seasons of time to discover what Dan learned about the offensive part of baseball and exactly how it came to him. How much and how fast did his knowledge grow?

Remember that the industries of that day, as well as each small town large enough to support it, each fielded a baseball team, for this new sport was rapidly gaining popularity, especially in Abner Doubleday's home state. These industrial or town teams were very, very competitive.

The townspeople and plant managers took great pride in their teams, the attendance was good, and feeling ran high at each game — in fact, on each of the plays of the game.

Now that we have set the scenario for the next four seasons, we look on the first day that Dan was the coach of the ADAMS COMPANY MILL team of eighteen men. To Dan, being coach was a great challenge and a real honor. But this man lacked experience in the role of coach. He had only played the game for other coaches.

Dan's only offensive strategy that he used, or knew, was HIT AWAY. He would use the sign, RUB ONE HAND ON ONE OF HIS HIPS, whenever he wanted this to be done. We can say that this was Dan's first offensive technique taught to his players. Hit to get on base, then hit the runners in. That's all you needed to do to win, to produce runs, wasn't it, Dan? Right? WRONG! Soon Dan found that not all of his hitters were good, reliable batsmen with runners on base. Some couldn't "hit water with a paddle if they were in a canoe." Dan sure did scratch his head a lot at home those first few months, wondering what he could do to add to his offensive attack.

Well, in his next four years of baseball coaching and managership, Daniel O'Rourke managed to discover and uncover all of the twenty-eight plays for offensive baseball. The young red-headed coach did not discover them, however, necessarily in a certain order. Month by month, Dan would use his baseball diamond as a laboratory, trying the timings of the various plays with his batter and/or runners. Then he would try them in the next games.

NEEDLESS TO SAY, IT WAS NOT LONG BEFORE THE ADAMS MILL COMPANY BASEBALL CLUB BECAME A POTENT SCORING MACHINE (ALMOST SCORING AT WILL) AND THIS CONTINUED DURING THE SEASONS OF 1896-1897-1898.

DAN O'ROURKE WAS NOW 29 YEARS OLD, A HEALTHY, ROBUST FAMILY MAN, AND HIS LIFE WAS COMPLETE AS A MILL FOREMAN AND A "BASE-BALL COACH EXTRAORDINAIRE." A YEAR LATER, AT THE TENDER AGE OF 30, WE ARE SADDENED TO INFORM YOU BASEBALL FANS AND READERS THAT DAN DIED OF AN UNKNOWN CAUSE — SOME STRANGE MALADY. JUST AT THE END OF HIS LAST YEAR AS MILL COACH, DAN CAME UP WITH THE "GEM OF HIS CAREER." HE CALLED IT THE "DELAY STEAL-BASES LOADED." This last play of his life, Dan developed quite by accident, as many of his creations had been born. THIS IS TODAY KNOWN AS BASEBALL'S "WEIRDEST PLAY" OF OFFENSE. IT FEEDS ON THE "COMPLETE ELEMENT OF SURPRISE."

One day, while kicking back and resting at home, Dan was asking himself if there might not be another possible running play which he might have overlooked in his four years as coach. He thought he had discovered and tried them all. With pencil and paper, he sat down to sketch the baseball diamond as he had done before. He loaded the bases on the field sketch and peered at it, wondering if there might not be a different timing for a TRIPLE STEAL. The thought shot through his brain in a flash. Of course, just combine the standard TRIPLE STEAL with the concept of DELAY STEALS. Putting two and two together, he came up with this absolute "WEIRDO." He noted, when bases are loaded, there were so few things a coach could call! Teams almost had to wait for the runners to be knocked in by base hits. So, he asked himself this provocative question: "What is the very last thing another team would expect you to pull on them with bases loaded?" The "ridiculous answer" shot back in this form: "They do not expect a first base runner to try to steal second. Of course not!!" Second base is already occupied. What a dumb move!! But the opponent would be completely baffled if you did it. What would they do? The next day, the play was born - it went from a piece of paper to the diamond laboratory again. They tried it ten times and scored a run and a catcher's triple steal on it - each time they tried. Dan wondered if any coach in the past had tried something so "counter to good baseball." But what is good baseball? Anything that works well!

This is how the play worked. Dan had the first base runner run hard down to second base, head down, and get within 25 feet of the base, then look up, look real shocked to see his teammate standing on second base. The second base runner yells at the dumb first base runner, "Get back, get back, I"m here."

To the spectator watching this play, it seems that "all hell breaks loose" on the diamond, particularly around second base. The startled first base runner and the second base runner"s yelling "unnerve the defense." The catcher is now holding the ball and is wondering what to do. The defense, never having seen this maneuver before, reacts in exactly the wrong manner. Since two runners are near second base, and the baseman down there is yelling for the ball, it looks like they might tag both runners for a double play. THE CATCHER FIRES TO THE SECOND BASE AREA. AND THAT IS HIS FATAL ERROR! The diversion at second base by the two runners has been created for the benefit of the third base runner to score. This third base runner has edged off his base just enough to be safe. As the ball leaves the catcher's hand toward second base, the third base runner breaks for home, sliding. He beats the return throw home from the second base area. As the throw starts home from second base, the second base runner, who has stayed close or on the bag up to that point, breaks for third, stealing that base, sliding. the original "dumb" first base runner is already twenty feet from second, so he moves a few steps and steals second.

WHEN THE DUST CLEARS AND TWO THROWS HAVE BEEN MADE, THE OFFENSE HAS SCORED A RUN, STOLEN HOME, STOLEN THREE BASES, AND DEFENSE HAS NOT GOTTEN ANY RUNNER OUT.

Yes, whoever heard of stealing second base with the bases loaded? Only Dan O'Rourke, our Irish redhead, could dream up such a weird one!

REST IN PEACE, COACH DANIEL. WHAT FUN YOU AND YOUR TEAMS HAVE HAD ON THOSE BASES!!

It was time for Stuart to take his leave, to head to the West coast and find out where his ship was operating. Was it in Pearl Harbor or in the South Pacific area?

The young Ensign bent down to hug Sam around the long white hair on his neck, and Stu planted a firm kiss on that right cheek (the cheek an 11 year old, years ago, that had felt the cold biting wind at Springfield, Illinois). That January morning of 1861, while young Sam went high on his dad's shoulders to get a last glimpse of their favorite son, Abraham Lincoln, stepping aboard his Inaugural train to Washington, D.C. Just as it was Springfield's last look at Lincoln, so it was Stu's last look at grand-dad Samuel Southworth.

Five years later Stuart was married to a brunette coed at the University of Washington in Seattle. They had been married for three years, and their one year old boy, Michael Stuart, was their pride and joy. Ensign Harold S. Southworth was recalled into the Korean conflict, leaving the two loved ones behind for a long year. Shortly after landing elements of the First United States Marines at the beach at Inchon, Korea, on September 15, 1950, now Lt. (jg) Stu Southworth learned of his granddad Sam's death. Will had written the sad news to Stu, that Sam had died in St. Louis, at the age of 101 years.

That long Korean winter, standing the long watches, day and night, on the conning tower of that USS LST 715 ship, Stu often recalled his two visits with his granddad, and he recounted the wonderful baseball lore passed down in so many unusual accounts of days gone by on the diamonds of America.

It was during that long period that Stu Southworth decided to be a "master collector" (and teller of) baseball's most unusual happenings throughout the history of the game. And, to this day, he has continued to do so. This very collection of fifty-two tales from thirteen decades of baseball attests to this.

PART TWO

Baseball's Greatest Moments 1900 - 1940

Narrator of Baseball Tales:

WILLIAM D. SOUTHWORTH
(1895 - 1976)

THE SECOND NARRATOR DISCOVERS SAN DIEGO, CALIFORNIA JUNE, 1929

IF THE CASUAL OBSERVER WERE to have viewed the large crowd at the ticket line on that August Sunday afternoon at San Diego's Lane field, he would have seen a rather tall gentleman with a pinstriped suit, straw hat, and a cravat tie. As this silver-haired man of 43 years purchased his game ticket, he would find his favorite seat above the field level over near the first base area. When seated in this particular spot, the good "Padre" fan would look about in the crowd for several of his good baseball buddies, for he had a real entourage who attended these games with him. They were always seated together in this area of the grandstands.

On this particular Sunday afternoon in 1938 the tall observer, Will Southworth, as his immediate family referred to him, found Abe Stolzoff, a Jewish co-worker and acquaintance, and soon they were in a discussion of the main topics of the day - most notably the San Diego "Padres," who were about to take the field against "JoJo" White's red hot Seattle "Rainiers". The Padres were doing quite well that season, and attendance was high at each game.

From this point on in this story let's refer to Will Southworth as Bill, for that is the name that his former wife, Hazel, liked to call him, as well as his nieces and nephews. "Uncle Bill" was one of their favorite relatives on his yearly St. Louis visits. Bill had been born in 1895 in St. Louis to Samuel and Emma (McKinney) Southworth. Living in a German section of that large city, the young Bill attended the grammar school then on to junior and senior high schools near his home. Young Bill had worked long hard hours in a grocery and meat market near his high school, and, upon graduation from the 12th grade, wanted no more of it. The young Southworth had become fascinated in electrical apparatus, so he took a good job with the Maloney Electric Company of St. Louis, for two years prior to World War I.

Soon Bill was a 23 year old private in Uncle Sam's "I Want You" Army, headed for the trenches of France. Emerging unscathed from this "War To End All Wars," this soldier came home victorious, only to suffer the loss of his precious Mother, Emma, from the flu of 1919's epidemic. The loss of Emma hit the family very hard, and Bill was soon leaving St. Louis to attend the Kansas State Teacher's College, Pittsburg, Kansas, from 1920 to 1924. This World War I veteran took advantage of the "GI Bill" (as it was offered at that time), so in the Spring of 1924, Bill Southworth not only graduated as an electrical engineer from Pittsburg, but he also wed his college sweetheart, Hazel Bolinger, a farm girl from nearby Fort Scott, Kansas. The two of them rode the "interurban," a "Toonerville Trolley" type of single car train (used to haul mail, milk cans, and people between the larger towns of that part of Kansas) getting off at Independence, Kansas, for the marriage ceremony - in the parsonage at the Methodist church there.

The newlyweds lived in Joplin, Missouri, and there Bill took his first good position in the power plant of Joplin. On to Dallas, Texas, and the young engineer advanced to a better position in a substation.

With the arrival of their only child, Harold Stuart, April 19, 1925, at Dallas, the marriage "went on the rocks" and was soon dissolved. The ex-wife, Hazel, trained to teach elementary schools, took her six month old baby, Stuart, and began a long tenure of teaching in the western Kansas town of Liberal. She and the child stayed in that community until 1941, a period of sixteen years.

With the divorce settled, Bill then tended to roam a lot, holding down several jobs in various cities. Jobs at Dallas, Denver, several other cities did not seem to satisfy this Veteran and father. Each year he did write Hazel, asking that they spend a couple of weeks in Denver in order that he could see Hazel and the boy. And so the three Southworths enjoyed each other, yearly, in the Rocky Mountain scenery.

Health problems (primarily bad sinus trouble) caused Bill to seek California and an ideal spot for sinus sufferers. The great crash of 1929 left the man with little money and no job. He actually rode the freight trains West that summer, landing one hot morning in San Bernardino, California, at the foot of the steep Cajon Pass. There he was attracted to the climate, the broad valley rimmed with high mountains, so he stayed three weeks in a board and room place near downtown San Bernardino. Within one week he found that this town had little to offer the working man, except those who were in the citrus or railroad industries.

Bill moved on west to Los Angeles, didn't like any of that area, then headed south along the beach to San Diego. He had heard that the city by the big bay was a paradise. Sure enough, it was as if he had been dropped into heaven. Everything in that Navy port agreed with him, and especially the damp air. Soon Bill had gotten himself an excellent job with the San Diego Gas and Electric Company, at a power plant, but several years later moved to door-to-door selling of Real Silk Products, (a large firm in Indianapolis, Indiana). Later he sold expensive bed pillows and comforters in wealthy sections of Coronado, Imperial Valley, Phoenix, Arizona. He had an exclusive, rich clientele.

All of this while, from 1926 to 1938, his son, Stu, had grown from six months to thirteen years of age. He had managed to see Hazel and Stuart the Summer of 1935 in Wichita, Kansas, for a brief reunion. Then came time for the first trip that Stu and Bill had made together to see Granddad Sam Southworth that June of 1938. What a pleasant reunion it was for young 13 year old Stuart, finally to meet all of his Dad's side of the family. And those darned baseball stories which grandpa Sam had spun during that visit. Sam seemed to have hundreds of them saved from years past. They served not only to cement the grandfather-grandson bond, but the old man had stimulated Stu's interest in the game of baseball.

That hot August afternoon Bill Southworth was reminiscing all of these things in his mind as he was half-heartedly discussing baseball and some politics with congenial Abe Stolzoff, his super salesman friend. Abe and Bill were born salesmen and excellent in door-to-door saleswork.

It was now time for the game batteries to be announced, and soon the first pitch was thrown to Seattle's leadoff hitter, a lightning fast runner. As that cagey leadoff batter worked the count to three balls and one strike, an odd thing occurred down at home plate. Bill, Abe, and the crowd were treated to a real rarity in baseball. The incident brought down the house.

The baseball uniforms of that era were rather baggy, not close fitting to the body at all, and some players wore their belts somewhat looser than others did. Flannel shirts were tucked in loosely at the beltline.

Ball four was delivered to the hitter. No one knows how it happened, but the last pitch, thrown away inside, popped out of the catcher's mitt, rolled up on the chest of the batter dodging away, then rolled down into his pant leg, settling way down at the elastic band where the socks were held up. The ball was held in there by elastic only. On ball four called, the hustling leadoff man trotted down to the first base while the dazed catcher looked for the ball. He looked everywhere around the plate. No ball to be found. The umpire joined the search. While the search was on, the runner at first sprinted for second, would have gone further had it not been for the umpire's yelling "Time out," throwing up his hands. At this moment the catcher realized that the ball must be on the person of that little leadoff hitter. He appealed for a search of his person. A somber procession of catcher and umpire marched side by side to the second base, and a frisking procedure ensued. The ball was soon discovered at the bottom of those baggy pants. The crowd was at first wondering what was happening down there on that diamond, but they soon caught on, and, when the ball rolled on the ground, after the elastic was opened up, pandemonium reigned. The crowd had mixed emotions, with anger, surprise, but the laughter didn't die down for several minutes. What a way to begin a ball game. Oh man! The old "hidden ball trick," but this time it was pulled by the team at bat. That was sure a new one.

The umpire ordered the runner back to first base, and the play resumed. Many years ago, near the turn of the century, the rule was changed that, if a ball was caught up in the clothing or lodged on the person of a base runner, that runner and all other runners advanced only one base.

Bill Southworth wondered how many times this scene had been reenacted on a baseball diamond. Then, when the confusion died down, Bill turned to Abe and related a story told him by Sam, his dad, years and years ago. Strangely, it was a tale of almost the same parade of events. Incidentally, the next Seattle hitter rattled the boards out on the centerfield fence with a stand up triple, scoring that cagey leadoff hitter who had tried to hide the ball. (I suppose that first runner would have come all the way around the bases and scored, if the umpire hadn't called "time"?)

BASEBALL STORY NUMBER SEVENTEEN - 1902
THAT LOGGING CAMP BASERUNNER CERTAINLY
"CARRIED THINGS WAY TOO FAR"
OR
IS THIS AN "OFFENSIVE HIDDEN BALL TRICK?"

AT THE TURN OF THE century, the mining and logging communities and camps of the Idaho panhandle were represented by pretty fair to middlin' baseball teams. In fact, each of them vied for the college talent, far and wide, who were willing to work four or five hard days, practice a couple of times a week after work, and play Saturday and Sunday games before large vehement crowds of people.

On one occasion the lumbering town of St. Maries was engaged in an important contest with the miners of Kellogg - both Idaho towns boasting the best team of the year in that league, the year being 1902. Each of these communities were "rough spots". The battle went on in the heat of that Summer afternoon until the bottom of the seventh inning. Kellogg, the home club, came to bat trailing by a score of 3-1. The St. Maries pitcher was the better of the two, and he had been mowing down Kellogg batters in rapid succession. But in the seventh inning this superb pitcher had the bases loaded on a walk, a single, and a walk. Up to the plate stepped the best Kellogg bunter, a Bart Gibbon. Now Bart shouldn't have been bunting, two runs down, in the seventh, with bases loaded. On the first pitch he surprised the whole ballpark, trickling a little squibber bunt about halfway to first base, right on the line.

The St. Maries first baseman fielded the bunt, reaching into the path (between the chalk lines) of runner Bart Gibbon. Bart hesitated to run into the tag for a second or two, then proceeded. He slightly collided with the first baseman on the tag movement inside the runner's legal base lane. At the moment of collision, the baseman reached in to tag Bart up high on his shirt, above the letters. The ball jarred loose and bounced a short distance up in the air after the tag, so the umpire then signalled "Safe". That darned baseball also came down quickly inside Bart Gibbon's uniform, which shirt was gaping open, as he was tagged. No one viewing the play, the baseman or the umpire could possibly see where the ball finally wound up after the collision. BUT BART FELT THE BALL INSIDE HIS SHIRT.

Of course, one run had scored on the bunt, but the runner who had been on second was now scoring while the defense was looking around for the "phantom" ball. Still no one could spot where the ball was. Had it been kicked hard by the runner or

defensive baseman to the sidelines?

The runner who had stood on first base at the start of this strange play, now he scored, giving Kellogg the lead momentarily, 4-3.

Since Bart Gibbon realized from the start that the ball was lodged on his person, he nonchalantly circled the bases, touching home plate with the fourth run of the play. Lord, this was just like hitting a grand slam home run! Four runs batted in? The play ended with the score now 5-3.

Upon crossing home plate, Bart Gibbon reached inside his baggy shirt, extracted the ball, handed it to the plate umpire, exclaiming, in a most surprised tone, "Oh God, here the ball is. It must have dropped into my shirt after the collision near first base. Here, ump, take it."

Actually, Bart should have kept it and had it signed by his team members in remembrance of this wacky occurrence. But he gave up the ball.

After the worst rhubarb in baseball that Idaho's panhandle has ever seen, brought on by the umpire's ruling "All runs score. The defense is responsible to know where the ball is at all times," the game was then resumed, with neither team scoring in the eighth or ninth innings.

Readers should know that this could not happen in modern baseball. Soon after this incident, rules committees met to change the rule to read "If a ball gets hung up in the clothing or on the person of a batter or runner during a play, runner or batter are allowed one base only, the one which they are proceeding to."

One Saturday afternoon several weeks later, Bill Southworth was comfortably seated on his rented cushion at the same seat in Lane Field, surrounded by five die-hard baseball associates.

Lane Field was built backed up against a triangular building with barely enough between the two for a spur railroad track to run down to the harbor's edge. In this odd shaped corner building was a big fish market, with several other fish markets right down on water's edge. It was close to a big pier where many fishing boats were tied up.

There have been, down through the thirteen decades of baseball, many wild tales of the game involving or centered around the antics of a dog. One of those fish markets owned a big brown dog, breed unknown. Several of the Portuguese and Italian fishing boat owners also kept dogs aboard, breeds also unknown. Games were too often inter-rupted by a stray dog - or many dogs in a pack. In fact, the management of Lane Field had not repaired the big vertical boards making up the outfield fences. Several holes could be seen at the base of these barriers large enough to admit a curious dog of a smaller size. Or, occasionally, a canine would tear right past one of the ball parks' gatekeepers, into the grandstands, and was soon out on the field cavorting around.

Recalling granddad Sam Southworth's tale of the earliest St. Louis baseball game of 1861 (broken up by the ball ending up in the mouth of a Union soldier's playful dog) we must again be reminded of a dog's natural bent to retrieve something the shape of a ball, grab it in its mouth, then play keepaway with any and all chasers.

Well, Bill Southworth and the five cohorts had just settled down to enjoy the first half inning of the game on that cool day. The rivals were the Padres versus the

Portland Beavers. Out of nowhere emerged this big brown dog from the fish market adjacent to Lane Field. The dog found a loose ball, just rolling loose from a Portland player warming up on the sidelines.

Of course, into the dog's mouth went that white baseball, whereupon he circled the bases and the field before coming to rest up on the top of the pitcher's mound, sitting with his paws on the rubber, the hind legs behind the slab. His head and ears were erect, and the dog was peering at home plate. He could almost have been mistaken for the starting pitcher.

Bill, his cohorts, all the Lane Field crowd were again amused by a "dog act," but more at the resting spot the animal had chose, and, before the groundskeeper could chase away that specimen, a San Diego Union photographer ran out within twenty feet of the sitting dog and snapped a good shot. It was a great pose and found its was into the sports section the next morning.

Finally two groundskeepers caught the big dog, trying to remove the ball from the huge mouth. It was finally pried loose by one of them, amidst a chorus of cheers, boos, and catcalls. Bill's friends gathered around were really surprised to hear him laughing at the top of his voice, shortly after the whole incident was resolved, and the team was taking the field for the first inning of play. Before his pals could quiz Bill about his delayed humorous reaction to the dog chase, he told them that the brown dog reminded him of a great baseball story his father, Sam, had laid on him when Bill was around seven years old. This tale wasn't about a baseball in a dog's mouth, but actually featured an innovative player who had to carry a baseball in his mouth - all the way into the mouth, held tight by his teeth. "Oh, come on, Bill," they doubted him in saying, "Why would a ball player want to do such a thing in a ball game?" Bill started, "Well, actually, it was way up north in the state of Maine, it was." Bill added, "In the year 1902. (The ball was hit into a shallow river near the ball park..) The case of an outfielder who shagged a long fly ball and swam with it - in his big mouth." They roared with laughter, chiming in together, "Oh, Bill, that Maine ballplayer must have had a big mouth."

But the pals weren't laughing after Bill told them all the details of that big day in Northern Maine.

After this session of hilarity from an old baseball story, up to the plate, in San Diego's Lane Field, steps the one and only Lou Novikoff, for the Los Angeles "ANGELS," the hitter was better known in that era as the "Mad Russian". Boy, could he get mad, and could he get beet red. He was a newly obtained outfielder for L.A., usually in left field. A trademark of Lou's was this - after a catch of a fly ball (with no runners on base) he would quickly "underhand" the baseball (yeah, underhand) to the cutoff or relay man. Lou had been discovered a few years earlier in Orange County (somewhere near Santa Ana or Anaheim) hitting softballs in "fast pitch," out of sight! Several were measured over 450' in distance from home plate! So the Chicago Cubs (and Mr. Wrigley) signed him to their CLASS "AAA" Pacific Coast League farm club, Los Angeles "ANGELS". It was hoped that he would develop into the Chicago Cubs cleanup man, their long-awaited home run hitter.

The Mad Russian chose the fourth pitch thrown to him to swing from the heels. Good Lord, thought Bill Southworth, a line drive shot into the left field stands. However, the San Diego outfielder, fleet afoot and very agile, an athlete in every sense, took off on the crack of the bat, never stopped for the low 3' fence, separating the fans from the left field area, dived into that bleacher crowd, as if into a swimming pool. In midair he caught the ball, after it had left the field, or beyond the actual plane of the left field barrier, landing on a hard bleacher seat. He also jumped back over the fence, fired the ball with an accurate throw to his relay man, and was wildly cheered, as Lou Novikoff pompously did his slow "home run trot". The plate umpire saw it all and yelled "yet out" as Lou reached home. He informed the slugger that his fly had been caught. The Los Angeles Angels manager and Lou Novikoff were both "hopping mad".

They both followed the umpire around a few minutes, called him bad names, argued the ball was out of the park when caught, and, in general, both ended up booted from the game. When we say "hopping mad," we mean just that! For, you see, Lou Novikoff had this strange habit, similar to a child that has been told "NO". Lou would not only argue, scream, turn beet red, etc. HE WOULD ACTUALLY STAND IN HIS TRACKS AND JUMP OFF THE GROUND SEVERAL FEET, CONTINUALLY LIKE A SPRING TOY, WHILE YELLING WITH THE UMP. This had to be one of the funniest demonstrations every seen on a ball diamond. Each jump must have been at least two to three feet off the ground, requiring a tremendous expenditure of energy. The man would literally wear himself out for the next inning's play.

But the umpire's call stood — "YER OUT, LOU". FLY WAS CAUGHT. Now we know why this fabled character of 1940's Pacific Coast League baseball was called the "MAD RUSSIAN".

Bill Southworth, now taken over as the "designated Southworth story teller of baseball oddities," then told his cronies nearby, a story of the year 1903, narrated to him years before, by his father, Samuel.

Bill actually told two tales of this type. In one, the umpire called the home run hitter out on the hit beyond the outfield wall. In the other case, the umpire signalled "Home Run," and missed the call badly, for the outfielder was practically sitting in the bleacher seats with his glove ready for the descending ball to plop into it. He could have been eating a bag of peanuts with one hand and caught the fly ball with the other.

BASEBALL STORY NUMBER EIGHTEEN - 1902 SHOWMAN ERIC BURNS WAS THE KIND OF OUTFIELDER WHO "HAD HIS FEET ON THE GROUND" OR PERHAPS ERIC WANTED TO SEE A HOME RUN FROM A SPECTATOR'S ANGLE

THE BASEBALL PARK AT VALLEY view in the season of 1902 was the pride of the village and country — well-planned, well-built, no skimping on materials or labor in putting that park together, fenced all the way around, with an up to date grandstand, holding well over 1000 baseball fans, and having a long protruding overhang on the roof for good shade on those hot Summer days.

The planners, however, made one major error. The outfield fence was built only 4' high, with a walkway and short rising bleachers on the other side of the mini-fence.

The first few months after Valley View's model ballpark was completed, there were several instances where home run balls were caught for outs by hustling outfielders. The fielder had to reach over that low fence to catch the ball, when it had actually left the playing field by three or four feet. In two of those sparkling plays, the defensive man had dived over the fence and caught the ball on the fly - "the ball was flying and so were those fielders". In those two cases, the fielders landed after the ball was caught. One day early in the season, one big outfielder landed in the laps of a gentleman and his lady, but missed holding on to the ball. How embarrassing to land in the laps of fans and still miss the catch. The man and woman had just gotten themselves seated, with beer in one's hand, a bag of peanuts in the other's hand. When the big fielder returned over the fence to the playing field, he was wet with beer and covered with peanut shells. Of course, he was yelled at and cursed some by those two fans, but all others sitting around them lauded the man's hustle and sparkling play - even if he did drop the ball in his sail over that four foot barrier.

The question now arises, "If the out is made by any outfielder going over the fence, out of the playing field, must he return quickly to the outfield, throw the ball in, if the runners tagged up on a fly ball and were allowed to proceed to the next base after the catch?" The umpires in those two 1902 instances ruled that the ball was dead, since it had left the field, even if it was a caught fly and an out. Dead ball rule.

Perhaps Eric wanted to see a homerun
from a spectator's angle.

The Valley View coaches knew that one day this would lead to a very important and deciding call in a close game. It did, and quite soon. Valley View was playing the town of Hardin late in the season. The score stood 6-3 for Valley View. Late in that game the Hardin hitters loaded the bases, and up to bat came their eighth hitter. The pitcher had easily disposed of this poor hitter, Radford, twice before, and he saw no cause for being especially cautious this time, even with the bases full. The Valley View chucker "hung a terrible curve ball" to Mr. Radford.

This poor hitter straightened out the pitch, and away it flew, wind blown some, into those low left field seats.

Now Valley View had a clever left fielder by the name of Eric Burns. Eric, fearing that this might happen at this point in the game, saw the ball headed for the low seats, and he planned his leap, but somewhat prematurely. HIS FEET TOUCHED THE WIDE WALKWAY IN FRONT OF THE BLEACHERS A SECOND OR TWO BEFORE THE BALL WAS SNAGGED IN THE AIR IN HIS GLOVE. Then Eric Burns made no effort to quickly return the ball to play in the form of a long and hard throw to the relay man. Therefore, all the runners tagged up and advanced one base after they saw the ball was a catch.

The nearest umpire signalled out on the catch, then he allowed all runners to advance their one base apiece. THAT UMPIRE MADE TWO GROSS MISCALLS ON ONE PLAY. The ball should have been ruled "HOME RUN" by the umpire calling the play, since Eric Burns jumped that fence before the ball was caught. His foot or feet touched that walkway before the ball touched his glove as it was caught. No play should have been allowed then.

The second error the umpire made in judging the call was this - the rule book at that time stated that, if a catch carried the defensive man out of the playing area, it was a dead ball until it was returned to the pitcher. Hardin lost the game, eventually, but, after that one inning the score should have stood 7-6 in their favor. The ball should have been "grand slam home run" and the catch disallowed.

It was the summer of 1940, as Stuart Southworth recalled years later, he had another year of growth, was now 15 years old, and was, by this time, getting better and better in all phases of the total game of baseball. Beside that, he had met "Solly" Hemus three years earlier. Solly had taken him under his wing and really made him learn how to hit fastballs, curves, drops, and knuckleballs - in their weekly "Over The Line" marathon games.

Solly and Stuart caddied (as well as hunting golf balls and selling them to players right there on the golf course) at the Balboa Municipal Golf Club course. In fact, the golf course was adjacent to the baseball parks.

After that summer of 1941, Stu Southworth was becoming quite a dangerous hitter in the lineup, playing summer league game on Saturdays.

In Class AAA Pacific Coast league ball, the Los Angeles Angels were very classy that year, and "Ripper" Collins led the LA pack into Lane Field one Sunday afternoon. Bill and Stu found their usual seats in the first base area at Lane Field, but this day they saw a new face among all of Bill Southworth's ballpark cronies. The middle aged man was from Long Beach, California, just up the Pacific Coast (and a relative of one of Bill's baseball friends gathered about him). After the man was introduced to the group near Bill Southworth, this fellow, in the course of the conversation, announced to all, "Yeah, I was a semi-pro baseball player in the Long Beach area for quite a few years. Recently, our finest diamond was bought by a large oil company. It sat on the edge of the Signal Hill oil field there. Soon after, a crew drilled an oil well right out near second base. It came in, a big producer, too. We had to find a location and build a brand new ball field quite a way from Signal Hill there in Long Beach. No one was too happy about doing it, but we sure got a good price for the old land."

Down below, on the Padre diamond, those poor L.A. Angels were suffering another embarrassing moment. With the score 1-0 for the San Diego Padres, in the seventh inning, with a man on first and no outs, L.A. tried a sacrificed bunt. It moved the runner over to second base, was a great bunt, but when the play ended, the plate umpire suddenly yelled for all to hear, "Dead ball. Batter is out. He stepped on home plate." And he certainly had done that. All could see it plainly. The first base runner was called back to first base.

In a moment, true to form now, Bill Southworth had to tell the "classic old baseball story," as told him first by good old Sam, of the 1903 incident in the Eastern USA, where the home run hitter, with bases loaded, stepped on home plate as his home run swing connected. It was his first ever "grand slam," too. Bill's friends "oohed" and "aahed" at such a sad account of a hitter, whose hitting error cost him four runs.

BASEBALL STORY NUMBER NINETEEN - 1903
HOWARD HOLDEN HAD BEEN TOLD TO "WATCH HIS STEP" WHEN IN THE BATTER'S BOX
OR
THE DEFENSE WAS SERVED "A GIFT ON THE PLATTER" BY THE PLATE UMPIRE THAT DAY

HOWARD HOLDEN WAS A BIG farm lad who could swing a mean bat for his locals, the 1903 town team from Fall River. We have heard tales, or perhaps even seen games in person, or on television, in which the great defensive outfielder goes back, back, back, ...even climbs the fence a few steps (we have the set of cleat marks on the wood to prove it) and leaps high to catch the home run ball, ending the inning and thus saving a grand slam home run, four runs, and perhaps the old ball game. On that daring catch, the ball might have actually sailed beyond the plane of the fence and the playing field, really beyond the ballpark, but somehow that gloved hand flags down that fly ball, and ball and outfielder slide down the fence and fall to the ground, amid cheers from all the fans and his team mates, alike. Thus we relate the cases of out-fielders who take away four sure runs with a great leaping catch.

Howard Holden didn't need such heroics, by his opposing outfielder, to take away four runs from him, and his team, one day in 1903. Howard did the job himself. His act that day at the plate did the same trick. You will say, "How could a batter rob him-self of a grand slam home run?" He did just that. Listen to this account.

Howard was a late hitter, notorious for banging long hard drives to the rightfield and right centerfield. He did this all the time, for he had the bad habit of stepping over the white chalk line that defines the batter's box. His foot was on that line near the plate, or often over it. Much too close to the plate. The various umpires working the games in which he had played that season, warned him of his infraction of this rule. Howard Holden merely persisted in doing it his way.

As all bad habits do, this one caught up with Howard in a game with Millbrae late in that 1903 season. The score that warm day stood 0-0 in the fifth inning, at Millbrae. The home umpires for Millbrae were known far and wide for not being too good with visitors in their calls. We wouldn't say they were dishonest, but definitely the calls went to the home club. Sure enough, the bases were loaded, two outs, when our slug-ger, Howard Holden, stepped into the batter's box, one front foot already touching the chalk line. Howard was determined to break up the ball game with one ferocious

The defense was served "a gift on the
platter" by the plate umpire that day.

swing. On the first pitch, in fact, the cleanup hitter connected. It sounded as a cannon shot was ringing reverently through the streets of old Millbrae. Howard started his home run trot as he saw the ball drop over the right field wall. Now, this hitter was a careful base runner, certain to touch each base in order as he rounded each one.

The pitcher had fed Howard an outside pitch, a good three inches outside the plate - just where he liked them. To hit such a pitch, Howard's front foot had landed on the left half of home plate. He could feel the springy rubbery sensation on the sole of that foot, but he thought little of it in this moment of triumph. The plate umpire saw this very definite infraction of the rules of batting, and he let the four runners cross the plate, after which he turned to the crowd and both benches, declaring loudly to all, "The batter is out for stepping on home plate as he hit the ball. that is the third out. The inning is over. No runs score. The game is still a scoreless tie."

Howard Holden and the Fall River "Bears" heard this late announcement with disbelief, disgust (plotting murder of the umpire, we are sure).

Thereafter, during the game, the local Millbrae police doubled their guard in the stands and near the playing field. There were suddenly four officers patrolling and keeping the peace.

To add insult to injury, Fall River went home that day the eventual loser, 3-1.

Several weeks later, on a hot Saturday afternoon, "the Lane Field aggregation," clustered around Bill Southworth, saw the Padre cleanup hitter, Dominic D'Allesandro, hit a long home run over the right field fence, a very high fence at San Diego's park. The short but powerful Padre rounded the bases after the mighty blow, but he barely failed to touch second base. The Seattle shortstop saw this failure to touch, and so did the umpire nearby. After the home run trot was completed, and the defensive appeal play was executed, the umpire signalled to the Padre bench, "That hitter is out. Failed to touch second base. No run counts."

Manager Cedric Durst was irate, Dominic D'Allesandro was irate, Bill Southworth and his pals were irate. After the ensuing argument, still won by the base umpire, the poor umpire was wondering, "Just where do 'I-rate' with this San Diego crowd?" But it was a correct call. The cleanup hitter was still "OUT".

After Bill Southworth had recovered his aplomb, and hushed the more than "murderous mob" around him that day, he related the story of Larry Speaker, a 1905 sandlot star, whose triple was taken away from him, and so were three RBI's. Tough luck, Larry. Rules are rules in the ole ball game, buddy.

At least poor Dominic D'Allesandro was relieved of only one RBI - just himself. There was no one else on base at the time of his long homer.

BASEBALL STORY NUMBER TWENTY - 1905
THE BIG SLUGGER BELIEVED THE TRIPLE
"WAS IN THE BAG"
OR
HOW TO LOSE THREE RBI'S, A TRIPLE, AND
YOUR "BASEBALL DIGNITY" IN AN EXCITING
TIME AT BAT

LARRY SPEAKER'S WIFE AND FOUR kids were in the stands that day in 1905. This ball player stepped up to the plate to face the best fastball pitcher in the league. Larry was noted for his vicious (but late) swing from the heels. His opposing right fielder was not aware of this heavy hitter's lateness of swing, so the outfielder shaded over much too far toward centerfield. There were two outs, the home fans cheering loudly for the Larry, Larry, Larry.....

The opponent was leading in score 5-3, and Larry's team was playing a rough opponent, tough to beat on any day. On the third pitch, a one and one count on Larry Speaker, his bat found the high velocity white sphere (up high in the strike zone). Larry's solid hit was parked in the extreme right field corner, barely fair, at the base of the fence. Larry wasn't too fast afoot, but he knew that this was a stand up triple, if he put out an extra effort. That must have been what was on his mind as he swung out "down the line" to round first base, for he failed touch to first - by about six inches. He barely reached third, should have slid, but didn't. The big man was probably out of gas and too tired to drop down into a slide.

The home crowd went wild, when they saw what he had done to that outstanding fastball pitcher. Larry doffed his cap and bowed slightly to their mad cheering. Apparently the score was now 6-5 for the home club, for three runs had scored ahead of that triple of Larry's.

But wait!! Both the first baseman and second baseman (as well as the first base ump) saw Larry fail to touch first base on his dash to third. The pitcher went into his stretch, stepped off, threw to first base. As the first baseman touched the base, holding the baseball, the umpire signalled with raised arm, "The runner is out. Failed to touch first base. Inning is over, and no runs score. Game score remains 5-3."

Larry Speaker's baserunning error not only caused the end of that inning, none of the three runs scored, Larry was not credited with a base hit, and he was deprived three

How to lose three RBIs, a triple,
and your "baseball dignity"
in an exciting time at bat.

RBI's. You see, when a batter has missed first base (even with a home run with two outs) he has actually reached no base - yet. All runs are negated, if the defense sees the foot miss the base, the umpire has seen the infraction, and the appeal play is made by the defense - to the umpire.

This story has a happy ending, however, for Larry. His team went on to win the 10-8, but there was "no joy in Mudville" for awhile when Larry and the three base runners drew a blank to end that bad inning.

Larry's wife and four kids felt like "crawling under the bleachers" after their man made that offensive boo-boo, but Larry's family finally became more forgiving than did Larry's team coach - who lectured for weeks after - on the old adage "touch every base in order".

Mr. William D. Southworth, as related earlier in these accounts, was educated to become a graduate electrical engineer in 1924. His work at power plants, hydroelectric dams, electrical substations, etc., had created within the man a great respect for electricity and all things electrical. It was natural then, that when the Grand Coulee Dam was constructed on the Big Bend of the Columbia River in 1940, West of Spokane, Washington, Bill Southworth was fascinated by the size of that project and made a vow to visit it at the first possible opportunity. Any person, of course, would have been awed by a man-made object of the magnitude that is three times that of the Great Pyramids of Egypt (by far the largest structure erected by man). Over a mile of concrete barrier stretched across the flow of the mighty Columbia. The mightiest river of the western United States and furnishing enough power to transform, absolutely, the lives of all the people living in three states of that area.

By 1944 Bill's son, Stu, then turned 18 years of age, had left San Diego, for Hazel and Bill divorced a second time. The ex-wife and son moved to the city of Denver, Colorado, in February, 1943. As a freshman, Stu pitched his first year of college baseball for the University of Denver "Pioneers". He enjoyed a fine baseball season, World War II had been going on for almost two years - the United States involvement, that is. The draft caught up Stuart Southworth in the whirl of affairs on April 19th of 1943, his 18th birthday. By September he was in "boot camp" at the United States Naval Training Station, Farragut, Idaho. After twenty weeks of Quartermaster School following boot camp, Stuart found himself a Naval V-12 trainee, assigned to the unit at Whitman college, Walla Walla, Washington, and perusing a rigorous program of twenty month duration to become a Navigator of Naval surface craft, graduating as an Ensign USNR. Experts believed that the war would end around 1948 or 1949, perhaps, and only after the bloody invasion of Japan. This young man's luck was doubled at Whitman College when he was coached in baseball, Spring of 1944, by Coach "Nig" Borleske, himself a former All-American and truly a legend in the Pacific Northwest. "Nig"'s name and record as coach and player in football and baseball are now enshrined in the NAIA Hall of Fame at Kansas City, Missouri.

Stu Southworth won his first college varsity baseball game on the mound for Whitman College early in May, beating Washington State college 5-4, pitching all 14 innings of a four hour contest, in 103 degree heat and scoring the winning run, after having driven a deep double into right centerfield to lead off the 14th inning.

In about a week's time, Bill Southworth appeared in Walla Walla to visit his son and see him pitch his third game of that young season. Settling himself in the beautiful Marcus Whitman Hotel in downtown Walla Walla, Bill dropped over daily to see Stu between classes at the campus and to watch each day's baseball practice. Bill was, of course, also on his way North to see the incomparable Grand Coulee Dam for the first time.

The following Saturday morning dawned warm and clear in Walla Walla that day in mid-May. The warm wind swept across the waving wheat fields adjacent to Borleske Stadium. Stu was given the starting pitching nod that day, for Coach "Nig" knew his dad had come to see him throw for Whitman. They were scheduled to play the U.S. Army Air Force Base of Spokane, and Stu was placed to bat fifth in the batting order by Coach Borleske. He was then batting .412 early in that season. Bill Southworth had come to the stadium early, watched the teams warmup, and he had gotten acquainted with some of the spectators near him in the stands directly behind home plate - farmers, merchants, parents of other ball players, and in no time at all Bill had his usual cluster of baseball "addicts" gathered around him. For Bill was at it again, telling outlandish but true baseball tales. Just like old Sam, who was still alive that day, way back in St. Louis.

Grandpa Samuel was probably listening to his favorite St. Louis Browns or Cardinals on the radio in the rocker, looking out of that big bay window. Bill Southworth had grown to like Walla Walla, Washington, the Whitman campus, its school spirit, and he enjoyed its people to the utmost now. But he found that it surely wasn't San Diego.

In the first inning Whitman's leadoff hitter had stolen second base, after getting on base with a hard line drive single. The catcher had hardly gotten the ball out of his glove, and the speedster had stolen the base. In fact, the poor Spokane receiver didn't even bother to throw down to the base, for he knew it was stolen. One "farmer-ball fan" who never missed a Whitman game, yelled down on the field, after the steal, "Yahoo, hey, I'll bet that runner could turn around and steal first base again on the next pitch, that catcher is so slow." Another fan nearby, a Walla Walla merchant, replied to this outcry, "Hey, fellow, you know better than that. He can't even try to steal first base on the next pitch. It's against baseball's rules to run bases backwards, in reverse order."

In the second inning, a Spokane Air Force Base slugger ripped a low liner at Stu's feet. The ball missed his feet and toes, luckily, but it did catch an exposed corner of the pitcher's rubber. (Nig Borleske, the Whitman Missionaries' baseball coach, had told that darned groundskeeper to pack dirt evenly, up to the level of the pitcher's rubber - but he did it only within a few inches of the top of the rubber, leaving the corner exposed to the flight of the low liner).

The baseball, ripped hard and low - caught the corner of the rubber, veered off to the left and into the air slightly. The shortstop caught the ball, on the fly, but the ball was still a grounder, and had to be thrown to first base to get the out. The runner was safe by a mile, for the soft fly came down into the glove of the shortstop much too late for a throw at all.

Shortly after this freak "grounder-fly incident," Bill Southworth recounted to that crowd of wheat farmers and Whitmanites a choice tale of a 1911 baseball game he had seen in Southern Missouri, when he was barely 16 (ending the game with a freak play similar to that witnessed just moments ago below on Borleske Field). The 1911 deflected "grounder-fly" had won the game for the home club.

BASEBALL STORY NUMBER TWENTY-ONE - 1911
HOW COULD A HARD GROUNDER SUDDENLY BECOME A FLY BALL
OR
THAT HARD "GROUNDER-FLY" SURE SET A RECORD FOR "HANG TIME," AND SCORED TWO RBI's TO BOOT

ONE DAY IN THE 1911 season, a baseball game was coming into the ninth inning on a diamond in a southern Missouri town. The score was close, and the home club, behind in the score, got the bases loaded. In fact, the winning run was standing on second base, with two outs. A good base hit would score the tying and winning run. Just a good solid single was all that was needed.

Up to the plate in this situation was the team's weakest hitter. The ninth hitter in the lineup, a fellow by the name of Jim Derryberry. He was hitless in the game, to this point. On the second pitch, this exceptionally inept hitter swung with tremendous effort - but very late. The pitch was hit so late that the ball was lined right to the front edge of first base, and it struck that hard canvas bag's upper edge in such a way to deflect the ball into a towering high fly ball. The hit was inches from being a foul ball, but all in the ballpark could see that it had been a line drive grounder-turned into a fly.

That baseball was sent into the air in such a manner that it soared directly over the pitcher's mound. In fact, the pitcher remained just motionless while standing on the rubber, waiting for it to descend. The ball hung up at its highest point of the arc for what seemed minutes to the defense. The pitcher called for the catch, and he waved his infielders, now in a circle around the base of the mound, away from the descending ball. All infielders and the pitcher (and everyone in the ballpark, staring in disbelief) waited and waited for the ball to come down.

In to score came the third base runner, to tie the game. Around third base came the winning run from second base. This second runner could see that he didn't have to hurry home, for the ball just hung up there. So he didn't hustle at all, just peered at the ball up there as he practically walked to home plate, touched it, and ended the game.

The two runners who crossed the plate on Derryberry's freak "grounder-fly hit," were celebrating with the whole team around them by the time the ball came down into the pitcher's glove.

That hard "grounder-fly" sure
set a record for "hang time,"
and scored two RBIs to boot.

To make matters even worse, the losing pitcher had to catch that airborne ground-ball. What a way to lose a baseball game. But there are so many freaky ways to lose a baseball game, aren't there?

The weakest batter on that Missouri team became an instant hero for swinging hard and late to produce such a glancing grounder-fly. I'll bet they are still discussing that hit and that game in the little Ozark village.

In the third inning, with the score locked up 1-1, Stu came to bat, with no one on base. He led off the third with a deep triple, almost a home run by a couple of feet. The ball was pulled down the left field line and bounced off the high stone wall erected many years before, all the way around Borleske Field. (Yes, this was really built of solid cement and stone. A menace to hustling outfielders.) On that 350' shot Stu pulled up at third base. On the very next play, a hard grounder came to the third baseman. The Spokane team had Stu trapped off third base now. At the end of the ensuing run-down on the big pitcher, the big black Spokane Air Force Base third baseman stepped on Stu's left foot, driving a long shoe spike all the way through the shoe, sock, foot, the shoe sole, and out the bottom of Stu's foot. The shoe soon was filled with blood. Stuart limped to the dugout, and there they doctored that spiked foot - by running a swabbed iodine applicator all the way through the foot wound and out the underside of the foot. The young pitcher then changed bloody sox, laced that left shoe again, and told Coach "Nig" Borleske he would be okay to pitch the rest of the game. His foot bled the remainder of the contest, but he emptied the blood at the end of each inning, washed the shoe with water, and put it on again. He pitched those Whitman "Missionaries" to a 4-1 victory that day. He wanted Bill, his father, to see him perform and pitch the best varsity game he had done to date. Stu allowed three hits to the opposition. Of course, Bill was proud, and he let his crowd around him know that his son had pitched a "gem". And, of course, Stu had hit that triple, too.

During this same game the crowd was treated to an unusual and theatrical sight. Certainly not the usual run of event found in most baseball contests.

A Spokane Air Force Base outfielder had gone deep to the wall to left centerfield and hauled down a long fly hit by a Whitman batter. He hauled it in just as a freight train was passing by, the rail line bordering the third base side of the stadium. The crowd could see the engineer and fireman in the cab.

The engineer and fireman were high enough to see the game, crowd, all of the field, in fact. They fully viewed and appreciated the great catch made by the Air Force fielder just a moment before. Just as the outfielder released that ball to the waiting infielder, the engineer and fireman simultaneously let out a loud cheer, clapped their hands, then the train whistle was opened up, full blast. TOOT - TOOT - TOOT. This shrieking sound lasted perhaps ten seconds. That crowd covered their ears.

Not to be outdone, certainly, that outfielder, himself a born "ham," then stood erect, facing the crowd and the passing train, took a deep bow, but removed his cap first. This caused a hilarious roar and cheering of real approval from the huge crowd assembled, with Bill Southworth leading the wild applause to the fielder's gesture. The performer-outfielder held his bow for a very long time.

Bill was, by this time in the game, also visiting with two high school baseball coaches from the Walla Walla area.

In inning number five, another rather unusual baseball incident occurred. It brought all kinds of comments from Bill Southworth and his "Monday morning quarterbacks".

Spokane Air Force Base had a man on first base, and their batter, a lefty, bunted to the first base line. The first baseman fielded the ball just as the bunter ran toward him. Suddenly, the bunter stopped and backed up a couple of steps. That Whitman first baseman followed the runner two steps toward the catcher to put the tag on him.

Just as Coach Nig Borleske yelled, "Go tag first base," the first baseman realized his temporary mental lapse. Then he ran to first base and touched it, with his foot, while he held the ball.

Near to Bill, one high school coach laughed hard and turned to Mr. Southworth, "Here's one for your collection of baseball stories. I read about a game, I believe it happened in 1912 between two very novice teams, they had hardly played the game before. The bunter laid down a bunt near first base line. The bunter stopped and forced the catcher and first baseman into a rundown between home and first, with runners on second and third bases too. The catcher stayed at the plate okay, that bunter yelled loudly at the two defensemen, and rattled them both unmercifully. Here is the rest of the story that Bill heard that day while sitting in Borleske Stadium in Walla Walla.

Baseball Story Number 22 - 1912
The Crazy Rundown Play Between Home Plate And First Base
OR
That Baserunner Was Sure Smart, Going "Down The Line"

Mighty odd things can happen in a baseball game when the players are either inexperienced, or are not knowledgeable about the rules of the game, or both.

Such a case developed in a game in 1912, played by a bunch of high school age boys against an opponent in New York State. Several of the lads that age had hardly ever been on a diamond, and it was early in that new season. Their coaching had been meager in just a few short days of practice, but each boy eagerly held on to all the knowledge imparted by the small town coaches.

One rule that they had learned was "never run into the baseball when it is being held by a baseman, ready to tag you." They were told to back off and get into a rundown situation.

Another skill they had worked on was that of dropping a bunt softly just inside the first and third base lines.

What happens when the combination of two things learned from coaching sessions suddenly are found - on the same play - in a game situation? Well, let's see. One of the most humorous plays in all of baseballdom ensued as a result of this coaching.

CAN ANY READER HONESTLY SAY THAT HE OR SHE HAS WITNESSED A RUNDOWN OF A HITTER BETWEEN HOME PLATE AND FIRST BASE - AT ANY LEVEL OF BASEBALL?

The author can't remember it ever being reported to him.

So on a Saturday afternoon in this little New York village we recount the following events, exactly as occurred, in 1912, with players from ages 13 to 17. Follow these events, one by one.

The home town had runners at second and third bases, with one out. Apparently, the coach told the next batter to bunt, just inside the first base line. He did that, but the bunt was too hard, so the runners did not try to move up on the play. The bunt was right at the creeping first baseman, right near the line. the bunter ran to first, but he saw the first baseman coming down the line to tag him - or wait for the runner to run

That baserunner was sure smart, going
"down the line."

into the ball and tag himself. THAT DARNED FIRST BASEMAN FORGOT THAT ALL HE HAD TO DO WAS TOUCH FIRST BASE WITH THE BALL IN HIS HAND (AND WATCH THE OTHER RUNNERS - TO NOT TRY TO SCORE ON THE PLAY).

The bunter-runner now recalled the axiom, "Don't run into the ball when they are to tag you. It gives up an easy out." So the runner backed away - back toward home plate from whence he came. This must have unnerved that first baseman, for he tossed the ball back to his catcher. The catcher was thoroughly shocked to be drawn into a play of this type, and he barely was able to get the glove up to receive the first toss in the rundown.

After two of these tosses between first baseman and catcher, on the third toss, the first baseman uncorked a wild throw that soared about five feet over the catcher's glove, and the ball rolled to the deep backstop. This caused the runners on third base and second base to score, for the angry catcher didn't hustle after the ball.

When the dust had cleared, and spectators were again gaining control of themselves from the shock of seeing the play (and the laughter it created) the bunter had legged it all the way to second base, and two runs had scored on the error - all of this on the "home and first base rundown".

A weird play, an unusual story. A tale such as this one makes us wonder, just wonder, if this play, created from a mental error or two, had ever happened anywhere in baseball since 1869, and at what level? Has it ever happened at a higher level of the game, where players really should know better? (We even imagine it occurred, maybe one time, in major league baseball.)

If ever there was a college game filled with unusual events, Bill had chosen that one to see in Walla Walla that May day. This Saturday game of 1944 he could use, certainly, to add to his baseball repertoire of tales. What baseball lore for future telling.

The very next inning of that game at Whitman, the contest was stopped suddenly when the Missionary centerfielder ran in toward the infield and yelled, "Time, time, time." As he ran, he had an object held in his two hands cupped in front of him. The crowd stood up to see what it was this player was cradling so carefully. When he reached the pitcher's mound, it was plain to see by the crowd that the outfielder was carrying a small bird. In the dugout he told "Nig" Borleske that the bird had dropped to the ground helpless. A flock of birds had flown over the stone wall out in his area and this smaller one was flying with them. As the others had circled around the wall and poles out there, this specimen had, for no apparent reason, clipped its wing against a light pole near that wall. Here it was now in the dugout with several sub's doing its doctoring. By the end of that half inning they had administered first aid and had a home for the unfortunate one, built in a shoe box they found near the team equipment. From this point on in this event the fate of the bird is unknown.

The fellows around Bill Southworth that afternoon were complimenting the young Whitmanite for his humanitarian effort toward the small creature, when Bill turned to all of them, asking, "Do you recall that story of the great day at Ebbets Field, Brooklyn, when Casey Stengel, player, had an injured bird in his hat?" None had heard this side of old Casey, but they knew plenty of other accounts of Casey's wacky adventures. Their ignorance of this "bird in the hat" incident resuscitated Bill to give the full account. The story teller from Southern California reminded the crowd of listeners that there were actually two versions of this memorable baseball event.

Not missing the chance to be the first master narrator, Bill spun both versions of Casey that day in Brooklyn. Listen to the two accounts of the same incident and tell us which of the two you believe.

BASEBALL STORY NUMBER TWENTY-THREE - 1918 – CASEY'S "BIRD IN THE CAP" IS WORTH "TWO IN THE BUSH" OR THE TRUE VERSION, OF THE TWO, IS LEFT UP TO THE READER, SINCE NONE OF US WERE THERE

CASEY STENGEL, THE "BIRD MAN OF THE BROOKLYN DODGERS IN 1918" – VERSION NUMBER ONE (Take your choice)

The story of Casey Stengel and the sparrow had been told in many variations. Usually it is warped around so that it becomes a piece of screwball behavior on the part of Stengel. Newspaper accounts of the incident, written in 1918, right after it occurred, would seem to contradict these versions.

Stengel was a great hero in the few years he played with the Dodgers. Then he was traded to the Pirates. On that day in 1918 he came back to old Ebbets Field in Brooklyn as a member of the Pittsburgh club. Technically, he had now gone over to the enemy, which was anyone who did not cheer for "dem Bums," yet the Brooklyn fans held him in such high esteem that it was a sure thing they would salute him with cheers on his return.

Casey did not bat in the top of the first inning for the Pirates, but he was the first hitter up in the second inning. He walked out of the dugout when the time came, selected a bat, and strode to the plate. The Brooklyn fans got to their feet and cheered him mightily.

This was to be the dramatic moment. Arriving at the plate, Casey Stengel turned and faced the stands, lifting his cap from his head in acknowledgement of their salute, and a bird flew out of his hair, circled the diamond once and then disappeared into the sky.

A gigantic roar went up from the multitude, for old Casey hadn't disappointed his old fans. The fact appeared that day that Mr. Stengel was as greatly startled as were his fans, when the bird flew out of his thatch. For the moment, however, he made no effort to disillusion his admirers, being content to think that he had rigged the "bird trick" in their honor.

The true version, of the two, is left up to
the reader, since none of us were there.

Later on he told his story of what had happened. When he had gone to his position in right field after his half of the first inning, he saw an injured sparrow wobbling along at the base of the wall. He walked over, picked it up, and he was then deciding what to do with it, when he noticed that the ball game had been resumed, and Casey needed to get down to business. He could do nothing but place the stunned bird under his cap and went to work as an outfielder. Casey swore later on that he had completely forgotten about the sparrow when he came in from the field and had to go to bat immediately.

Nonetheless, this bird story has been widely repeated as an example of Stengel's showmanship.

✪   ✪   ✪   ✪   ✪

"A BIRD IN THE CAP IS WORTH TWO IN THE CROWD" VERSION NUMBER TWO
(The reader may take his choice as to which version to believe)

There have been so many humorous tales of salty old Casey Stengel, of his playing and coaching and managing days, but this one is surely one of the earliest. It is certainly typical of this unusual character on the diamond.

Casey was a professional baseball player in his twenties. He had been so popular among his Brooklyn fans, and when he was traded to the pittsburgh Pirates, his fame lived on in Brooklyn. This clown and player who had such a good and lasting relationship with his Brooklyn and Pittsburgh fans, hit a triple deep to left field one afternoon in Brooklyn. When he pulled up at third base, the home team gave Casey, now a visitor, a thunderous roar of acclaim. Casey had knocked in a run or two ahead of him.

Now came the "magic moment," perhaps never before or since duplicated in the history of the game. Casey, also the kind and sentimental type, always a crowd pleaser, in order to acknowledge the roaring acclaim afforded him, stood on third base, and with a slight bow, slowly took off his cap and tipped it toward the crowd. In disbelief to the fans there observing, and to the utter surprise of Casey himself, on Casey's shock of thick hair, stood a small sparrow.

This sparrow, God knows how it ever got under Casey's cap and onto his head at that moment, flew off into the air, but in a weakened condition, it appeared, and disappeared into the crowd. Perhaps it landed on something after a rather short slow flight?

Casey now became the object of both hilarious joking and laughter, and some ridiculed the ballplayer at the same time. Fans turned to each other, just gasping for breath from prolonged laughter, and were heard saying one to the other, "That sparrow was under Casey's cap when he went to bat. Why, he ran all the way around the home to third with that bird under there."

Casey was totally puzzled, then it came to him, and the fans could see the look of enlightenment appear in his eyes. He remembered what had happened. He had run out to his outfield spot the inning before, stooped down to pick up his glove, and he saw a sparrow on the grass. As it appeared injured, Casey then admired it, placed it on his finger, stroked it. "Play ball" was called, and he did not have time to take it over to the foul line to deposit it until the inning was over. He could do no more than to place it on his head, under his cap, and he was going to take it out when he got to the dugout, examine it, and maybe doctor the poor bird, examining its condition more carefully.

But alas. Casey forgot it was even there, so engrossed in the game was this pro ball player. Now, how many people could or would forget that a bird was on their head and under a cap? but old Casey could.

And so we apparently have the full explanation of the "sparrow in the cap". Was there ever a more colorful man in this long line of colorful characters of our great national game?

Late in the game, the eighth inning, the Whitman second baseman had managed to make it to third base with one out. Coach "Nig" Borleske called for a suicide squeeze bunt, to score another insurance run. The base runner was off with the pitch, but the hitter, usually a fine bunter, got a curve ball offering, and he missed the ball completely. That little second baseman running the bases saw the missed bunt and knew that he was "hung out to dry".

Instead of sliding hard to avoid the tag at the plate, he chose to try to "take out the catcher" and jar the ball loose. A 140 pound infielder taking out a 200 pound catcher? Really, now! What a mistake in judgement that was!

As that runner sprinted into the range of the catcher's reach, the large defensive man merely pushed his big arm (and the ball it held) out into midair and not only tagged that poor runner, but the force of that arm suddenly plunged straight out (in a "stiffarm" manner) stopped the runner's momentum, knocking him back about two steps. The runner looked as though the catcher had "Stamped a brand on him," as with cattle at a roundup. An examination of his ribs later would verify that comparison. His ribs were probably branded "Spalding" with the seams of the ball showing as well.

The Whitman crowd leapt to their feet in defense of their player who was out (and buffeted). Bill Southworth did not, however. After they sat down, claiming a "damned cheap shot," Bill reassured the fans around him that, in that case, the catcher had the right of position and to block the plate, and the littler player "chose him off," matching weight versus weight. Bill commented that the runner had used poor judgement, and then most of those present finally agreed with him.

Referring to this controversial play which came in that game (which Stu won for Whitman on the mound) that May day in 1944, Bill Southworth closed out his visit to baseball in the State of Washington as the result of an amusing last inning play. This was an event that occurred in the stands, and not on the field.

On a mighty swing, the Whitman Missionary cleanup hitter had fouled off a fast moving high fly ball, quickly descending among the fans all huddled up directly behind home plate, in about the fourth row up. One family had brought food galore, and were consuming it in large quantities. One family was eating, drinking, watching the game in that group there, when the high foul tip dropped into the lap of the unsuspecting Mother, the ball spinning around oddly. The ball spilled her Coca-Cola all over her small boy beside her. No one was injured, but they could have been, very easily. The Mother was visibly annoyed as the neighbors watched her clean up the liquid spilled, dabbing at her clothes and her son's overalls.

One old farmer leaned over to Bill Southworth and volunteered, "If that ball had landed in the middle of the big cup of Coke, she would have been cleaning up everyone all around her. The ball missed the cup a few inches."

A very vivid memory came sliding out from the far recesses of Bill's baseball mind - a memory of his dad, Sam and him (age 20) in St. Louis' big league ballpark, a warm day in 1915. As Bill told the events of that day to all around him, he wondered what Sam was doing at that very moment in old St. Louis?

BASEBALL STORY NUMBER TWENTY-FOUR - 1915
THOSE BIG LEAGUE BALLPARK BEER VENDORS ARE SURE TO "HAVE A BALL" WORKING THOSE GRANDSTANDS ON HOT SUMMER DAYS
OR
THEREAFTER, ALL BEER VENDORS WERE EQUIPPED WITH FIELDER'S MITTS. THEY COULD BE USED TO CATCH FOUL BALLS OR COINS

ONE VERY WARM DAY DURING the 1915 baseball season in St. Louis, Will Southworth and the old gentleman, Samuel, were enjoying a BROWNS game in the shade of the big grandstand.

In those days the builders of major league ballparks hung wire screen to protect the spectators directly behind home plate and all the way down along the stands for a considerable distance. This prevented any real hard foul tips or foul line drives from hitting a paying customer. Some backstops were as far as 120' behind the plate, so that the catcher had to really hustle after a passed ball or wild pitch. These light screen sections seldom extended back as far as the fan who sat directly behind first base or third base. In some parks, screen ran only 60' down from the point behind home plate. Many people in the big ball parks did receive painful injuries from hit or fouled balls.

Will and his dad, Sam, were fully engrossed in the tight contest going on between St. Louis and Boston that afternoon. The crowd was sparse, for the Browns were in a slump at that point in the 1915 season.

In the vicinity of Will and Sam's grandstand seats was a beer vendor, with his big box of beer bottles strapped in front of him, uniformed in a strached white coat with a cap to match. This enterprising seller of brew was hawking his wares with cries of "Cold beer. Cold beer here."

The vendor was quite tall, and he had just bent over to his right side, slightly toward a person who had ordered a cold beer. Down on the field the St. Louis batter

Thereafter, all beer vendors were
equipped with fielder's mitts. They could
be used to catch foul balls or coins.

swung hard, had just lifted a high foul popup which sliced in an arc toward the stands. It was obviously going to land near Will, Sam and the beer vendor. The vendor was in the middle of pouring beer into a cup, but Will and Sam were watching the ball arc even closer to them. The ball descended into the stands with a lot of velocity, so Will yelled suddenly to the vendor, "Heads up. Look out." Neither the fan getting the beer or the vendor heard Will's shouts, for the baseball slid down the side of the vendor's bulky white coat, smack into the middle of the bulging open pocket, filled with change, of all denominations. When the white ball hit and lodged into that big white coat pocket, it dislodged some folding money and lots of coins. They scattered in all directions, and for quite a distance. Of course, all the nearby fans swooped to bend down and pick up the coins and bills. Some were given back to the vendor and some were not.

Father and son did not move. Will and Sam just reared back and roared with laughter at all the sudden activity before them. Those fans didn't miss getting every coin and bill. Fans all agreed, "That beer hawker sure lost money on this game." Sam leaned over to Bill and said to his son, "We could come to a ball game a million years and never see that happen again. A ball dropping into a vendor's big pocket!"

Say, pro ball players talk about a baseball "having eyes" when it is hit between or just out of the reach of two or more defense men, ending up a base hit. Maybe a baseball does "have eyes." Will and Sam would have attested to this fact after witnessing the weird "stop" the beer vendor made.

By 1974, exactly 30 years had passed, too quickly, it seemed. In the lives of Bill and Stu Southworth, so many events changed the lives of father and son that the reader will be referred only to several which are important to move the continuing Southworth narrative up to the year 1974.

After that memorable Whitman game of May, 1944, Bill bade his son goodbye, traveled north to see Grand Coulee Dam, returned to his job at the U.S. Navy Air Station, North Island (Coronado) on San Diego Bay. Bill held that job for 25 years, from 1940 to 1965.

Stuart left Whitman college and its baseball there, was transferred to the University of Washington at Seattle, where he pitched varsity baseball for the "Huskies" in the spring of 1945. He returned after World War II ended, to attend that large university, from 1946 to 1949. From the University of Washington, Stu Southworth studied at Columbia University in New York City, U.S. Navy Midshipman's School, graduating as Ensign USNR, on November 2, 1945. On assignment with the United States Seventh Fleet, Shanghai, China, Stu became Navigator of USS LST 846 at Shanghai, serving for a year on the north China coast, hauling personnel and cargo north.

Stu married Liane Foster, a University of Washington professor's daughter in 1947, the same year that Bill, his father, remarried to Ethel Weniger of San Diego. Stu's wife, Liane, died in 1974, her family of two boys and a girl raised, but Ethel died shortly before this, in 1972. There Bill and Stu, father and son, were widowers, together in the world.

Stu went into teaching and coaching right out of college, and he had done this for six years when he accepted a position at Pacific High School in San Bernardino, California, in 1954. Near the Southworth residence was a short order malt shop, named "McDonald's," where high school kids could get quick lunches. The two owners, creators of an innovative "fast food system," had made this business, near the high school, into a real gold mine.

An experienced entrepreneur whose name was Ray Kroc heard of this new business venture, investigated it thoroughly, then bought the idea and system from the McDonald's owners. (The readers know the rest of the story of Kroc's success. He made McDonald's the world's newest food symbol, the "golden arches". "Mr. McDonald" made so much money so fast that he needed ready investment sources.) That baseball city of San Diego, California, and Ray Kroc applied for the new National League franchise one year - for the team to be named the same "San Diego Padres" (chosen decades before, when baseball came to the city at the turn of the century.) However, Lane Field was not the home of the new Padres, but the new Jack Murphy Stadium had been built.

So here, one sunny afternoon of the summer, we find Bill Southworth, again seated among baseball fans and eager listeners, but in a new setting. The beloved San Diego Padres were finally in major league baseball. To the North 120 miles away, now lived Stu and family, teaching (and coaching high school baseball) - teaching young men to play the game. Old granddad Sam would have enjoyed looking in on this scene in 1974, his son and grandson very much involved in the game that Sam first saw in 1861, in St. Louis, in its very primitive form.

Seated with his new group of baseball cronies, friends interested in the now "MAJOR LEAGUE - SAN DIEGO PADRES," and loving to hear his odd collection of baseball reminisces, in the middle of that Summer game, the crowd rose to its feet, stunned beyond words at the sight of that "big male streaker" - a big white nude body of a bearded man cutting across Jack Murphy Stadium in broad daylight. This man had jumped out of the stands, undressed, somehow was running rapidly from the right field foul line to the left field foul line - and was just as suddenly stopped, apprehended, and "covered" by groundcrew and police stationed in the stadium stands. He was bundled up with some kind of body covering and whisked off to the nearest San Diego police station.

All kinds of crowd response could be seen and heard, as the announcer at Jack Murphy Stadium made the following statement, "Pardon the sudden interruption, ladies and gentlemen, play will now resume." The umpires again signalled "Play ball" as if nothing had scampered across their field - or line of vision.

Many of the baseball fans around good old Bill Southworth surely believed this to be a "first" in baseball history, for this kind of human exhibition. Bill was quickly responding to this surmise, for he proceeded to inform all of them about him, referring to an incident, back in 1922, taking place in a Midwestern community. The fate of the "streaker" of that day was somewhat different than the San Diego version - that all in the big stadium had been entertained to recall for years.

BASEBALL STORY NUMBER TWENTY-FIVE - 1922
WE ARE CERTAIN THAT THE BATTER WAS THEREAFTER KNOWN AS A "STREAK HITTER"
OR
DID THE POOR "STREAKER" BEAR A MARK, FOR LIFE - A REAL "TATTOO" IN THE SHAPE OF A BASEBALL, WITH SEAMS SHOWING, AND LABELED "SPALDING"?

IN 1922, IN A MIDWESTERN town of good size, three young men were plotting a very daring "caper" - daring for those days, at least. It was done while imbibing at the local "beer hall - pool hall - recreation center." It all centered around the big Saturday baseball doubleheader in which that town was playing the next village down the road in that county. This match was for the League Championship, too. This game would bring everybody, from baby to grandma, out to see the "locals" prevail over their arch rivals. What a setting to pull their stunt - these three "bad boys" were becoming more daring and cunning with each schooner of "suds" the bartender set up.

Why, what dastardly plan had this trio cooked up for the benefit of the local establishment? Finally, they all had the plans jelled in their collective minds. One boy would drive a second boy to the gate constructed there, where the right field line met the outfield fence. (This would be done in the very middle of the game, when the home club was batting). This second lad, let's call him "Bud" (for the gross amounts of Budweiser beer he could consume at one sitting) had drawn the short straw, to see who would do the more daring of the day's work - undress and expose himself to the crowd while "Streaking" across the ballfield in broad daylight. There had been a drawing of straws for this privilege. "Bud" would have a canvas bag over his head, with large eye, nose, and mouth holes.

Long before "streaking" became a fad in the 1970's (then seemed to die down just as quickly as it came in) here we have the original "streaker," and where would they get all the town together to observe their daring - at the big ball game of the year, of course? Surely no one would recognize "Bud" in his "natural state." They wouldn't see him long enough, anyway, eh? His stunt would be on people's lips for years to come, and all the local and nearby newspapers would say much about this "dash across the outfield" for days on end. Bud was to sprint, very fast, from the right field gate to its corresponding left field corner gate, built on that side of the fence, to form a perfect exit. The third boy would be waiting in a strange old car, unknown to anyone, rescuing the "streaker" from any possible pursuer or curious follower. The driver of the car would be hooded, also. They would disappear and be seen no more.

OH BOY! OH BOY! OH BOY! THREE BOYS OFF ON AN UNUSUAL MISSION! These three non-baseball enthusiasts would "break up the ole ball game," and they weren't even ball players!

On the big game Saturday, at the assigned time, the plan was set into action. With the aid of moderate amounts of alcoholic beverages to bolster their collective courage, the three boys proceeded, unafraid. The entry of the "bare one" was made at precisely 3:12 p.m. of that hot afternoon, while everyone was watching ball, feeding their faces, and drinking untold quantities of any kind of wet beverages sold at the park. By the time the nude streaker, 1922 model, was into centerfield and centerstage, seen by all the grandstand, screaming commenced, but not before the pitcher had released his best curveball to the home town slugger. The batter up then was a real "ripper," a specialist in low line drives that would easily behead infielders who were quite unaware.

The pitcher's fabulous curve ball was quickly converted into a very straight ball by this murderous line drive hitter. THE BALL WAS HIT, RIFLED TO WHAT SPOT ON THE FIELD, DO YOU THINK? NONE OTHER THAN THE EXACT SPOT WHERE THE LEFT RIB CAGE OF THE "EXPOSED STREAKER" WAS AT THAT PRECISE MILLISECOND. OF COURSE, THE BALL COULD HAVE HIT OTHER PARTS OF "BUD'S" ANATOMY, SO HE GOT OFF LUCKY.

The hard hammered baseball and the lily white left side of the exposed rib cage met each other. Having slightly greater velocity than the boy's nude body, the ball won the contest for the moment, moving the fast runner about five feet back toward the outfield fences, and IN PAIN.

Needles to say, all the team in the field, as well as all in the dugouts, stood or sat transfixed. No one moved to witness such a new sight as a "streaker." All in the ballpark were frozen. Only the running boy was in motion at all. This is easily explained. How many people had ever seen a nude boy (or girl) running across a ball diamond in the middle of a crucial game?

The injured lad kept up his pace, grimacing beneath his hood, a few tears now running down from his eyes and down his warm body. The brave nude made it to the third hooded boy, waiting for him at the gate, and he was soon whisked away down the hot dirt road out into the country, for a quick change - and some more beer, no doubt. They got away in an old 1910 "flivver," and they were "chugged away" before the crowd came out of their hypnotic spell. It was over - almost too quickly.

In the crowd there were two young high school age girls sitting directly behind home plate, and about halfway up the seats toward the top of the grandstand. One of the two girls had stepped out of the seating area to get a soda pop, when all the "streaking" began. She just made it to the grandstand walkway, when she saw this white body disappear out of the left field gate, and she wondered what in the world had occurred during her brief absence.

Did the poor "streaker" bear a mark, for
life – a real "tattoo" in the shape of a
baseball, with seams showing,
and labeled "Spalding"?

Her girl friend, who had witnessed the whole escapade, was standing up at her seat, mouth open wide, looking somewhat puzzled. The other girl now heard the screaming, talking, and wild remarks coming from the crowd, pointing to the field, and she finally asked her girl friend, "What was that out on the field that created all the commotion? What did I miss? I saw someone running out of the left field gate."

Her bright eyed young friend, who had stayed through it all, said, in a strange tone, "I really don't know, Helen. I'm not sure, but I think it was a boy."

Baseball is a game peculiar in this way - occasionally an observer will see the "same pattern of throws, overthrows, etc., with a man or men on certain combinations of bases." If this explanation does not suffice, let us give the reader a specific example - an incident which Bill and his cronies (who had seen or played hundreds of baseball games) had observed occurring in exactly the same sequence.

The sequence, referred to, goes something in this order: A man is on second base, ground ball hit through the middle for a base hit rather slowly, centerfielder makes the throw home, but the throw is somewhat wide and deflects off the catcher's glove. Runner at home scores. Catcher next throws down to second base, and the throw is over the head of the infielder covering second base, rolls way out between outfielders, while the man who hit the ball to begin the play is now rounding third and being waved home. Outfielder picks up the loose ball, throws it miles over the head of the catcher. Everyone scores, no one has been thrown out, defensive coach or manager is ready for the insane asylum. The ball is now resting next to the screen behind home plate. The foregoing pattern does occur quite often.

One month after our first story in the new Jack Murphy Stadium (and Bill's fine story of the line drive off the pitcher's rubber), this exact sequence of throws and runs did occur in a big game. Padres versus Cincinnati Reds. Major League ball.

This time, and at this point in our story of that afternoon, an old ball fan, well over 85 years young, turned the tables on Bill Southworth and told him the strange happenings which follow, an example of 1924 style baseball in New England. Bill and his fan friends were the listeners.

After hearing this humorous account in a manager's life, the "red hot ball and the manager's water bucket," William D. Southworth found himself wishing that the big red water bucket was again a part of the modern scene on the diamonds of America.

BASEBALL STORY NUMBER TWENTY-SIX - 1924
THE "RED HOT BALL AND THE MANAGER'S WATER BUCKET"
OR
I WONDERED IF THAT MANAGER "DROWNED HIS SORROWS" AFTER A CLOSE LOSS

ONE DAY IN 1924, A major league ball game was progressing nicely with neither team committing an error into the seventh inning. With no score for either team, the home team stepped up to the plate. The leadoff hitter whacked a double to right centerfield. Immediately following that beautiful double, the next hitter lined a single between right and center field. The centerfielder had a great arm, and his throw should have beaten the second base runner out by a mile at the plate. As the runner slid into the catcher, the strong outfield throw took off many feet over the catcher's outstretched glove and hit the backstop screen, dropping to the ground. The hitter had stopped at first base, not trying for second when he saw the throw coming through. But, seeing the overthrow, the hitter headed for second base. The alert catcher hustled to the overthrown ball and fired it to second. His throw was miles over the infielder's head, whereupon the sliding runner at second moved on to third and rounded the bag there.

"They say that history repeats itself." The centerfielder then picked up the ball and made his "second brilliant throw on the same play," firing it a mile over the catcher's head again. Of course, the runner going into third now scored easily, whereupon the manager of the defensive team ran behind the home plate, picked up the baseball there, ran over to his dugout, and there stuck the ball into the visiting team's water bucket, announcing, to all of the crowd, at the top of his voice, "There, this damn thing is hot enough."

Of course, the crowd and both teams laughed with ferocity and ridicule.

The next season, 1975, found the San Diego crowds much larger, and the interest in major league baseball had increased considerably. From his perch high on the upper deck of the new Jack Murphy Stadium, Bill could see the Mission Valley to the east. The old San Diego Mission, the first of the chain built by Father Junipero Serra, was almost lost to the viewer. It was hidden by shopping malls and new tall high rise buildings. The same congested scene met his eye to the west, toward Mission Bay.

About midseason, in a close game with the Los Angeles Dodgers, Bill's ever improving Padres took a step backward, only temporarily, that is, in the fourth inning.

I wondered if that manager "drowned his
sorrows" after a close loss.

With the score 4-2 for the brown and gold clad San Diego club, the Padres had the bases loaded again. They were threatening to blow the ball game wide open.

Suddenly, with one out, the first base runner thought he saw the steal sign flashed. Not thinking to look again toward second base to see if there was a team mate occupying it, he forgot it was occupied. Head down, running full blast toward second base, he slid safely into second base as the stunned defense looked on in disbelief. The San Diego crowd now screamed and ridiculed the runner and probably the manager and coaches. As the Los Angeles catcher threw the ball down to the second baseman covering the bag, the perplexed runner who slid was tagged out for "playing two on a base." Now, the second base runner, equally as confused by this bizarre act, forgot and stepped a few feet off second base toward third. The infielder was about to go after him for the third out, ending that inning, when his team mates yelled at him that the third base runner was breaking for the plate. He had a good break, but the second baseman had a better arm. The throw narrowly nailed the sliding runner at home, while the second base runner successfully stole third base - all to no avail.

Oh, how Bill enjoyed that "super colossal bit of base running exhibited." In jest, and in disgust, he turned to a couple of cronies and yelled, "That last play could be topped only by Babe Herman and the zany Brooklyn Dodgers of 1926. Do you recall that fiasco at Ebbetts Field? Every man sitting there with Bill nodded in the affirmative. After all, who doesn't? It's such a legendary bit of baseball lore that it has become a "fixture" in the game's long array of odd incidents.

For those of you readers who have never heard the true account, you'll see that Babe Herman's honor topped the "San Diego lapse of memory." Readers will further relate it to Abbott and Costello's baseball puzzler, "Who's on first.........." all too well.

Baseball Story Number Twenty-Seven - 1926
The "Daffy Dodgers" Get Three Men On Base
OR
Thereafter, When Brooklyn's Dodgers Had Three Men On Base The Common Question Asked By Everyone Was: "Which One?"

THROUGHOUT SPORTS THE HISTORY OF team games are filled with accounts of men and women who have achieved national fame - of infamy - totally beyond their control, absolutely unpremeditated, and usually to their complete surprise. These events can bring on much anguish. Such things as mental lapses, misplays, faulty judgements, or transgressions and ignorance of the playing rules or code. These occurrences could all be grouped into that category known as "boners."

Such miscues have served to spotlight certain persons overnight, making them national and international celebrities or "putting them behind the eight ball." The fame thrust upon some of these athletes was, in most instances, unwelcome and classified as a form of notoriety, causing them distress and some lasting humiliation. (Will Mickey Owen ever live down his dropped third strike in the crucial game of that World Series with the New York Yankees, especially since the Yankees went on to win that game and the series later?)

However, in most cases, it did them no lasting harm and it may have led, in some instances, to greater success than they otherwise could have dreamed of.

In 1902 a baserunner named John Anderson became famous overnight by trying to steal second base in a game at New York City with the Highlanders (Yankees) (Hey, our San Diego runner wasn't the first man in history to make that awful boner, was he?) For, you see, the bases were loaded at the time of the steal!

In 1926 occurred the "play to end all plays," at least in the area of baseball's baserunning, for the slugger Babe Herman created the most famous chapter of the zany antics of Dodger's baserunning boners. This mental lapse occurred in a game with Boston, at Ebbets Field. His pitcher, Dazzy Vance, and teammate Chuck

Thereafter, when Brooklyn's Dodgers had
three men on base, the common question
asked by everyone was "which one?"

Fewster, were sitting safely on first and second bases, respectively. The Babe drove one of his murderous long shots to right centerfield. Vance, on second, was undecided as to whether the ball would be caught, so he stood waiting half way between second and third bases. Fewster stayed on the bag, upon reaching second base. However, the hitter, Babe Herman, had "triple on his mind. Three bases."

His head down, instead of looking up to see what was going on in front of him, Herman rounded first and tore for second base. Fewster saw him coming, so he had no other option than to head for third, unless he wished to get trampled. As the ball dropped safely, Vance Proceeded 45 more feet to third base.

Should we call this story "THREE RUNNERS IN AN APPARENT FOOTRACE TO SEE WHO COULD REACH THIRD BASE?" The footrace became nearly a tie - a dead heat. Fewster and Vance arrived at third almost simultaneously, stood looking at each other in bewilderment, while Babe Herman was hurrying to join them, head down.

What was the defense doing all of this time? Well, the deep ball had been picked up, relayed to the second baseman, the cutoff man, who whipped the ball to the third baseman, touching the bag. The amazed third baseman perhaps had envisioned an unassisted triple play, and he could go down in history? so he tagged all three of them, "plunk, plunk, plunk." (Like three rubber stamps.) The three base runners, although stunned by the tags, remained on base to hear the umpire's calls. Of course, Vance was safe, for he was the advance runner. Fewster and Herman were tagged out - "a spiffy double play" without too much effort on the defense's part.

Would you believe that Vance died there? Did not score that inning. That Brooklyn Dodger side had been retired in what should have been a triple with no outs, scoreless for the inning. Probably, pitcher Vance wished he had really died there.

For years afterwards, fans in all of baseballdom have said two patented things about the Dodgers. First, "It could only have happened in Brooklyn" and second, "When ever anyone reports that the Dodgers (now residing comfortably in the confines of Chavez Ravine, Los Angeles) have three men on base, all fans within earshot ask the obvious question, "WHICH BASE?"

Oh, these never forgiving fans have forgotten about Anderson in 1902, for the St. Louis Browns. And how about that San Diego runner Bill Southworth saw in San Diego in 1945?

Triple plays are one of baseball's rarest oddities. Has a baseball fan ever wondered how many different types of triple plays could occur in a ball game? I suppose that the numberpossible combinations of different infielders or outfielders handling the ball, or various runners or men on bases, running and scoring, would be in the thousands - perhaps ten thousand.

Well, at Jack Murphy Stadium our old (80 years old by 1975) ball fan and story teller, Bill Southworth, saw a real strange triple play in a game with the San Francisco Giants. There were runners on first and third bases when a slicing fly ball, a soft one, was hit in back of first base. It was obvious that it would land fair if it were allowed to drop. The first base runner was far enough off base to try for second it if dropped, but he quickly hustled back to the bag to be safe. The momentum of the hustling second baseman carried him a few steps beyond the foul line after he did make the shoestring catch. That was out number One. He stopped and faked a hard throw home. The first base runner thought that he had actually thrown the ball, so he started for second base. The third base runner retreated back to third on the "bluff throw." Of course, now the second baseman's throw went, instead, to second base where the shortstop was covering. The defense found that they had "first and third base rundown play" going. They ran down the slow first base runner, applying the tag to him just as the runner on third base broke for home. The alert shortstop turned, fired a perfect strike to the catcher at the plate. That was the Third out of a continuous triple play. It had begun as an innocent fly ball base hit dropping near right field foul line. A very alert hustling second baseman had turned it into a 4-6-3-6-2 triple play. Not an unassisted one, to be sure, but a very unusual sequence of events. Bill Southworth had never seen that one, and he probably never would again. And he'd been watching major league games since 1900, 75 years of it. For five minutes or so after the play, Bill's pals gathered around, discussed triple plays, when one of them then asked Bill, "Have you ever seen an unassisted triple play in big league ball?"

Bill Southworth had the answer right on the tip of his tongue for that question. He blurted out in response, "No, but there have been only eight of them since 1869, in major league history." Whereupon Bill told the crowd the story behind all eight of these rarities.

BASEBALL STORY NUMBER TWENTY-EIGHT - 1927 AND OTHER DATES AN UNASSISTED TRIPLE PLAY IN A WORLD SERIES?
OR
THE OFFICIAL SCORER RECORDED 2B TO 2B TO 2B????

RECORDS SHOW NO MORE THAN eleven major league pitchers who have performed what we call "the perfect game." Nine players have belted four homers in a game. These feats are obviously so rare that they are sensational for fan, player, or the teams involved. But a mere eight men in baseball have performed the "unassisted triple play." They are:

NEAL BEAL SS	CLEVELAND INDIANS	JULY 19, 1906
BILL WAMBSGANSS	CLEVELAND INDIANS	OCT. 10, 1920
GEORGE BURNS	BOSTON RED SOX	SEPT. 13, 1923
ERNIE PADGETT	BOSTON BRAVES	OCT. 6, 1923
GLENN WRIGHT	PITTSBURGH PIRATES	MAY 7, 1925
JIMMY COONEY	CHICAGO CUBS	MAY 30, 1927
JOHNNY NEUN	DETROIT TIGERS	MAY 31, 1927
RON HANSEN	WASHINGTON SENATORS	JULY 30, 1968

Of these eight infielders, the feat of Bill Wambsganss was certainly the most famous, for it came in the 1920 World Series played between the Brooklyn Dodgers and the Cleveland Indians. The unassisted triple play certainly has to be made by either the shortstop or second baseman? It is difficult to imagine a man in any other fielding position being able to even complete the feat? Yes, it has always been around the "keystone sack" - or has it? Let's see.

Bill Wambsganss' feat, being the one and only one in World Series play, makes him the most memorable of the eight. That, of course, is just a matter of luck. The play can happen at any time in which there are no outs and men on first and second (or possibly with the bases loaded).

Strangely enough, the unassisted triple play Number Seven followed unassisted

The official scorer recorded
2B to 2B to 2B????

triple play Number Six by only a matter of a few days. It is odd to relate the player who performed Number Seven had read in the papers (a few days before) about Number Six being executed, and he happened to make the remark to his teammates at the time, "I'm gong to get one of those, one of these days." And he was a first baseman. So there is one exception to the "keystone rule" mentioned above. Johnny Nuen was a first baseman who took a line drive hit right at him for out number one, "doubled off" first base runner eight steps away from the bag. Even though he had to run over to first base eight steps, he saw that the second base runner had broken to third on the pitch, forgetting the number of outs. So Neun ran 90' over to second base to "triple off" the errant baserunner, rather than to toss the ball over to second baseman Charlie Gehringer.

Of course, the usual chain of events in the "unassisted triple play" goes like this, as it did for shortstop Ron Hansen, the last major leaguer to perform the feat for the Washington Senators in 1968.

1. SHORTSTOP HAS HARD LINE DRIVE HIT TO HIM AT EYE LEVEL - IS OUT NUMBER ONE.
2. SHORTSTOP THEN STEPS ON SECOND BASE - DOUBLES OFF THAT RUNNER - IS OUT NUMBER TWO.
3. SHORTSTOP THEN RUNS TOWARD RUNNER COMING HARD DOWN THE LINE FROM FIRST BASE - WHICH IS OUT NUMBER THREE.

It will be interesting to see, in the baseball years ahead, whether some player, playing at another position other than those mentioned here, will ever be able to come up with his own "special brand of the unassisted triply play." I just hope that I am there to witness this unusual baseball phenomenon.

After Ethel, Bill's wife of 26 years passed away in 1972, and Liane, Stu's wife of 26 years, passed away two years later, Stu and Bill saw each other more often, visiting each other in either Stu's apartment in San Bernardino or at Bill's small flat over the garage of a friend in North Park, San Diego, near the Balboa Golf course. Father and son really had not spent many days of their lives together. A good game of golf was their most common activity when they visited one place or the other.

Bill had been seeing his family doctor and also an internal specialist for five years. an operation in 1973 removed a small malignant growth in his small intestine. The doctors thought that the operation had gotten the cancer before it spread (metastasized) to the organ's of Bill's body. This hope and assumption proved to be false, for Bill began failing fast in 1974. The cancer took him in May, 1976, one and a half years later.

One beautiful day in the spring of 1974 Stu and Bill were golfing. It was a warm day, and they had covered 10 or 12 holes on the municipal course. They talked about many items and events of importance to both of them. It was a welcome rest taken on a bench there in the shade of a big tree.

Bill began the conversation by asking his son, "Stuart, did you ever think of baseball umpiring as a sideline occupation? There is good money in it." Stu nodded vigorously, in the negative, and replied to his dad, "No, dad, I never cared to be a baseball ump. The job never interested me at all. I was also so busy coaching (and having lots of fun with the kids on the diamond) that umpiring never even entered my mind. It's a tough job, and I've never tried to give them a hard time. And I've never been booted out of a ball game yet."

We must pause in the ongoing story of Bill and Stu at this point to relate an interesting coincidence which occurred the very next year in the lives of Stuart and his son, Michael.

The first spring after Liane's death, 1974, Stu did not coach a sport. There were many affairs to be handled in regard to the passing of the wife, and the man did not have the spirit to do the job. The following year, 1975, found Stu assisting Coach Bill Kernen in baseball at San Gorgonio High School, in San Bernardino. Mike, Stu's older son, was given the position as Junior Varsity Baseball Coach. When they played games away from home, the two teams traveled together. On the spring day that the San Gorgonio High "Spartans" journeyed to Chaffey High School, Ontario, California, they knew that both teams were in for tough ball games. Chaffey was perennially a baseball power of the Inland Empire area.

The two diamonds were very close to each other, almost overlapping. Stu charged out on the field in the sixth inning of the varsity game, when the Chaffey Tiger catcher applied a vicious tag to a trapped baserunner. With the entire Chaffey bench entering into the argument, Stu yelled a few "choice words" in their direction, comments which he later regretted. One of the varsity umpires took Stu by the arm and led him to the gate, saying "You're out of this ball game, for using such language." Dejectedly, Stu had nowhere else to go but down the foul line to the Junior Varsity diamond and sit there, watching his son's game. While walking, he noticed that his son was nowhere to be seen in the dugout or on the field. He asked one of Mike's J.V. players where their coach was, and he replied, "Mr. Southworth, Mike was "booted" by a J.V. ump a few minutes ago, for arguing a call at the plate, on a high pitch to his batter." Smiling to himself, Stuart found Mike sitting behind the plate, up in the stands. Michael learned of the circumstances of Stu's ejection, and the two of them suddenly broke out in loud, raucous laughter at the same time. They were both thinking the same thought - they both were kicked out of baseball games almost the same moment at the same place. "What would Mike's Mother have thought of the two of them?

Stu finished his discussion of baseball umpiring with Bill by closing, "Well, I never wanted to start umping, although it does look like an interesting job to me. You sure have to know every rule well. These umps sure take a lot of flak from players and manager, though."

By that time Bill Southworth handed another little treasure to Stu - one which he had been saving for many years. It was an old brown enveloped postmarked 1931, with a red 2¢ stamp on it. As he handed it to him, he told his son, "Your grandfather sent this news article, from a paper somewhere around St. Louis. He always admired the good umpires very much, and this is a news article about what some people in a midwestern town did for their umpires. They had an "Umpire's Day" for their local men in blue that year. You may keep this one to add to your big collection of baseball stories. This is a great one. Can you imagine someone doing this today for their umpire crew?"

Stuart took the article from his old dad's hand, read it aloud, and thanked him as they both howled in glee at the events of that tale. The two novice golfers just sat on that golf course bench, laughed and laughed at the reporter's version of "nice treatment the home folk afforded those upstanding umpires." What a day it was, one not to be forgotten by all present.

One of the zaniest stories handed down to Stu and Bill, the father (the last year Bill was alive, 1976) involved a 1931 game that the old man had heard described by one of his friends at the time.

What makes the baseball incident so bizarre is that it begins as a standard "infield fly situation," then it quickly degenerates into a triple play.

The reader may now enjoy this circus of mental errors and circumstances totally beyond the control of some of its participants. Even "old Sol," bright sunlight, gets into the act to "complete the triple play."

BASEBALL STORY NUMBER TWENTY - NINE - 1931
THE "INFIELD FLY" FINDS THE SECOND BASE RUNNER'S BALD HEAD, SOMEHOW
OR
HOW CAN WE GIVE THE FIRST BASE RUNNER A "PASSING GRADE" FOR HIS ERRATIC BASERUNNING?

HAVE ANY BASEBALL READERS EVER seen a triple play in a game - one of which the defense never handled the ball at all? In other words, the hitting and running team committed all of the outs against themselves?

It sounds incredible, but this very play occurred in 1931 on a semi-professional league diamond in the Northern part of the United States.

Chatham was playing Darrington on an unusually hot Summer afternoon. With Chatham enjoying a 16-1 lead in this "laugher," this bunch of heavy hitters got runners on first and second bases to lead off the seventh inning. None away. It was at this point in the game that batter Art Barrow lifted an unusually high popup to the infield. Barrow had taken a full cut at the pitch, swung from the heels, and disgustedly banged his bat down on the ground. He ran to first base, but didn't have to, for he was out on the infield fly rule, as the plate umpire alertly called the play, yelling "Infield fly, batter is out." A guy by the name of Hurley was the first base runner (and proving to be not too intelligent a runner at that). He either forgot the number of outs or had a real lapse of good baserunning sense. Hurley broke full speed for second base, head down, rounded the base, and then passed the second base runner, Brown, who had moved about 10' off that bag.

One out had been made - the hitter flying out (under the infield fly rule). The excellent second base umpire there that day saw Hurley pass Brown, then he saw that the first base runner realized his gross error, tried to correct or hide it by repassing Brown, heading back to first base. This good umpire yelled out, loudly, "First base runner is out for passing another baserunner." Now we are down to two outs in the inning. Now, where does the third out of this bizarre inning come in?

Brown, an older man, was baldheaded, but it was covered with his baseball cap. He stepped back on second base, not wishing to advance "at the runner's own peril" (as

How can we give the first base runner a
"passing grade" for his erratic
baserunning?

part of the infield fly rule). By this time that high hanging fly ball was coming down. But where? Right on top of second base! It was a blazing bright day and the sun was hot and glaring through a slight lid of thin clouds. Although the second baseman didn't have to catch that popup fly (the batter was already out when he hit it), instinct came into play, and he moved right on top of Brown's body, so to speak, and reached up to field the fly. Brown, that runner, was looking up at the same second. The ball got in the sun. Both men, at the very last second, had to turn their eyes away from the sun. The baseman and base runner moved off the bag slightly as they were blinded, and Brown's cap fell off, exposing a complete baldness. The swiftly moving baseball dropped right onto the middle of Brown's forehead as he looked up at an angle. He crumpled on the ground, lying on second base. Immediately the alert second base ump shouted, "Runner is out, the batted ball hit him." That was the third out. Inning over.

Not only had poor runner Brown had his head and his dignity wounded, but he had been the victim of the rules - the third out of one of the "most bizarre triple plays in baseball history." DURING THIS WHOLE FIASCO THE DEFENSE HAD NOT TOUCHED THE BALL. THE OFFENSE COMMITTED ALL THREE OUTS.

Brown's team mates carried his dazed body to the dugout to revive him quickly, while the plate and base umpires were explaining this "one in a million series of events" to both teams and managers.

During those last two years that Bill was alive, Stu clearly recalled many incidents and events - both humorous and tragic - that he had experienced with his dad during ball games at Lane Field in San Diego. The saddest one was on a warm August day in 1940, the summer Stuart was a sophomore in high school. Bill and Stu had barely gotten to their usual seating place in the old wooden ball park, when they were stunned by the announcement, by the game commentator over the PA system, that Cincinnati Reds catcher, Willard Hershberger, was found dead that Sunday morning. An apparent suicide. All spectators were asked to rise and bow their heads for a silent moment in Willard Hershberger's memory. The complete story, as written in that day's San Diego paper, follows:

"Willard Hershberger slit his throat with a razor blade after a game, said the reporter, referring to the Reds' catcher. He had replaced the great regular Reds catcher, Ernie Lombardi, in the second game of a double-header. The Reds lost that close game, and I understand that Hershberger took the responsibility for calling the losing pitches. Hershberger, who had also gone hitless in that game, returned to his hotel room in Boston and, over the bathtub, did himself in."

It is recalled, though, that there may have been more to his darkness of mind than baseball. As a boy, Willard Hershberger supposedly discovered the body of his father, who had also killed himself by slitting his throat. (And other mental and emotional burdens may have been carried by the catcher.) It is never just one thing that precipitates suicide, according to Loren Coleman, a research associate with the Human Services Development Institute of the University of Southern Maine." Since Hershberger's suicide, 77 major leaguers or former major leaguers have done themselves in. It has been studied extensively, and researchers have found that it is invariably a number of interwoven factors.

Fortunately, the memories of tragic or sad moments were few for Stu and Bill. For the game of baseball is a fun game, especially exciting and relaxing and uplifting to the spectator.

Certainly the most memorable of these many days together in Lane Field would be the summer of 1937, when the young slugger, Ted Williams, hit the classic tape measure home run over the right field wall which ended up down at the Santa Fe train station. The San Diegans still refer to that one as "the home run." Has any slugger anywhere ever hit a baseball as far? It is doubtful that they have. Bill and Stu, father and son, jumped to their feet as the hit ball rocketed skyward, just stared at each other in a state of complete awe. Here are the legendary particulars of that one.

BASEBALL STORY NUMBER THIRTY - 1937
TED WILLIAMS' "WELL-TRAINED" HOME RUN AT SAN DIEGO'S LANE FIELD
OR
THE "SPLENDID SPLINTER" REALLY "TOOK THAT PITCHER DOWNTOWN," DIDN'T HE? IN FACT, ALL THE WAY TO THE TRAIN STATION

T HEY CALLED HIM "THE SPLENDID Splinter," for this batter, whom many in the baseball world claim to be the "greatest left-handed hitter in the history of baseball," was a lanky build - not heavy and stout as was Babe Ruth. But what perfect timing Ted did develop on that picture perfect swing of his. It was "poetry in motion." And his eyes - they must have been one of the most unusual sets of eyes in the history of baseball players.

Few other baseball hitters have ever claimed to be able to read the manufacturers name label on the ball as it sped toward the plate. He supposedly could count the seams on the ball, too. This gifted San Diegan combined "hawkeyes with perfect swing" - and careful pitch selection, for he studied his strike zone so well. He almost intimidated the plate umpires with his "laying off of bad pitches." They were afraid to call close strikes on him.

The combination of these perfect factors for baseball hitting could produce just one thing - long, long balls, hit with regularity.

But this story is not a discourse on Ted's attributes, but rather, a tale that many fans may not know about one of his many home runs. (It was the classic ball he hit the summer he was breaking into pro ball.)

He really was just a kid, the year was 1937, and he was nineteen years of age. Ted had already become the home run hitter and the great drawing card for his hometown San Diego Padres, the Class "AAA" club and the last step to the major leagues (of course, all fans know that he has become "the legend" of the Boston Red Sox and is in the Hall of Fame.)

Lane Field was just a little distance from the San Diego harbor, and, the highway running North and South, paralleling the right field fence at Lane Field was wide, well-traveled Kettner Boulevard. Beyond that wide thoroughfare were the Santa Fe

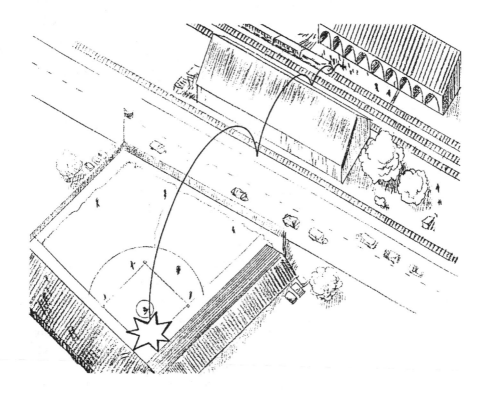

The "splendid splinter" really "took that
pitcher downtown," didn't he? In fact, all
the way to the train station.

Railroad tracks, then the large Santa Fe freight depot and warehouse lay to the East of those. Finally, there was a series of passenger train tracks on east and the beautiful San Diego passenger train station, built in the Spanish mission style. An architectural beauty.

On that day, a beautiful San Diego summer afternoon, sometime between 1 p.m. and 5 p.m., the monstrous blow was struck by Ted, the boy slugger. Theodore Williams really parked that ball!

Working the count carefully on the opposing pitcher, that opposing hurler let go of the pitch Ted was waiting for. With one gigantic sweep of the bat, Ted Williams wrote himself into the baseball history books. At the moment of impact, that large crowd gasped, Stuart and Bill Southworth among them. THE BASEBALL DISAPPEARED OVER THE RIGHT FIELD WALL, STILL RISING AT THE 340 FOOT MARK!

Witnesses over near the freight station, across Kettner Boulevard. say that the projectile finally dropped to the asphalt pavement, from its parabolic arc, in front of the long, wide freight warehouse. The home run was hit so high, when it descended to the ground, its first bounce off the pavement was high enough to clear the high-peeked freight building. The second bounce began on the other side of the freight platform, several tracks beyond. The San Diego - Los Angeles Streamliner was loading for its early evening run up the coast. Passengers were mounting the steps of the scenic chair cars.

That baseball which was sent into orbit by Ted took its third bounce just in front of some of the passengers Los Angeles bound, bounced up, hit the side of the train, and finally came to rest between some tracks near the train. The ball grazed a few passengers on its last rebound.

One passenger loading at the time, who had actually been grazed by the white sphere, ran over and picked up the ball, gazing at it in a complete state of puzzlement. He was wondering who had thrown it at him, when the brakeman, conductor, several passengers, gazed to the West toward the ball park, heard the roar of the crowd as Ted trotted around the bases. They knew immediately, agreed simultaneously what had happened, and told the male passenger. It is said that the man who picked up the home run ball was a native of San Diego. Several weeks later, upon his return to town, he attended a Padre game and related the story to all present.

Not only that, but the man related the story to the Padre team, and he offered to give the ball to Ted. But the young hitter told the man "Thanks," autographed the ball, and handed it back to him. (Try to imagine the value of "that classic ball" on today's market, among collectors of baseball memorabilia.)

Now the awesome conclusion to this 1937 tale of baseball heroics. Several people measured the distance from home plate in Lane Field to the spot of the first bounce - where the ball finally settled to earth. The distance is approximately 616 feet. The next two or three bounces cleared another 200 - 300 feet. Stu recently visited the exact spot where home plate was (it is now a big parking lot area near San Diego harbor, there is no trace of Lane Field at all). Using an auto speedometer once, then pacing it off on foot the second time, Stu Southworth has come to the conclusion that the total path of the ball was over 900 feet from point of impact. The spot where a railroad passenger still could have been "laid out cold" by the impact of Ted's home run ball.

The latter half of 1975 had rolled around, and, by this time, Bill Southworth, then age 79, had married Mildred Murray, herself age 76, a long time resident of Chula Vista, California. They were wed at the town of Bonita, nearby, in Glen Abbey's "Chapel of the Roses." A small English country church, an exact replica of Alfred Lord Tennyson's church in England. Bill and Mildred lived happily together in Mildred's lovely home high above Bonita canyon, just six miles from the waters of San Diego Bay. Stu had never seen two happier people during the year and a half of marriage. Just like two young kids who had discovered love for the first time.

Bill wasn't able to go to the ball park much that year, attending the Padre games at Jack Murphy Stadium perhaps three times that season. His deteriorating condition tired him badly. Bill and Mildred were desperate to try anything to arrest the cancer, which had spread to many areas of the body - even tried laetrile in a Mexican clinic down at Tecate, Mexico, on the border. But Bill Southworth was failing fast, and no type of treatment (radiation, chemotherapy, miracle drugs) seemed to arrest the effects of the condition. Stu's visits to the San Diego area that year usually found his Dad comfortably content to lean back in the big easy chair in Mildred's living room. Stu and Mildred would occupy the other rocker and lounge chair, talking to Bill by the hour.

On one occasion, Bill reminisced about two of Stu's best boyhood friends of Golden Hill Playground, and high school days at Grossmont High School. Mention was made of Albert Taylor, with great memories but with real sadness, for Al died in World War II, in 1944, with Colonel "Chesty" Puller's First Marine Division at Peleliu Island. The other buddy that Bill recalled, Solly Hemus, was surely a great favorite of Bill's from the early years. Mention of Solly's name brought a smile to Bill's face.

Stu and Bill traced Solly's career, that quiet afternoon, from the confines of Golden Hill Playground, Balboa Municipal Golf Course, to San Diego High School, to Pocatello, Idaho, on to the Class "AAA" Columbus "Redbirds" farm club of the Cardinals, and finally to the St. Louis Cards as a player and manager. They were spanning the period of 1938 - 1961. Bill was soon rolling with laughter in his big white easy chair when he retold the story of the first time he came down on Saturday morning to watch our team play in the Junior American Legion games, and in watching Solly Hemus "steal first base." Although Bill had seen this happen, and had often heard the hilarious tale from Stu, who was Solly's pal at the time, he asked Stu to again relate the events as they happened that morning.

BASEBALL STORY NUMBER 31 - 1939
WHAT A "SOLLY" WAY TO STEAL FIRST BASE
OR
I WONDER IF DON BAYLOR AND RON HUNT
TRIED THIS TRICK WHEN THEY REACHED THE
MAJOR LEAGUES?

HAVE YOU EVER HEARD THE baseball myth "You can't steal first base?" Don't you ever believe it, for there are actually three or four methods of pilfering that "first base of the circuit" around the 360' pathway. One of the sneakiest methods that Bill and Stu ever observed of getting away with this feat was tried by none other than that hustling, peppery second baseman of the St. Louis Cardinals, Solly Hemus, in the early 1950's.

Stu, of course, as related earlier in this volume, met Solly Hemus at the Golden Hill Playground area of San Diego, the summers of 1938-1939-1940. They would play "OVER THE LINE," the old hitting game, for hours on end. Hour after hour, day after day. What fun!

Solly was a member of an American Legion Class "B" team, all of whose members aspired to someday soon graduate to the POST 6 or POST 201 Legion Class "A" teams of San Diego. All the teams played at Golden Hill park. Solly was Stu's hero, and he would watch his every move, on and off the diamond. In addition to playing "OVER THE LINE" and baseball together, the two lads would caddy at the Balboa Golf Club, and Solly taught Stu the difficult art of hunting golf balls and selling them on that course. They would hunt and hunt - in the ravines, canyons, the most difficult places to get into and out of - where golfers refused to go to rescue a lost ball. Stu, age 65, returned to that golf course, 50 years later, walked the ravines of those 18 holes - and actually found 34 balls!

Back to the ball diamond. This is the way that our friend, Solly, very early in his career, learned to "con" the umpire and the opposing pitcher into "stealing first base."

Today's baseball spectators must realize that in the 1930's and 1940's most ball uniforms were made of flannel, a very hot material to wear in the summer, but in San Diego's cool sea breezes, it was comfortable. The shirts and pants of those days were not form fitting, but the shirt could be baggy around the middle and the pants could be ballooned out to resemble real knickers. In fact, baseball pants are really nothing but knickers.

I wonder if Don Baylor and Ron Hunt
tried this trick when they reached the
Major Leagues?

This brings us to our leadoff left handed hitter, Solly. Right handers had a tendency to pitch inside to little left handers anyway, so Solly took extreme advantage of this fact. While in the on deck circle taking his practice swings, Solly would, little by little, pull out on this shirt at the front, just grab a handful of it at the navel, and pull some.

When Solly strode up to his position in the batter's box, there he would be, short, with a small strike zone to throw to, but looking like a woman three months pregnant. In addition to this, our friend would crowd the plate. This probably confused the pitcher some, causing him to throw more toward the center of the plate. Invariably, though, one of this hurlers pitches would be just inside the strike zone, it would either strike Solly's shirt (and drop to the round) or just graze his shirt. At the instant that either of these would occur, "injured" Solly would bail out of the batter's box, look wounded, grimace, and look up to the umpire for pity. More often than not, he was awarded first base, recorded as "hit by pitcher." As he trotted to first base, there would be the inevitable argument by the catcher or the opposing coaches. Solly would but smile and prepare to steal second and third bases on successive pitches.

In conclusion to this tale of trickery in baseball, let us inform the reader that there are two or three other ways to "steal first base." Oh, yes!

It was early December, 1975, that Stu and his dad enjoyed their last visit. The cancerous cells were now throughout the body of Bill, but he still got out each morning to do some light work in the sunshine. He loved his final home high on the hill at Camino del Cerro Grande Street in upper Bonita, a suburb of the city of Chula Vista, California.

Stu had come down to present his dad with a new Christmas present a few days early. It was a new pocket-sized computer, battery operated. When Stu handed his gift to his dad, Bill accepted it with wonderment, as a child would with a new toy. Bill Southworth had never done even the simplest kind of math problem on an electronic computer. This graduate electrical engineer had done any needed calculations during his entire 1920 - 1965 career on either a slide rule or the electronic calculating machine. Stu watched his dad run through some basic arithmetic problems, and this new calculating tool sure brought a sparkle to his eye, a very hearty "Thanks, Stuart," and a sudden realization of the "computer age."

That last stay with Mildred and his dad was an especially good two day visit. Stu, Mildred, Bill did several things to bring the Christmas spirit in a little earlier than usual, and especially a good sea food dinner at Anthony's sea food restaurant in Chula Vista. Mildred had become an integral part of this family by now.

It was there that day, seated at Anthony's for lunch, that Bill then disclosed his final baseball tale to the two of them as they listened intently. Mildred and Stu chuckled so loudly in the dining room that other diners might have wondered what created this stir of mirth among the party of three seated near them. Surely Bill had saved one of his best for the last. For everyone present around them would have been both amused and in disbelief to hear the Father's last baseball tale - a real true story of a "Reverse Triple Play" - Nebraska style.

Baseball Story Number Thirty-Two - 1939
Triple Plays Are Rare Enough, But A "Reverse Triple Play"? - Really, Now
OR
Was This A Game Of Baseball Or "Tag"

THE BASEBALL FAN OR PLAYER knows that a triple occurs rarely at any level of baseball. If we researched the statistics of every game ever played, what would be the "micro-percentage" that a triple play occurs, for all innings ever played?

If we agree that a triple play is an infinitesimal percentage, what would be the percentage for a "reverse triple play"? How many of you have ever seen one?

Strangely enough, this is one play which could occur equally well at nearly any level of baseball. Of course, the play must go from first to second to third bases. Let's explain that, for such a very rare play to occur, the conditions must be perfect, or as follows:

NO OUTS, FIRST BASEMAN MUST BE PLAYING ON FIRST BASE LINE, THERE MUST BE RUNNERS ON AT LEAST FIRST AND SECOND BASES, AND THE BALL MUST BE HIT HARD, JUST INSIDE THE FIRST BASE LINE.

During the years that millions of ball games have been played, the author has heard of it occurring just one time, although, of course, it may have occurred more frequently than that. We just don't now, or have those kinds of records.

It was during a 1939 game of town team ball in Northern Nebraska that we heard of this happening as follows:

It is in a rural setting, and with runners on first and second bases, no outs. A heavy hitting left handed slugger - a pull hitter - stepped up to the plate to make history that day. On the first pitch, his bat met the ball squarely, and the screaming "grass cutter" he smashed was in the first baseman's glove as the first base runner, who had a good lead then, broke for second. The first baseman stepped on first, being left handed and a quick arm, fired the ball to second base to shortstop covering. As he threw the ball to second, first baseman yelled loudly, "Tag." The fast first base runner was tagged-fast. This completed a "lightning double play." Now the stage is set for the third out of this "reverse triple play."

To make this rare defensive play in baseball work right, you must have the second base runner hesitate somewhat when the ball is hit, then head for third with some delay.

Was this a game of baseball or "Tag."

The second base runner on this day thought that the low "grass cutter" might be a caught low fly ball, but then saw his first base runner advance - so he advanced, too, but with a hesitation. His late start gave the shortstop just enough time to tag the first base runner, then pivot, fire to third base, and he also was alert enough to yell, "Tag" to the third baseman covering that bag. Third baseman heard the call and complied. That completed the third out, triple play in one sequence. All base runners were wiped out, and the inning was over.

Odd? Unusual? Yes, no doubt about it, although the conditions are such that this type of triple play is waiting for any defense that has no outs and runners on first and second. It could happen any time. Maybe tomorrow, who knows?

So - the order of events in this "reverse triple play" were: FORCE, TAG, TAG.

Whether this rare triple play ever occurred in the history of the major leagues is doubtful, for the base runners would be smarter, quicker, and faster.

The day that Stuart had to return to San Bernardino and prepare for Christmas with his three children there, he cheerily bade "so long" to both Mildred and Bill. They had arisen early, had their favorite breakfast and Mildred was finishing the dishes. Bill slid over to his favorite chair and was soon nodding as Stu carried his luggage to his car.

Stuart gave Mildred a huge squeeze, then he went over to see his dad in the big chair. Bill's head was resting slightly to one side of the back of that easy chair, asleep. His son looked down at the old man, and he seemed so at peace that he didn't want to awaken him. Mildred was about to say to him, "Bill, Stu wants to say goodbye," but Stu put his finger up to his lips to indicate "Shhhhh" to her. Instead of awakening his father, Stu bent down, kissed his high forehead, just as he had done that cold November morning of 1945 in St. Louis, when he said his last goodbye to granddad Sam. He looked at that hairline that had been pure silver since his dad was 25 years old. Over 55 years ago. As Stu stood up, after the last kiss, he slowly murmured to himself, "I love you, Dad."

At that instant there probably flashed through Stu's mind each of the events of their lives together. So many of them had been fun. His dad had the great gift of knowing how to have fun each day. And - Stu's father had taken him to the boy's very first baseball game.

Mildred and Bill later decided not to tell Stu how bad Bill's cancerous condition was. Bill went into the hospital several times, but the two of them did not want Stu to see Bill in that condition.

On May 12, 1976, Stu Southworth was in his math classes - midmorning. He was called from his classroom at San Gorgonio High School by Mildred on the phone. She informed Bill's only child that the old man had died that morning.

The legacy of baseball story "collector and narrator" was that day passed on to the 51 year old ex-Whitman pitcher - from Samuel Southworth (1860 - 1900 tales) and William Dallas Southworth (1900 - 1940 tales) to Harold Stuart Southworth. So, the final third of this volume of stories will be composed of twenty "modern baseball incidents" dating from 1940 to 1990, the last half century of the great game. These final tales will really differ very little from the past, for each of the twenty, though new to the baseball fan and the reader here, could have, and probably did, occur somewhere in the 130 year tenure of the game.

We, the narrators of this book of thirteen decades of baseball, hope you are having many laughs, fun, great enjoyment and enlightenment in discovering these "unusual days in baseball history." Pass every one of them on to your children and grandchildren. Don't let them fade away.

PART THREE

Baseball's Greatest Moments 1940 - 1990

Narrator of Baseball Tales:

HAROLD S. "STU" SOUTHWORTH
(1925 - 20??)

THE THIRD NARRATOR "KEEPS THEM ALIVE" AND INCREASES THE REPERTOIRE

W ELL, THE DODGERS HAD MOVED to Los Angeles in 1956. Of course, the Los Angeles Memorial Coliseum, used as their home field, was a big joke, but it was the best they could find and it did have 100,000 seating. With a left field wall less than 300 feet away, the Dodgers, and some of the National League opponents, learned to chip little "moon shots" over that high wire barrier in left field (for home runs?). Then a clearly hit home run, a tremendous blast in any other ball park, would be rising, hit the screen so hard that it would drop down into the left fielder's glove. The home run hitter would be held to a single and most times be thrown out trying to stretch a hit into a double. It was truly weird. The new Los Angeles Dodgers suffered through it for four seasons, including a World Series, which they won, against the Chicago White Sox. Imagine a World Series played in a football stadium? Finally America's most beautiful major league baseball park was completed in Chavez Ravine for the World Champions to move into.

That old Wrigley Field in Los Angeles, home for years of the Los Angeles Angels, the Cubs' farm club, Class "AAA" baseball, was soon chosen as the playing site for Los Angeles' new American League baseball team, the California Angels. Gene Autry had become famous earlier with his singing and acting, with "Rudolph the Red-Nosed Reindeer" and others, and had accumulated holdings with wise investments. Autry and others had brought the American League to town. The Dodgers had some drawing card competition.

By 1962 Stu was coaching in San Bernardino, and his two sons, Mike and John, were 13 and 10 years of age. Both boys and Stu wanted so badly to see those new "Angels" play. Stu and family were still struggling on a teacher and coach's salary, so it was decided that Mike, the oldest boy, (and a Pony Leaguer that summer), should get the one ticket affordable.

John and Stu took him to the gate at Wrigley Field and saw him inside. They then retired to a corner cafe nearby to see the game on TV. The two baseball fans ordered supper, watched the telecast. Soon an old friend of Stu Southworth, a man who had played ball with Stu as a kid in San Diego, joined them, and they were into a lively discussion of the years past and their favorite topic - baseball. Little John's eyes were wide as he listened to the two old baseball buddies swap tales of glory on the San Diego sandlots. That evening the announcer of the TV program kept making repeated referrals to "handicapped baseball players of the past."

Soon Stu and his ex-player friend were comparing "one-armed and one-legged major leaguers of past years." The following comparisons were made of this unusual group of baseball competitors.

BASEBALL STORY NUMBER 33
MAJOR LEAGUE BASEBALL'S AMPUTEES
OR
THE ONE-ARMED AND ONE-LEGGED
BRIGADE OF COURAGE

ONE OF THE MOST INTERESTING accounts in the history of baseball is to chronologically attempt an accurate summary of all those men, since the art of professional baseball has been practiced, who have tried out for the teams of the big leagues and who were missing an arm or a leg. More fascinating is the knowledge that even one of those brave and disabled souls landed a starting spot on a big league club.

The following is a cursory examination of these who would not let their lack of one arm or one leg prevent them from being written in the history books as major leaguers.

Probably the most famous one was Pete Gray. His story begins very early in his Eastern Pennsylvania town of Nanticoke. At six years old, hitching a ride on a farm wagon, he fell to the road in such a way that the right arm was mangled in the spokes of the wagon's wheel. It required amputation to save his life.

His name was Peter Wyshner in early life, and he was resolved that this early accident was not going to prevent him from being an unusually talented ball player. He not only switched to left handed batting, but he taught himself to handle himself in the field, catch and throw with the same hand. He got very fast in his "catch-throw timing." Following is his record in pro ball:

Three Rivers, Quebec, Canada	
Semi-Pro Club	Late 1930's and early 1940's
Three Rivers, Quebec, Canada	
Professional	1942 - Age 25
Memphis "Chicks" Tennessee	
Professional	1944 - (Most Valuable Player
	in Southern Association)
68 Stolen Bases	
Stole Home Ten Times	
Batted .333 with one left arm	
St. Louis Browns	
Major League	1945 - Age 28

The one-armed and one-legged
brigade of courage.

At the end of World War II, players were scarce, and St. Louis Browns management wanted a drawing card. Pete was a great box office attraction, and he knew it. PETE PLAYED FOR THE ST. LOUIS BROWNS, SALARY $20,000.

Gray would not be the first big league player with such a severe handicap. Hugh "One-Arm" Daily had pitched from 1882 to 1887 in the National League and the Union and American Associations (the latter two also considered to have been major leagues), compiling a 68-80 record and once striking out nineteen batters in a single game.

Pioneer or not, Gray was, of course, a curiosity item. As he worked out with the Browns during their 1945 spring camp at Cape Girardeau, youngsters would imitate him, playing ball with one hand. Manager Luke Sewell picked up Gray's glove on one occasion and tried to catch and throw using one hand himself. Sewell, meanwhile, would wait and see. "He's just another ballplayer in my book, he'll stand or fall on what he shows," the manager told reporters at the training camp.

Gray made the team and there were some good moments: five stolen bases, six doubles, and a pair of triples; cheers from a crowd of thirty-six thousand when he trotted out to left field for the first time at Yankee Stadium; a presumably inspirational display of his batting technique before amputees at Walter Reed Army Hospital; the opportunity to give some confidence to four-year-old Nelson Gary, Jr., who had lost his right arm in an electrical accident (and hoped some day to be another Pete Gray).

But the major leagues, even in the last wartime season, were too difficult for a one-armed ballplayer. At the plate, while he was tough to strike out, Gray had little power and the infield played in to take away the bunt. He would manage only 51 hits in 234 trips to the plate, a .218 average. And however deft, Gray couldn't avoid giving the runners an edge in that brief extra moment it took to transfer the ball for a throw back to the infield.

Gray knew he was in the majors primarily as a gate attraction and, inclined to be an introvert, he found it was hard to avoid a feeling of exploitation. There was friction, too, with teammates who felt he might have cost them some games in a tight '45 pennant race that would wind up with the Browns in third place, six games behind the Tigers.

After the season, Gray went barnstorming in California, playing against a team featuring a one-armed black outfielder names Jesse Alexander. The next stop would be the Toledo Mud Hens of the American Association. When the war ended, so did the brief major league career of Pete Gray. Gray played a few more years in the minors, then went back home to Nanticoke.

We have mentioned an earlier player, Hugh "One Arm" Daily, who pitched in the majors from 1882 - 1887. It is hard to imagine Hugh striking out nineteen batters in a single game one afternoon.

There was Bert Shepherd, an ex-fighter pilot, a property of the Chicago White Sox when he was drafted in 1942. Bert lost a leg, but came back to attempt to resume his pro career. He was in Walter Reed Hospital when it was learned of his ambitions to return to professional baseball.

The twenty-four-year-old was convalescing at Walter Reed when his ambitions came to the attention of Undersecretary of War Robert Patterson. The official got in touch with Larry MacPhail, who had served as his aide prior to being released from the military early in 1945. Together they arranged for a tryout at the Senator's College Park spring training base, not far from the hospital.

On March 13, a few days after being fitted with a more efficient though still temporary limb, Lieutenant Bert Shepard arrived at the Senators' camp.

"This is the one thing I dreamed about over there for months," he told reporters after going through a three-hour drill, displaying a slight limp noticeable only to those who might have been watching for it. "Sure I'm serious about playing ball. I can still take a good cut, throw well, and then I get a special leg instead of this temporary one, I'll do okay."

While it was questionable whether Shepard could make the Senator pitching staff, an incident that occurred a few days later made it clear the ball club prized the south-paw, if only for the goodwill he could bring.

Soon after his initial appearance in the Washington camp, Shepard told Patterson he wanted to work out with the Yankees. An Army plane was provided to fly him to the team's Atlantic City training base and along for the ride was MacPhail, who had just bought the Yanks in a partnership with Dan Topping and Del Webb. When Clark Griffith heard that Shepard was gone, he became extremely upset, suspecting kidnap.

Hollywood has featured a full length film of the "Pete Gray Story" and also starred Jimmy Stewart as Monty Stratton, the Chicago pitcher who did quite well with the White Sox. A hunting accident on his farm caused amputation of a leg. Monty was very despondent, but with encouragement by friends and relatives, Monty did make a brief comeback in baseball. He even learned to move that artificial leg to cover bunts.

During that same Yankee-Angel game (around the corner at Wrigley Field where Stu and John were passing those 2 1/2 hours), the Angels were behind in score and desperate for outs in late innings. The inning previous to this one, there had been a big "rhubarb" between the second base umpire and the third base coach (being ejected from the game). After the ejection, that umpire kept looking over toward the home dugout in an effort to locate the player who was doing further heckling. While in a gaze away from the field of play, the Angel tried a pickoff throw to second base, beat-ing the runner back to the bag by a foot or two. The call was "safe," for the umpire never saw the play until it was completed. The poor man could not very well call the man "out." He really couldn't call anything. The Angel manager, Bill Rigney, came charging out onto the field, and soon he was ejected from the game. His comments about the "derelict umpire" were anything but complimentary. Over the radio and TV, Stu and John in the cafe could see that the announcers were nearing heart attacks over the "no call."

Stu's friend from San Diego, Carl Wilson, reacted by asking Stu, "Say, remember that famous 'disallowed pickoff play' by Bob Feller to Lou Boudreau in the Cleveland Indians - Boston Braves World Series game in 1948? The umpire completely missed seeing the out on the play, and it cost Bob Feller his only World Series victory. Poor Bob, that fastballer, never won one World Series game in his career."

Stu Southworth sat in that corner cafe reminiscing that famous incident of the 1948 World Series - one which is still discussed by old fans of the game of baseball.

BASEBALL STORY NUMBER 34 - 1948
BOB FELLER'S FAMOUS "DISALLOWED PICKOFF THROW"
OR
FELLER'S FIRST WORLD SERIES GAME - AT BOSTON

IT WAS IN THE 1948 World Series, the opening game, and in Boston, where the Boston Braves (under Manager Billy Southworth), National League Champions, were trying to wrestle that first important game from the Cleveland Indians (under Manager Lou Boudreau). The tall fastball pitcher from Van Meter, Iowa, was on the mound in his stretch position. There's a runner leading off of second base. Suddenly that tall pitcher whirled, fired a perfect pickoff throw to second. The shortstop was there in a flash, catching the ball and making the quick tag, all in one quick movement. It was obvious to everyone anywhere within sight that the Boston runner had been caught off too far and could not get back in time to beat the ball. EVERYONE WAS AWESTRUCK WHEN THE UMPIRE SIGNALED "SAFE." He simply "had not been looking at the play" and seen it. Incredible! Following this rhubarb which the Cleveland manager started on the call, Boston lashed a single, scoring that second base runner, the only run of the game, and Boston won that game 1-0.

Actually, it mattered little to the final outcome of the Series, for the Indians finally won it 4 games to 2. However, it prevented Bob Feller, one of the several fastest pitchers in baseball history, winning one World Series game.

For an exact account of the events leading up to this famous "disallowed pickoff play" of 1948, here these words from the authors Danzig, Allison, and Reickler in their co-authored book THE HISTORY OF BASEBALL - ITS GREAT PLAYERS, TEAMS AND MANAGERS:

It happened at Braves Field in Boston, where 40,135 fans had turned out for what promised to be a pitcher's duel between Feller and Johnny Sain, the Braves' right-handed ace. The promise held true as the two craftsmen worked carefully on each batter. Feller hurled hitless balls for four innings. Sain gave up only one hit, a single by Ken Keltner in the second. Boston got its first hit in the fifth when Marv Ricert opened with a single to center, but Feller disposed of the next three batters easily. No other Boston player reached base until the eighth, when Bill Salkeld opened

Feller's first world series game –
at Boston.

with a walk and Phil Masi, sent in to run for him, was sacrificed to second by Mike McCormick.

Eddie Stanky was the next batter. As he stepped to the plate, manager Lou Boudreau called time and came in from his shortstop position for a conference with his pitcher. "Walk Stanky," Boudreau ordered.

Feller shook his head. "I'd rather pitch to him," he said.

"If anybody's going to break up this game," the manager replied, "I don't want Stanky to do it."

Feller reminded Boudreau that Stanky had a bad leg and that he hadn't hit the ball hard the previous two times up.

Bob also mentioned that the next two hitters were Sain and Tommy Holmes. Sain wasn't a bad hitter, and Holmes, a left-hander, led the National League in hitting.

"I know," Boudreau said, "but if we put Stanky on, maybe Sain will hit into a double play."

"You can say," Feller recalls now, "that we had a firm discussion out there on the mound. But he was the manager."

Stanky was walked intentionally, and Sibby Sisti ran for the scrappy second baseman. Feller couldn't induce Sain to hit the ball on the ground, but he got the pitcher to lift a fly to right field for the second out.

With Holmes at bat, Boudreau hovered at second to keep Masi close. Masi refused to stay put, however, and edged off the bag. On signal Feller wheeled and let fly directly to second. Boudreau, who had timed the play perfectly, was there. He speared the ball and slapped it on Masi driving desperately back to the base. Umpire Bill Stewart made his decision without hesitation, spreading his arms in the "safe" motion. Boudreau's protestations did no good. Feller resumed pitching to Holmes. With the count one ball and one strike, Tommy signaled to left, scoring Masi. Alvin Dark grounded out, but the damage was done. The Indians failed to score in the ninth.

"I knew Boudreau was going to call the play." Feller says. "It was a perfect pick-off. Everybody in the park saw it except the umpire. Sure I was disappointed, but I wasn't bitter against Stewart. You can't win if you don't get any runs."

A few weeks later, in a high school baseball game on the Pacific High School diamond in San Bernardino, a varsity Citrus Belt League game was underway with Colton High School. In fact, the great Freshman Ken Hubbs (later to be rookie of the Year in the National League for the Chicago Cubs) was the shortstop for the Colton Yellowjackets. It had been an unusually rainy spring for the San Bernardino area, and the infield and outfield were still pretty wet and slippery. The game really should have been called off because of wet grounds.

As a Colton second baseman dashed over to cover second base (on a straight steal play that Stu had signalled for), the ball was hit to the left of the second baseman, through the hole, on a well-executed hit and run play. The momentum to the right, and then having to reverse to the left, caused the player's feet to gain no traction on that slippery surface, leaving him in midair, going nowhere but down. The unfortunate Colton second baseman just flew up in the air, hung there a second, remaining parallel to the ground, and he fell to the field below "flat like a board." All of his body hit the slightly muddy field around second base with such a thud that the earth shook. When he slowly got up, that player was mud from bill of cap to toes of shoes. Time out was called, fresh towels were brought out to clean up the poor fellow, mud was finally removed from his face, hands, glove, and little else, but the deflated player stayed in the ball game, unhurt to be sure. Just that his gray traveling uniform was so black with mud that no trace of the red and gold letters spelling "COLTON" could be seen anywhere.

As Stu peered out from his position in the dugout, he had to chuckle several times, not at the crazy situation or poor condition of the opponent at second base, but there crept back, from his first baseball season of 1949 at Toutle-Lake High School, Washington, a very similar incident as this.

It was also an incident in baseball caused by a muddy field in the part of the state of Washington where rainy springs are common. There had been a hard rain the night before at the town of Napavine, the small town where Toutle-Lake traveled to play that day. Games such as this one recalled in Stu's mind should definitely be postponed, for the field conditions caused the outcome of that contest, in favor of Toutle-Lake.

The Colton player's misfortune, his midair acrobatics, caused his Yellowjackets no runs in that game, but the poor Napavine player, about which we are to relate his untimely misfortune, cost his Napavine varsity four runs. There can be no occurrence in baseball costlier than a four run miscue. Has the reader ever seen a similar play in a baseball game, one in which field conditions cost the defense all four runs?

BASEBALL STORY NUMBER 35 - 1949
THE "ABORTED THROW" IN FROM
CENTERFIELD
OR
"THE OUTFIELDER PREPARED TO
UNCOIL BASEBALL'S FINEST OUTFIELD THROW"

IT WAS MY FIRST BASEBALL coaching job, in 1948, at Toutle-Lake High School in Southwest Washington state. On that particular day we had travelled to the little logging community of Napavine. Both Toutle-Lake and Napavine were not near the top of the league in standings, so it was not an important game from the standpoint of league standings.

The field was in good playing condition, except the area in deep centerfield. It had rained several days previous to the game, and the area mentioned was very slippery and soggy. So, the stage was set for this unusual and unfortunate event about to take place. That poor centerfielder.

In the middle of the game, one inning we were leading by a score of 5-0. We had the bases loaded. One of our heavy hitters clouted one deep to centerfield. Of course, the runners tagged up, because the fly was caught. When the centerfielder caught the ball, his two feet were planked squarely in the middle of that muddy, oozy, grassy area. He had no real footing.

As he caught the ball, he set his feet to throw into the infield. Although he was miles from the infield, he was going to throw that guy out at the plate, he thought.

He reared back with that arm, cocked his body, and he was ready to "uncoil with Baseball's greatest throw ever."

As he started to throw, he slipped, and his feet were in the air under him. The ball, instead of going forward, travelled a mile-a-minute in reverse and landed near the base of the wall.

All I recall seeing at that instant was his feet go flying out from under him, his hat flew in one direction, his glove came off in his hand and flew in another direction, the ball flew backwards, and he landed belly down on the grass and water puddle, face in the mire.

Neither outfielder backed him up or was over to help, in case. He was all alone there.

The outfielder prepared to uncoil
baseball's finest outfield throw.

All four of those runs scored before he could extricate himself form the mud puddle, wipe the water from his eyes, go get the ball, throw it in and relay it to the plate.

The score was then 9-0 for us.

Coach Stu Southworth not only loved the game of baseball, but he faithfully followed his high school's football fortunes as well. Stu and the family seldom missed a home game when his Pacific High School or San Gorgonio High School teams performed. In fact, Stu was the home school's football timer - for a period of ten years.

One evening, at an early season football game with a strong team from the Orange County area, the opposition not only brought over their team mascot, a huge, fierce-looking bulldog on leash, but that school also provided Stu Southworth with a "check timer" (a teacher or an athletic coach to sit with the home timer (Stu) to see to it that the scoreboard and clock were kept correctly - and honestly). Stuart thought nothing of this, as it was customary to provide timers from the visiting team. It also gave the lonely timer, at his table on the field, some company to pass the duller moments of the game.

During the football games, the check timers, usually coaches of one of the team sports in that high school, discuss anything and everything along the athletic line.

That evening the discussion led to baseball, and the Orange County pride, The California Angels.

Stu Southworth and the Orange County coach began to compare baseball oddities - "games so unusual that they defy the laws of percentages."

Finally, to top all stories told that evening, Stu was treated to the unbelievable account which follows - all about an American Legion team which had left 27 men on base (27 LOB) in a nine inning game, but the team had been held scoreless, and outhit their opponent 10 to 3.

Three weeks later the coach from Orange county sent Stu the article taken from a newspaper in a Northern USA town, verifying that, in 1949, this had, indeed, occurred.

BASEBALL STORY NUMBER 36 - 1949
TWENTY-SEVEN RUNNERS LEFT ON BASE AND HELD SCORELESS - THE ANATOMY OF BASEBALL'S MOST UNUSUAL SHUTOUT
OR
DOES LOB REALLY MEAN "LOSING OUR BALL GAME" WITH STRANDED RUNNERS

THERE ARE NO ACCURATE RECORDS kept in the history of the sport citing the number of managers who, having lost a ball game in a most bizarre fashion, went out and commit suicide as a result of their extreme depression. There are some sad stories about major leaguers who contemplated or actually succeeded in doing away with themselves after a bad game of baseball. Willard Hershberger is one name which comes to mind. This author was sitting in the stands of the old "AAA" Lane Field in downtown San Diego, with Will Southworth, his father, in 1939, when a Pacific Coast League game was interrupted to announce the death of Hershberger by suicide that morning. A tragic memory for your writer.

If ever, though, there was a reason to contemplate suicide as a coach or manager of baseball teams, it would have to be after the tale which is about to be unfolded in this story of a shutout.

After extensive research on this statistic, we finally come up with a game so statistically unbelievable that it "defies the odds." In fact, if asked what the odds would be that this could happen, we would, perhaps, reply, "Oh, about a 'zillion to one'." It is a record, a percentage, a statistic which the author has never even heard discussed until he began tracking it down.

THIS STORY CONCERNS A BASEBALL TEAM, AMERICAN LEGION LEVEL, UP IN THE NORTHERN PART OF THE USA, WHICH LEFT BASES LOADED EACH OF THE NINE INNINGS, SCORED NO RUNS, LOST 2-0, AND OUTHIT THEIR OPPONENTS 10-3.

Whether this ever occurred again in the history of baseball is not known. One thing we are sure of - it probably couldn't happen on any level of pro ball.

Now follow the strangest line of innings you could imagine in the game:

INNING ONE - Bases loaded after three consecutive base hits. Two outs. Hard hit ball

Does "LOB" really mean "losing our
ballgame" with stranded runners.

in shortstop hole. Shortstop makes brilliant play for the third out. No runs scored.

INNING TWO - Bases are loaded after two outs. No runs scored. High fly ball to third baseman for the third out.

INNING THREE - Bases are loaded after two outs. No runs scored. Left handed hitter drills a hard line drive fly to the first baseman.

INNING FOUR - Bases are loaded. No outs. No runs have scored yet. A ball is hit to the third baseman, who touches his bag and fires a throw to catcher. Tag play for an out at home. Now there are two outs, men on first and second bases. the next batter drags down a bunt for a hit, in front of the third baseman. Bases loaded again. Next batter strikes out.

INNING FIVE - Bases become loaded with two outs again. No runs scored. Next batter hits a little nubber only five feet in front of catcher. Catcher tags home plate.

INNING SIX - Bases are loaded after two outs. No runs scored. Weak grounder is hit to the pitcher. He throws to the plate for the third out, instead of throwing to first base.

INNING SEVEN - Bases are loaded. No outs. No runs scored. Two high popups caught for two outs. Next batter strikes out.

INNING EIGHT - Bases are loaded after one out. No runs scored. Infield is in. Two successive grounders are hit to infielders who throw to catcher at the plate.

INNING NINE - Bases are loaded, after two are out. No runs have scored. The number eight hitter strikes out, ending the ninth inning and the game.

Now that we have examined the anatomy of such a possible game, but a highly improbable one, let's look at the line score of the two teams involved:

	1	2	3	4	5	6	7	8	9	R	H	E
TEAM A	0	1	0	0	1	0	0	0	0	2	3	5
TEAM B	0	0	0	0	0	0	0	0	0	0	10	3

After this American Legion game, there is no account of what went on in the team meeting, what words were said there, or of what the coach did when he left the scene.

We baseball fans would concur, however, if ever suicide were justified, this game would be the set of circumstances promoting that act.

TWENTY SEVEN MEN LEFT ON BASE IN A NINE INNING GAME. THAT MUST BE A RECORD. BUT TO ADD INSULT TO INJURY, THE SAME TEAM SCORED NO RUNS. TO FURTHER ADD INSULT TO INJURIES, THE LOSING TEAM OUTHIT THE WINNERS BY A COUNT OF TEN TO THREE, SHOULD THE DESPONDENT COACH DO HIMSELF IN BY HANGING, POISON, THE SILVER BULLET, OR DON HIS KIMONO FOR "HARI KARI"?

After reading this account, we Americans can only conclude that "baseball really is a crazy game."

As is customary, a national tradition at each football and baseball game in America, the crowd turns toward the flagpole and stands at a position of attention, singing the national anthem, "The Star Spangled Banner." Once more, Stu and the three young men standing next to him at Dodger Stadium that day, stood and sang. The year was 1961, the day of August 14th, son Michael's 12th birthday. What a sight. What a view of all of Los Angeles from that spot chosen by the planners and builders. Stu's sons, Mike and John, had looked forward to this day for so long, and Mike had invited his best friend. A boy his age, Ronnie Lawson, to help him celebrate the big day. The special attraction was that the day offered a doubleheader with Chicago's Cubs, and all in attendance had the double fun of seeing "Fergie" Jenkins pitch one of the games, and they loved the unpredictable antics of Manager Leo Durocher. His gyrations from the third base coaching box, his wiping out the chalk lines of that coaching box by the end of the first inning. Durocher was unusually active that afternoon, for both games went into extra innings, each lasting twelve or thirteen innings. The boys sure got their money's worth, for they were in their seats watching warmups at noon and left the stadium shortly before 9 p.m.

As was mentioned above, as the first game approached, the announcer asked that packed crowd to rise and sing the national anthem. After this ritual was completed, Stu entertained the three boys until game time - with the silly baseball tale of "Jose from Havana, Cuba." That myth has been around at least since the mid - 1950's, but not one of the three youngsters had heard the classic.

Stu really conned the kids into the tale by asking them, "Boys, did you hear about the visitor from Cuba, who wanted to see an American game of baseball so badly, he sat on top of the centerfield flag pole in Cleveland during the whole game?"

John, Stu's 10 hear old son, looked up at him and said, "Dad, how could Jose do that? He'd fall off after a while. There's not enough room to even sit." But Stuart was adamant with his younger son, and he turned and winked at both Mike and Ronnie, the 12 year olds, further insisting, along with the two boys that the visitor had, indeed, done this very thing for over 2 1/2 hours one afternoon." I guess John had never heard of "flagpole sitters"?

Between the time that the two clubs' starting batteries were being introduced and the throwing of the first pitch of the first contest, the father taught his kids (and friends) one of baseball's funniest myths of baseball lore. This tale is entitled "The Best Seat In The House."

As those three young fans have grown to manhood (Mike is now 41, not 12), none of them ever let the aging high school coach forget the fact that they were led down the "road to baseball myth" that important day in their lives.

Will you readers find yourselves disbelieving Jose's incredible feat - that day he came to Cleveland to see "Minnie" Minoso play?

Baseball Story Number 37 - 1950's Era
"The Best Seat In The House" In
Cleveland Ohio
OR
Would They Have Sung Some Other Song If His Name Had Been Pedro?

T HE BEST SEAT IN THE HOUSE"
(Do you really believe this is a true story?)

There once was a ball player named "MINNIE MINOSO." He had played ball all of his life and grew up on the sandlots of Havana, Cuba. "Minnie" was "picked up" by the Cleveland Indians. When this occurred, the people of Havana were so proud of their hero. But most of "MINNIE'S" friends were very, very poor. But, oh, were they proud of their buddy, "MINNIE," whose real first name was ORESTES.

One evening all of the poor buddies were drinking rum in their favorite tavern in the lower side of Havana. They said, "Gee, I wish we could go to Cleveland to see "MINNIE" play. But, alas, not enough money!" Suddenly, they had a bright idea. They would pool their available money and "draw straws." They had enough money to send one of them by plane to America. When the straws were broken, then drawn, who do you think won? Yup, it was Jose! Oh, he was so excited! He would get to go to Cleveland to see "MINNIE" play a ball game. He ran home and told his wife, Escuela, and she made him a shirt and packed some good food for his trip. Jose's buddies took him out in Havana, went to a good clothing store, and they carefully had Jose measured for a good suit of clothes.

On the appointed day of departure, Jose was taken to the airport, and they all waved to him from the airport terminal. Away he flew. But before he left, they made him promise that he would keep a diary, then share all of his experiences when he returned.

Jose flew to America without incident. He changed planes at Miami and on to Cleveland. Sure enough, there was "MINNIE" at the airport. They hugged each other, and "MINNIE" had rented a limousine to take them to the huge Cleveland stadium.

When they arrived, "MINNIE" told Jose that he had come to see the game on a day when all the seats were taken. SOLD OUT! But this was no dilemma, for "MINNIE" said he had saved the "best seat in the house" for Jose! He pointed to the tall flag pole out in deep centerfield. He said, "Jose, there is the best seat in the house. You

360 FEET

Would they have sung some other song if
his name had been Pedro?

'shinny' up that pole and you can see everything." "MINNIE" said "So long," and went in to dress for the ball game. Jose was delighted to have the finest seat in the house. From where he perched up high he could see the teams warming up, taking infield and outfield practice, then the game began. Cleveland won, in nine innings, and "MINNIE" Minoso turned in several sparkling defensive plays and got three hits - one was a home run which flew out of the park, near Jose.

Oh, what a great day! They had dinner out at a fine restaurant, and the next morning "MINNIE" saw Jose off to fly back to Havana. At the airport there, Jose's buddies greeted him. Away to their favorite bar they sped. They asked Jose to recount all of his experiences. He told them every detail, every minute he was gone on the trip.

He especially mentioned the courtesies that everyone at the ball park extended to him. "But," said Jose, "the finest moment in America was just before the ball game began. There I was perched way above the field on my flagpole. Suddenly, the entire crowd, players, umpires, everyone turned and faced me, and sang to me these words - "Jose, can you see?"

Coach Robert A. Webster was Head Baseball Coach at Pacific High School in San Bernardino from 1954 to 1955. Stu Southworth replaced Bob as the baseball coach in the years 1956 to 1959 inclusive. The two men had been college basketball and baseball players at USC and the University of Washington, respectively. During their years at Pacific together, they coached basketball at the same levels. It was in the 1960 season that both men produced championship basketball teams. Shortly before Easter vacation, it was decided by the two coaches that they should celebrate the titles won by treating themselves to a long auto trip to Colorado and Kansas. The day before Easter break, Bob and Stu got on the road for Palm Springs, Indio, Blythe, Prescott, Arizona, and on to Flagstaff, Gallup, Albuquerque, and at Trinidad they parted company for a few days. Bob visited in Colorado, and Stu had people in Western Kansas to see. The two had agreed to meet in Denver and drive home by Pueblo, Raton, Taos, Santa Fe, to Albuquerque, and home to San Bernardino.

This was the only trip the two took, of this length, in their very close friendship of 35 years or more. It was a while riding that first night across old Arizona that they opened up and told each other more and more about themselves. They should have repeated these trips every two years or so.

Bob Webster died in December, 1987, and Stu Southworth has dedicated the volume completed (prior to this collection of humorous tales) to the memory of Coach Bob. The title of the book is THE COMPLETE BOOK OF BASEBALL SIGNS.

Two of the most hilarious baseball incidents in Bob's playing days were shared with Stu that night, across the moonlit Arizona desert. About ten o'clock that evening the athletic stories, both playing and coaching tales, were flowing fast and furiously from the recollections of Bob and Stu.

Fresh off the USC campus, Bob told, he was drafted by the Yankees to Ventura, California, in the California League. The next season he was sent as a pitcher to Twin Falls, Idaho, of the Pioneer League. Bob Webster's pitching career in pro ball was looking up, until he received a line drive on the knee area. Soon his injury ended his pitching hopes and his professional career in the game. His season at Twin Falls was 1948.

The Pioneer League is spread wide over Idaho, Utah, and Montana. The Twin Falls Cowboys traveled to Montana through Yellowstone National Park. If any reader has been to the shores of Yellowstone Lake near the Fishing Bridge, he has probably stopped off for food or coffee at the large Yellowstone Hotel. It faces the lake, and the dining room windows face the lake.

On one trip through the park, some of the Twin Fall's team was just sitting at their tables relaxing, after the good food served them was consumed, when they looked to the lake front and saw, to their surprise, several of their team mates with baseball bats and balls. They got up and peered out the window at the sudden activity in that area. Their eyes, they thought, must be deceiving them. Some of the team members had gotten into the bus, dragged out the team equipment, and were actually fungo hitting good baseballs out into the lake to see who could win a bet (as to who would hit the ball the farthest into the deep water). Gil McDougald, Gus Triandos, Bob Webster, and a couple of future New York Yankees were on that team stopping at the hotel for the meal. Manager Charlie Metro, the team leader, was fit to be tied! What was said when he discovered the guys wasting baseballs will not be repeated. The reader will recall that in later years Charlie Metro was one of the "co-managers" of the Cubs when those Cubbies tried the "rotating manager system."

Stu never forgot those unforgettable moments that Bob shared with him.

As the old 1950 Ford sedan was being pushed across Arizona and New Mexico on that Easter vacation trip, Bob told of another baseball rarity, a game in Great Falls, Montana. As he told this one, both coaches wondered if such an odd event had ever been seen on a ball field.

Bob said he was pitching to the Great Falls team, and his catcher, Triandos, called for the curve ball. Bob objected and shook off the sign. Triandos called for it again. Oh, well. Bob threw it! The ball was mashed, it was hit so hard. Back went the centerfielder to the flagpole, and he leaped as high as he could, but the ball glanced off the tip of his glove. He really didn't see it after that. It didn't go over the fence. The ump and outfielder looked for it. The Pioneer League ump had to know where the ball was to really call "home run." It didn't go over. It didn't stay in the park. It never bounced off anything. Just disappeared. WHERE IN THE DEVIL WAS THAT BALL?

Finally, on a hunch, the umpire climbed the foot rungs of the flagpole. At the top of the fence the ball was found. Somehow it had curved around in flight, glanced off the fielder's glove, and had wedged itself way up high between the flagpole and the fence at that point. The flagpole also served as a lightpole.

Bob, the pitcher, was freezing out on the mound, waiting for the game to resume, there was a furious debate, miles from home plate, involving both managers, players, all umpires, and probably some spectators, too. When the rhubarb calmed down, the ball was ruled a double. One run scored, but no more that inning. The Great Falls aggregation was most unhappy, of course. Bob Webster chuckled when he told Stu how lucky he was on that decision. Both men agreed that the hitter was robbed of a scorching home run - by a light pole.

In remembering Gordo's great baseball team of 1956 and its fabulous base running exploits, Stu recalls his first time in successfully teaching the "fake throw - hidden ball play" to a baseball team. Stu and those '56 Pacific Pirates were amazed at its consistent effectiveness in "AAAA" class level of ball.

Of all the hidden ball tricks, this variety must be the most cunning - really a "dastardly trick," to be sure.

This sudden surprise to the base runner can be worked at any of the three bases. On a pitcher pickoff attempt, catcher pickoff attempt, or anytime that any runner on base has had to slide into a base on a close play from any defensive throw. The procedure is as follows:

The close throw comes to the base. The runner barely is called safe by that nearby umpire. the runner has slid in (the play works much better if it is a runner sliding in head first, for his head is faced down looking at dirt and bag. Now comes the trick that makes this play work. The baseman covering the bag who received the throw on the close sliding play, he immediately fakes a "quick snap throw" back to the pitcher, who has his glove out ready to receive the ball. The baseman never throws the ball, though, but he hides it in his glove right away after the fake toss. The pitcher catches on right away to what is going on, and he turns his back on that base.

If the sliding runner did not actually see the ball tossed back to the pitcher, but he only observed the baseman's arm motion (the quick snap fake throw) out of the corner of his eye, he may think that the pitcher actually got the ball. The pitcher, after seeing the quick fake throw, must carry out his part of the scam. He now walks toward the mound area, back to the runner, as if to take the position on the rubber. Pitcher must remember, however, that he is not allowed to be in the dirt area near the mound.

The sliding runner gets up, dusts himself off, then steps off his base a few steps to assume his normal primary lead, the baseman comes over to the runner and tags him with the ball he had hidden in the glove and yells over to the near umpire, "Hey, ump," holding the ball on the runner's body. The near umpire will see this, and yell, "Yer out." Or he certainly should.

If the reader of this story doesn't think that this cute trick works in a baseball game, up and down the baseball ladder, Little League to the major leagues, consider the following news article from the August 13, 1989, San Bernardino Sun newspaper. Yep, it happened to Padre Marvell Wynne, on that day. Jeff Treadway, the Atlanta Braves second baseman pulled it by faking a toss to pitcher Joe Boever and saying, "Stay off the rubber, Joe." Then Marvell got up, led off base, and you know the rest of the story.

The Padres manager, Jack McKeon said afterwards that he couldn't recall the last time he'd seen the play work in major league ball. But it does certainly prove one thing in the history of baseball - that any offensive or defensive play that has ever been worked successfully at any level of the game, can be worked just as well at any other level of the game."CAUGHT OFF BASE BY THE HIDDEN BALL"

"Marvell Wynne of the San Diego Padres forgot a simple command of baseball Friday night: Keep your eye on the ball at all times. Know who has it.

With Atlanta leading 6-5, Wynne led off the ninth inning of the opener of a doubleheader with a single and was sacrificed to second base. With Roberto Alomar batting, Wynne took a couple of steps off second, and Braves second baseman Jeff Treadway, who still had the ball hidden in his glove pocket, moved in for the tag. Wynne was the victim of the old hidden ball trick. Said Treadway, "I faked tossing the ball to the pitcher Joe Boever and told him to stay off the rubber," Treadway said. "I've tried it before in the minor leagues," Treadway said, "but it had never worked for me before. When you're playing the way we are, you do whatever you can do to win ball games."

Padres Manager Jack McKeon said that he couldn't recall the last time he saw the play work. "The base runner has to keep his eyes on the ball. The pitcher was not on the mound, anyway. There was no purpose in him being off the base. Where was he going?"

Back to the dugout, as it turned out. Beware of hidden ball tricks. There are several types, and each of them are mighty tricky.

One of Stu Southworth's favorite baseball plays was the "double suicide squeeze play." His teams from 1947 to 1979, for over 30 years in three western states, plagued the opposition with this tactic, one of complete surprise to the defense. Any opponent expects the hitting team to try for one run on the squeeze play, but to try for two? And easy, cheap runs.

This clever play is quite simple in theory. With base runners on second and third, or bases loaded, the coach gives the batter the suicide squeeze sign. Of course, the runners are all stealing on the pitch.

On the good bunt, of course, the runner from third base scores easily. Keep your eye now on the second base runner. He is the key man on this super play. He steals on the pitch, after getting a huge lead off base. That second base runner never breaks stride as he steams around third base, sliding home on what will always be a close play, but one which should go to the runner in percentages of success. This runner beats two throws, even if both throws are right on target. The defense will throw from the third baseman picking up the ball, to the second baseman, usually, covering the first base, followed by that second baseman's throw to the catcher at the plate. BUT WHAT MAKES THE PLAY WORK IS THAT THE SECOND BASEMAN COVERING FIRST BASE WILL USUALLY HESITATE SOME BEFORE RETURNING THE THROW HOME. That spells defeat for the defense on stopping this second run.

When the action is over and the dust clears, two runs have scored on one bunt (THE SAME DAMAGE AS COULD BE INFLICTED BY A SLUGGER HITTING A HOME RUN OVER THE FENCE WITH A RUNNER ON BASE).

Coach Southworth had an excellent, smart, willing group of baseballers, his Pacific High School Varsity of 1956. They were all good bunters and worked on it by the hour. The play shown above was worked several times - once performed twice in one game for a total of four runs. The opposition was stunned completely by this tactic - pulled twice.

Spectators began to expect two runs to score whenever a squeeze was called for. In their wildest hopes, however, none of the faithful Pirate fans ever expected to see three runs on one bunt. Neither did coach Stuart.

That very play happened one day against those Colton Yellowjackets - three runs on a bunt. For this to occur, let us make it very clear, the ball had to be bunted very hard, almost "push-bunted," the entire field had to be very smooth, hard, with grass new cut and low-cut.

Fans, now imagine yourselves watching the following feat performed.

BASEBALL STORY NUMBER 38 - 1956
GORDO'S LONG, LONG, LONG, ...BUNT
OR
THAT BALL WAS BUNTED AND PICKED
UP OVER 200 FEET FROM HOME PLATE

PACIFIC **HIGH SCHOOL OF SAN** Bernardino, California, was in its third year of existence in the Spring of 1956. I had just been appointed Head Coach of the Varsity squad and we were in the thick of the league race.

Our first meeting with COLTON HIGH SCHOOL in the "AAAA" Citrus Belt League was on our home diamond. The diamond had been prepared for the game, after a couple of days of rain and very overcast weather.

We played the game on a threatening day. Rain clouds hung low and thick over the field. occasional sprinkles fell all afternoon.

It was sure a close ball game until the bottom of the fourth inning. Then the "dam burst" on one unusual play.

We had the bases loaded with one out, score tied 1-1. Up to the plate steps my Third Baseman, Gordon Sloan, nicknamed 'GORDO'. He was a fine bunter and an excellent switch hitter, and our great team captain.

When bases are loaded, it is sometimes coached that the two inside infielders "peel out" and cover third base and first base on a bunt attempt. They leave second base area open, covering first base and third base for a pickoff attempt on a missed bunt attempt. Colton did exactly that. So I had Gordon fake a bunt on the first pitch. He was batting from the left side of the plate. Sure enough, the right fielder was dashing way over to the right field line behind first base to cover an overthrow at first base. The center-fielder was playing straight away. Second baseman dashed to first base to cover the throw there. I called time out and told Gordon to push a hard bunt past the pitcher, just out of his reach, to his left, to roll out near second base.

Gordon Sloan was an athlete who took great pride in following directions to the letter. On the next pitch, Gordon did exactly what I had asked. His bat was in bunting position, but he pushed the bunt harder than usual, more than a bunt. I had signalled all runners to steal on the pitch. Runners were going hard.

The ball was pushed just outside the reach of the pitcher; it rolled hard out to the spot where the second baseman had vacated. It kept rolling hard, for our diamond was hard and the grass was cut low. Would you believe the centerfielder and right fielder

That ball was bunted and picked up over
200 feet from home plate.

had to go get it out in medium right field? But both outfielders were shifted wrong, and they were both surprised. It took them a long time to get the ball. All the runners scored, and Gordon was on second base before you could bat an eye. As the outfield throw came in from the centerfield to the catcher, Gordon watched the throw go through, and he was sliding into third base, safe.

When the dust cleared on this play, everyone was in a state of disbelief - here a baseball player had bunted in three runs (three RBI's) and ended up on third base, on a long rolling bunt through the infield.

The score was now 4-1. We scored three more times in that inning, going away the winner 7-1."

Athletic history is filled with stories of the "superathlete," the high school or sand-lot young man or woman who has the secret desire to "land a certain position on a certain team" or "some great individual goal," these may be aspired to secretly, or the athlete may let it be known by everyone that he or she is driving straight for that target from an early age.

Coach Stuart Southworth was in his second year at Pacific High of San Bernardino. Down the road a distance of 30 miles to the west was Citrus High School (serving two towns, Glendora and Azusa, right at the foot of the San Gabriel Mountains). There also was located Citrus College, a junior college, still in existence. Today there is no Citrus High School, but the high school students are split between Azusa High School and Glendora High School.

In 1956, a Citrus High School senior excelled in three sports - more than excelled. He is today a legend at that school. Although this young man enjoyed a fantastic foot-ball season, Stu was unable to see him perform in that sport, nor did he see him in the spring in baseball. During the winter, several Pacific coaches did pile into a car one day and journey down the freeway to Fontana High School, and watched this "Adonis" lead his basketball squad to an overwhelming victory over the Fontana "Steelers." Stu and other coaches could but sit in their seats, watch the superb perfor-mance of this kid, roll their eyes around in the back of their heads, and dream about coaching such a young athlete with this much talent - just once in their careers - in any team sport. Once in a coach's lifetime.

This super senior went on to lead his baseball team that spring to the C.I.F. (Southern California Championship) in that school's division. Citrus High School won it 6-5 in the ninth inning, finding themselves behind 5-3 and losing to Central High School of El Centro, and a very fine pitcher.

Sure enough, in the clutch, this super performer came through - in the most unusual finish a baseball fan has seen. The slugger-athlete belted a score-tying double to tie the game, eventually win the playoffs, end his senior year and high school athletic career, and go on to his next goal, which was a lofty one. He aspired to be a quarterback for UCLA's Bruins. He enjoyed a fine college football career for the next four years at UCLA.

What made the last inning of that classic game so dramatic? This Citrus legend performed a feat that is well worth recounting to all baseball fans and readers.

Before we tell the reader of the unusual manner in which the game was won by our hero, we must stop to believe, however, that, of all baseball games played since 1869, probably at least one has been won by a hero of days long past, and in exactly the same manner. Maybe more than one game.

BASEBALL STORY NUMBER 39 - 1956
THE "SUPERSTAR" WHO
REFUSED TO BE WALKED
OR
THE SOUTHERN CALIFORNIA
CHAMPIONSHIP DECIDED BY
THE RUN SCORING DOUBLE, DURING THE
"INTENTIONAL WALK"

THIS STORY WAS TOLD TO me the day I played our first 1957 Varsity baseball game at Citrus High School in Glendora-Azusa, California. It has been so long ago that I am not going to vouch for names, team members, etc., except to tell the reader that it is a true story.

We had gone to the Citrus High School that day in late February, 1957. As we were waiting for the field manager to line the field, the Citrus Varsity coach told me this tale of his final game the year before. His Varsity baseball team won the C.I.F. championship the year before, but the manner in which they won the title will leave the reader speechless. What a finish to a season, a championship game, and to a superathlete's high school career.

He said that Citrus High School was playing El Centro High School for the title that day - at Citrus High School field. Now, in those days, out in right center field there was the corner of a tennis court sticking out quite prominently into the outfield area. It protruded enough to make a long fly ball not too long, excepting that it had to be high enough to clear the high fence.

The game had been a nip-and-tuck contest. In those days, all high school games were nine innings, not seven. It was the bottom of the ninth inning, and the score was 5-3 in favor of El Centro, the visiting team.

Up to bat steps Citrus High School for the last inning. Somehow they got one man on base, on second. I'm not sure of the number of outs at the time. El Centro had a great pitcher who had done a super job all day of holding down the strong Citrus lineup to three runs. (He later pitched for U.S.C.)

Up to bat came a heavy hitter for Citrus High School. He tripled the fourth run in, and the stage was set for the final heroics of our star of this tale. A base hit would bring in the tying run, and the hitter would represent the winning run.

The Southern California Championship
decided by the run scoring double,
during the "intentional walk."

With first base open and Citrus High School's great superstar coming to bat, the El Centro coach instructed his pitcher to intentionally walk the batter. This player is, to this day, probably the greatest athlete ever to graduate from the (then) Citrus High School district. Ball one - the catcher stepped out to receive the pitch. Ball two - the batter watched the second pitch go wide. He called time out and went to the batrack, and what he did we do not know. Perhaps just to throw the pitcher off, to worry him. While there he told his coach that the two pitches thrown were very close to the outside corner of the plate. He wanted to know if he could swing on the next one, if it was close enough? The third pitch was just barely outside the plate. The El Centro pitcher was not careful. Whamm! Sure enough. That strongarm athlete didn't just poke the ball on the end of his bat. He rifled a double off the tennis court screen. He had knocked in the tying run, and he was the winning run, standing on second base. At that point in the game this star had batted 5 for 5, had stolen second, third and home his first time up, and had stolen another base in another inning.

The Citrus coach gave him the sign to steal third on the next pitch. The good hitter at the plate then grounded one to shortstop as this superstar broke from second on the steal. As the shortstop made a long throw to first for the second out, this great athlete just rounded third and headed for home plate. The bewildered infielder covering first on the throw hesitated long enough for the star to slide under his throw home, and score the winning run, 6-5.

The game was over. Citrus won the Southern California Baseball title in the "AAA" class that year.

The great superstar who ended his high school career on this note was none other than Bill Kilmer, eventually the N.F.L. professional quarterback for the New Orleans Saints football club, and the Washington Redskins, as well. After high school, he attended UCLA.

Fans, how would you like to win or lose the "big game" that way?

The reader earlier was taken through the playing days of his third narrator, Stu Southworth. At that time Stu unfolded the nostalgia of his first baseball teams, the American Legion Class "B" squads, all sponsored in the decades when the only youth baseball in America was "Legion Ball." Little League and Pony League and the like - these had not formed yet. Does the reader remember the incidents told of Stu and his first playground pal, Solly Hemus, in San Diego?

For a moment, let's go back to the previous story of Bill Kilmer, the Citrus High School star athlete. We showed how a young man can strive onward, upward to a goal - often a secret one, but often achieving the dream he had.

From the earliest of his boyhood days, Solly Hemus would have aspired to reach the pinnacle of baseball, the big leagues. He wished to play in the Cardinal infield, which he eventually accomplished. But what of the dreamer who rises even above and beyond the expected level of his dreams? Probably never did Solly include (in this framework of hard work toward his goal) the possibility of filling the role of Cardinal manager from 1956 to 1959. If he had, we can be pretty certain that he would not have suspected some of the bizarre incidents which can befall a team and manager during his tenure in that position. Solly spent approximately 550 days in the capacity as manager of the St. Louis Cardinals.

When he arose one day to assume his duties and play another National League game, he could not have guessed that the day would bring to him and the Redbirds one of the strangest games in Cardinal history, if not all of baseball history.

Let us focus now on the utter confusion which would reign in the middle of a major league baseball game if, by accident or misunderstanding, or by intentional act, another baseball suddenly appeared on the playing field. We are playing the game with two baseballs.

Two balls being thrown around by the infield at one time. This new ball being thrown, relayed, caught, chased down, etc. Such an incident could be very dangerous to player, offense or defense, or the umpires. What would you do if you were an infielder and saw two balls coming your way during a play, after the ball was hit?

Such a thing could even occur in practice or pre-game warmups. Our good friend and coach, Robert A. Webster, mentioned earlier in a baseball tale in this book, recalls another incident in his playing days in the Pioneer League. The Twin Falls Cowboys had taken their pre-game warmups one evening at Ogden, Utah. The Ogden manager was at home plate with his starting catcher taking the throws coming in. Many teams use two balls in practice drills and pre-game warmups. Somehow there was a mixup in the drill procedure, for as the Ogden catcher reached out to catch one ball coming in from one side of the infield, another ball was being fired into home plate. This unfortunate catcher never did see the second thrown ball, thrown with great velocity. The second baseball struck the catcher on his chest, directly over his heart. He fell to the ground and passed out. An ambulance was summoned immediately, but the baseball player died on his way to the hospital. The impact of the thrown ball had stopped the heart beat.

We are happy to report that this is not what occurred one day at Wrigley Field with the St. Louis Cardinals battling the Chicago Cubs. See if you can "follow these two balls" as they became a part of the same play.

BASEBALL STORY NUMBER 40 - 1959
TWO BALLS IN PLAY ON JUNE 30, 1959
OR
SUDDENLY THE CARDINAL'S DIAMOND
"RESEMBLED A BILLIARDS-TABLE"

BABE HERMAN ONCE DOUBLED INTO a double play. Ed Linke began a double play by stopping a line drive with his forehead. Fred Merkle ran into the clubhouse instead of to second base as Moose McCormick crossed the plate for what should have been the winning run. (That one cost the Giants a pennant.) Germany Schaeffer stole first base from second. Grover Land hit a home run on a ground ball that rolled up a vent. Luke Sewell tagged out two men at the plate on Tony Lazzeri's double. Ranking with these as the strangest plays on a major league ball field is the episode of "two baseballs in play at the same time."

The most bizarre of diamond dramas had an estimable cast: Stan Musial, Alvin Dark, Bob Scheffing, Ernie Banks, Bobby Thomson, Solly Hemus - and of course, several umpires. The game was played in Chicago's Wrigley Field on June 30, 1959. The St. Louis Cardinals were the visiting team. It was the top of the fourth inning and Stan Musial was at bat. The count on Stan was three balls and one strike. Bob Anderson was the Cubs' pitcher, Sammy Taylor was the catcher, and Vic Delmore was the umpire behind the plate.

Anderson's next pitch was a ball and sailed past Taylor. But Taylor didn't bother to chase the ball, thinking that it had hit Musial's bat and therefore was a foul. The catcher stood at the plate, arguing with Delmore as the ball rolled back to the screen. Cubs manager Bob Scheffing and Anderson joined Taylor, contending that the ball had either hit Musial's bat or grazed his arm.

"The ball hit something," claimed Scheffing. "I know it did. There's no way it could have bounced that way without hitting something."

Delmore kept shaking his head, indicating that the pitch was a ball.

Musial, meanwhile, having taken ball four, was strolling down to first base. As he neared the bag, he heard his Cardinals teammates screaming from the dugout, pointing toward the ball, which had reached the screen. "Run," they shouted. Musial rounded first and sped toward second. Everyone has heard that expression, "Run, Stan, Run!"?

Alvin Dark, who was playing third base for the Cubs, suddenly darted after the

Suddenly the Cardinal's diamond "resembled
a billiards table."

ball. He realized that if it had been ball four as Delmore had indicated, then the ball was still in play and Musial would be entitled to as many bases as he could get.

But before Dark could get to the ball, the Cardinals' bat boy picked it up and tossed it to Pat Pieper, the field announcer. Sitting near the screen, as was his custom, Pieper took the ball, then dropped it like a hot potato.

Dark came rushing up, yelling, "Give me that ball!"

"I haven't got it," said Pieper, pointing to the ground. "There it is."

Dark spotted the ball, grabbed it, and threw it quickly to shortstop Ernie Banks at second base. But at that very moment, another ball flew toward second. Where did it come from?

While Delmore was arguing with Scheffing, Taylor, and Anderson, he unconsciously reached into his pocket and gave the Cubs' catcher a new ball. Seeing Musial racing for second, Anderson grabbed the ball from Taylor and threw toward second. The ball thrown by Dark, ball number one, and the one thrown by Anderson, ball number two, were in the air at the same time. Anderson's throw was high and sailed over Banks' head into center field. Dark's throw was low. Banks came in and took it on the hop.

Meanwhile, Musial was sliding safely into second base. The hilarious fans, wanting to get into the act, joined the Cardinals' bench in yelling, "Run, Stan, Run."

Musial looked up and saw the Cubs' centerfielder chasing a bouncing baseball. So, he picked himself up and started for third base. He hadn't taken more than three or four steps when Banks tagged him with ball number one. Ball number two had been retrieved by Bobby Thomson, who casually lobbed it toward the Cubs' dugout. Seeing one ball in Banks' glove and another in the air, Musial looked disbelievingly in both directions and stood on the base lines, unable to decide what to do.

By now, Solly Hemus, the Cardinals' manager, had joined the discussion at home plate. Soon it was a rhubarb. Scheffing kept pointing to the screen, Hemus to second, and Delmore to both benches in a vain attempt at ordering both managers back to the dugouts.

Al Barlick, the senior umpire, joined the huddle. After a while a decision was reached, or was it? First, they ordered Musial back to first base. Then they told him he was out. Hemus declared the game would be played under protest, a protest that became academic when the Cards won the game, 4-1.

At the end of the 1959 season, Delmore was not asked to return as a National League umpire. No explanation was given. The most suspicious interpreted Delmore's banishment as punishment for his part in the ludicrous occurrences of that June day.

The answer to the riddle of the "unidentified flying baseballs" should have been quite simple. As soon as the bat boy touched the original ball, it should have been declared dead, and Musial, who had reached first at the time, should have stayed there. But the dispute was never officially resolved, allowing would-be baseball jurists to argue the case without the burden of dicta from the league office. Baseball officialdom was obviously trying to forget the nightmarish matter.

Stuart was 36 in 1962, had taken time off the summer before to finish his Doctor of Physical Education and Recreation degree at the University of Oregon. Unable to complete this desired degree, upon his return to San Bernardino, he was assigned to teach mathematics and coach Jr. Varsity baseball at the new Eisenhower High School in nearby Rialto, adjacent to the large city. Since that time, both Ronnie Lott, defensive back for the San Francisco '49ers and Darnell Coles, infielder for the Seattle Mariners, have graduated from that school's athletic program. Stu's new assignment was a godsend (his finest year of high school teaching and coaching of a 36 year career). It was greatly brightened when he realized, at late winter baseball tryouts, what an outstanding collection of young men had been assembled on that Junior Varsity squad. A new school. A new town. Every coach in athletics has the "one team of a career." A group of young men who are so unusually talented, both in team and individual effort, that, while he is in the season experiencing it, the coach realizes that there probably will never be another as good in his career. This was all happening in Stu Southworth's life in the 1962 season. He finally cut the squad to 18 players, exactly two nines. They were two teams so equal that all players got into games an equal number of innings. Stu tried to downgrade the idea of any "athletic stars" on the squad. He was preparing as many of them as possible for the next two years of high school Varsity ball.

In their 20 games allowed, by C.I.F. rules, one of the nines would start, the other nine would sit. After four innings, the other nine would replace the entire team. Stu would usually sub only seven players in order to have one or two kids, just in case of injury or need for a quick substitute. No matter what opponent they played, this was the arrangement. The next game, the other nine would start, and the sitting nine would come in and sub.

That "wonder team" won 19 games, lost the last one (only because "everyone plays as they had substituted before"). Lost that game 4-3, away from home, insisting that all the kids get equal innings their last game. As the following story will reveal, this squad competed against an Upland High School squad that had Rollie Fingers pitching that year.

Before we tell the reader of one of the most exciting days in the lives of this squad, we should stop to consider where these young men went after high school to continue their education. At graduation time, from this one California squad of 18 players, this baseball team sent one player to the United States Naval Academy at Annapolis, one player to the United States Military Academy at West Point, one player to the United States Air Force Academy at Colorado Springs, and a fourth player attended Dartmouth University at Hanover, New Hampshire, an Ivy League school, being named Captain of "The Big Green" baseball squad his senior year. Could any coach ever be more proud of any group?

Of course, even with a highly superior talented group of athletes such as described, anywhere, in any sport, there will always be one individual who rises to the top of the group. Like cream rising to the top of milk. In sheer baseball ability only, in comparison, Stu soon realized that a boy named Mike Stipes was such a "charmed person on the diamond." Coach Southworth would coach 16 more years on the diamond, 1962 -

1978, before retiring, but Mike Stipes would be one of the four best baseball players that Stu had the privilege of coaching.

The unusual ability, charisma, team leadership abilities, and clutch performances are best summed up in this tale of that fantastic season and that "super kid."

Baseball Story Number 41 - 1962
Mike Stipes' "Measley" Pinch Hit Home Run
OR
Are We Sure He Wasn't Secretly Taking Batting Practice Daily?

ONCE IN A COACH'S CAREER he has a player like Mike Stipes. You know it during the season you have him. You keep waiting for another one, but you know he will never appear. And he hasn't yet - and that was 1962, 30 years ago.

In the Spring of 1962, at Eisenhower High School in Rialto, California I first saw MIKE STIPES at Spring tryouts. He not only made the team, but he was to become, in a few short weeks, all of these: switch hitter, best bunter, best pitcher, team captain, inspirational leader, best hitter for average. I could go on and on and on.....

Our team was so good that year (we won 19, lost 1, won our league three games ahead of the second place team) that we could have won nearly all the games without Mike. But, man, what a difference when he was in the lineup. But, alas, measles epidemics knock down the best specimens of humanity. About mid-season Mike got the measles. Two weeks out, the doctor said. No buts about it! Did we miss him? What a competitor he was! It was all they could do to keep him in bed. About four days before we travelled away to play Chino High School, Mike showed up each day and watched practice longingly. I told him to get on home toward evening before he got cold and chilled. Mike was most obedient. The doctor examined him two days before the game and said, "You can go to the game with the team, but do not play until a week from today." Mike's face brightened, and he came to school and dressed in his game uniform. He said he wanted to sit in the stands with him mom, but with his uniform on. As his coach, I relented. There he was, next to his mom, with warm jacket on, watching his team play.

Chino was tough that day. They hit the ball and defensed well. We were undefeated, and, in the fifth inning, it looked as though we might get beat. Down by 5-4 score in the fifth, we had men on first and second, and the next two batters weren't strong hitters. There was one out. A seven inning game.

I heard a commotion in the stands behind me. It was Mike running down to me. Through the fence he said, "Let me pinch hit. If I get on, just put a runner in for me right away." He had been in bed for two weeks, remember. With a right handed pitcher

Are we sure he wasn't secretly taking
batting practice daily?

up, I let him take his practice swings. He chose to bat from the left side of the plate. He must have been hitting over .500 from both sides of the plate at that time in the season. Mike hadn't seen a pitched ball for over two weeks. Mike steps up to the plate. Ball one. Strike one and he fouls it off. A clear, hot day and no wind at all. On the third pitch, the whole ball park "dropped their teeth." Mike Stipes hit a hard high fast ball dead centerfield, completely over the high tennis court fence, almost hitting a tennis player. His longest home run of the year. A tremendous blast that "jumped off the bat and carried forever."

I ran to the foul line and yelled, "Walk around, Mike." They all waited for him to walk slowly around. I told the umpires he had had measles, and I didn't want him to get a sweat up. Mike crossed home plate (winked at me) smiled and said that he knew he was going to get a good hit. But a pinch homer?

Score was now 7-5. That's the way the game ended. Mike got bundled up and sat in a car the rest of the game - then home to bed early.

Mike Stipes, two years later, went to Cal Poly College at Pomona and had a good college career in baseball under Coach John Scolinos."

Back at Pacific High School, San Bernardino, in 1962 -3, after the "dream year" at Eisenhower High School in Rialto, Coach Stu taught three more years at Pacific, then moved over to the east, two miles away, to San Bernardino's brand new San Gorgonio High School.

Before departing for SGHS, however, Stu and other coaches would fill a car and ride into Dodger Stadium to see the winning L.A. team. Stu did recall one trip with Dr. Kenneth P. Bailey, principal of Pacific High School, and three other baseball coaches, earlier when the Dodgers were still in the Los Angeles Coliseum. "Doc" Bailey was UCLA's first recipient of a Ph.D., degree, before moving into the educational field. He was very proud of his tall son, Ken, Jr., for excelling in three sports and holding down the first base position on the Varsity baseball quad for two years.

The evening remembered with "Doc" and others, the San Francisco Giants were in town, Orlando Cepeda being one of them, and Orlando had enjoyed a great career. In the first inning with Dodgers on first and second bases, Manager Walt Alston called for a sacrifice bunt on the first pitch. The bunter failed, fouling the ball off. In slowly crept the giant infield for the bunt attempt again. Orlando Cepeda, the first baseman, was in within 15 feet of the right handed swinger, who suddenly swung at the pitch from the heels. Orlando got that huge, tall frame of his flattened on the ground, hit the deck so quickly that the fans couldn't believe it. The big first baseman had been signalled to play right up in the batter's face, it appeared. I'm sure that Orlando could feel the draft of wind form that hard swung bat. Poor Cepeda got up, in one piece, fortunately, but was plenty wary. He looked over to the Giant bench and indicated a definite "NO." He wasn't going to do that again on this batter. If a ball can be thrown over 100 miles per hour by a human being, how many miles per hour does a batted ball travel, after being driven hard by a swinging bat? Orlando didn't want to know.

Stu Southworth recalled that moment, a few years later, when his Junior Varsity baseball team at San Gorgonio High School travelled to Riverside Poly High School

(Bobby Bonds' alma mater) for a league game. In this unusual account of a 1965 incident at Poly High, follow the action as the visiting Spartans from SGHS came to bat in the top of the sixth inning, and remember the tale just told, concerning Giant Orlando Cepeda.

Baseball Story Number 42 - 1965
Bunter Turns Home Run Hitter
OR
To This Day, Riverside Poly High Believes That Jim Missed The Bunt Sign

DURING THE 1965 SEASON, I was coaching the Junior Varsity baseball team at San Gorgonio High School in San Bernardino, California. One afternoon, late in the season, we were locked in a crucial struggle with Riverside Poly High School at Riverside.

I distinctly recall it being the top of the sixth inning. San Gorgonio High had runners on second and third with one out, and we were behind 4-3.

Jim Charles was the right handed hitter up. Everyone in the ball park knew that Jim was a great bunter. He had laid down a good bunt earlier in the game, beaten it out for a hit. So they thought we were going to bunt. They didn't know that Jim also was a very long ball hitter. His home run potential was great.

Riverside Poly's coach then did something that I have never seen a coach do. He called time out, went out on the field and told his third baseman and his first baseman to come and stand ten feet from the batter. I guess he thought that this would upset the bunter so he would miss the ball or pop up the bunt in the air so it could be caught.

I yelled at both the infielders who had been moved in, practically on top of the batter, "Hey, you guys better move back. One of you is going to get beheaded! I have no intention of bunting." They didn't believe me, but they would in a minute or two. The two infielders just ignored me, and the Riverside coach came out storming on the field. He told me to leave his infielders alone and to quit telling them what to do. I warned him that he was endangering the life of his players. The pitcher took his stretch and then delivered the ball.

Jim Charles connected with that bat and hit his longest home run of the year. It cleared the left field wall by twenty feet. But the ball took off of the bat and whistled by the head of that third baseman, missing him by three or four feet. I looked over at him, and his eyes were as big as saucers. He just stood there transfixed on the hit ball. He didn't even have time to react. I calmly yelled at him, "Son, I told you so." Their coach said nothing. Jim Charles made believers of them all.

The score was then 6-4. We won the game 7-5."

The last year was 1964 that Stu taught math classes at Pacific High School. By this

To this day, Riverside Poly High believes
that Jim Missed the bunt sign.

time the school had grown from an enrollment of 1200 at its opening in 1953 to nearly 4400, and this included only the top three grades of high school. Freshmen were still contained in the junior high programs. Needless to say, the class load was frightful for teachers, and the campus was so crowded that students could not pass through the central hallways, but had to go around the end of the long parallel buildings to go from class to class. In June there were nearly 1100 graduates, and the ceremony lasted for hours. Pacific High of 1964 was ranked the largest school in California. Fortunately San Gorgonio High School was finished that spring, ready for 1200 students in the fall. For Stu it had been a rough year, a rough baseball season, and the classload caused a great deal of work to be done after school, when time afforded it.

It was the afternoon of the last baseball game of the regular season. Stu Southworth walked out of his math room F-5, heading for the parking lot and home. He had no idea that the Junior Varsity baseball team was playing there at home. In fact, the Pirates were playing Chaffey High School of Ontario. As Stu locked his room door, he heard the loud cheers from the ball diamond, so he decided to take in a little baseball before going home.

The Junior Varsity team, coached by Larry Mercadante, was battling those Chaffey Tigers for the J.V. Championship of the Citrus Belt League.

As Stu approached the field he could see that the game was in its last half of the last inning -down to the wire, the score tied 2-2. The crowd was locked in a tense mood. Attracted to all this setting, as any coach would be, Stu stood behind the cyclone fence, behind home plate, on the first base side. Coach Stu had just put his fingers around the fence wires, leaned against that heavy wire fence, when he was treated to another crazy moment in baseball history at Pacific High School. Perhaps the Greeks and Romans were right. "The gods really can be against you." This is what Stu recalls.

BASEBALL STORY NUMBER 43 - 1964
PACIFIC HIGH SCHOOL'S "WET BLANKET"
OR
THE CHAMPIONSHIP LOST BY THE AUTOMATIC
TIMERS ON THE SPRINKLER SYSTEM

HAVE YOU EVER SEEN A game of baseball tied in the bottom of the last inning and called because of "sprinklers going on"?

That is exactly what happened one day late in the 1964 season. It was a classic Junior Varsity duel in baseball between the two powers of the league that year.

Coach Larry Mercadante was the Junior Varsity coach for Pacific High School. The score was tied, and Pacific, being home team, was batting last. Somehow, Pacific High got a man to second base. I'm not sure how many outs there were.

At that moment I walked up to the game. I had been working in my Room F-5 near-by the field, doing some Geometry lesson work for the next day's classes. Wouldn't you know that just as I walked over, put my hands on the fence behind the home plate, it happened.

It was one of the strangest happenings you could imagine! Up to bat steps the good hitter for Pacific High School. After a pitch or two, the pitcher releases the next ball to the batter. Just after the ball leaves his hand on the delivery, the umpire behind the plate steps back and yells, "Time out." The sphere sails toward the plate. The batter swats the ball for a base hit. The hit ball goes out between left field and center field. One of their outfielders picks up the ball and fires a good throw home. But the runner from second base was fast, and he slid in away ahead of the throw.

The game was over! Pacific High had won this crucial game by one run! Hurrah! But wait!! By this time the sprinklers all over the field were automatically getting everyone wet. People hurried to get off the field. They were getting soaked out on the playing field. But Pacific High players were delirious. The umpire yells "Game called a tie. The hit doesn't count, the run doesn't count, the field is too wet to continue. Goodbye."

Someone had forgotten to adjust the timing on the automatic sprinklers, whose controls were inside a corner of a metal shop building a few feet from the diamond.

I actually collapsed on the ground laughing so hard that my sides were aching. If I live to be 214 years old, I doubt if I'll see anything funnier than Coach Larry Mercadante standing near home plate with hands on hips, facing the building where

The championship lost by the automatic
timers on the sprinkler system.

the sprinkler controls were housed, saying very plainly and loudly, "This ——— —
—— school!" as if to say, "Is there anything else that could happen at this institution?"

I can sympathize with him. How many of us baseball coaches have ever been beaten
in the "big game" by a set of automatic sprinklers, after the winning blow was
delivered?"

In reverting back to that "dream season of 1962" at Eisenhower High School in
Rialto, California - another most unusual baseball rule sparked an incident, rarely seen
by the player or fan of the game. The interesting thing about the rare play, which
Coach Stu and his E.H.S. "Eagles" benefited greatly from, was the fact that this one
umpire's call turned the season around and won the key league game.

Baseball is such a strange game, for one break (for or against a team) can change
an inning, a key game, a season, and even a league championship. Let the reader be
very aware that in the game of baseball, complete knowledge of every rule is vital.
True, there are many rules, but failure to know just one of the many can really cost a
team. Rules for defense must be learned just as thoroughly as the rules for offense.

One section of the Official Baseball Rulebook deals with "appeal plays." Prior to
the 1962 campaign at EHS, Stu, the baseball coach, had read his rules fairly well, but
he sure hadn't learned about the "offensive appeal plays." There may actually be
several of this kind of appeals, but for certain there is one. THAT ONE IS RARE. It
is called the "trapped third strike by the catcher" appeal. Go to the rulebook and read
it carefully.

The coach, player, fan, will be advised to read the following story carefully. It is an
umpire's correct interpretation of that rule.

You can bet that the Upland High School Highlanders surely recalled this appeal
rule, years later, for it probably cost them the league championship. As Coach Stuart
Southworth recalls the Upland J.V. team that day, he believes that Rollie Fingers was
either a starter or a sub on the Upland Highlander squad.

BASEBALL STORY NUMBER 44 - 1962
THE "TRAPPED THIRD STRIKE" INCIDENT
VERSUS UPLAND HIGH SCHOOL
OR
ROLLIE FINGERS, THE ROOKIE, OBSERVES
UMPIRE "SCOTTY'S" STRICT RULES
INTERPRETATION

THE UPLAND GAME - APRIL, 1962
(A story about a "trapped third strike" with two outs)

"This is a great baseball tale with all the fun and excitement of the old American game, but it also points out how vital it is to know every rule in the voluminous Official Baseball Rulebook.

In 1962 I served one year as Junior Varsity Baseball coach at Eisenhower High School in Rialto, California. I happened to be gifted with such a talented squad of eighteen players that I soon realized that:

a. I had two men at each position. Exactly two men at each spot.
b. I had such intelligence on the team that, I decided to 'overcoach' and see just how much 'running game' could be taught to a high school squad. From this team we sent four boys to top scholarships at the end of their senior year. One went to U.S.A.F. Academy, one went to Annapolis, one went to West Point, and the fourth became Captain of the Dartmouth College baseball team.
c. The eighteen men were of equal ability. We decided to start nine players, let the other nine sit. At the end of four innings, the other nine came in, no matter what the score. In the next game, the nines would switch. At the end of the year, each of the eighteen man squad had played the same number of innings. We won 19 and lost 1 game and won our league three games ahead of the second place team.

This tale has to do with our toughest game of the season. We were playing Upland High School and ROLLIE FINGERS, who later played for Oakland, Milwaukee, and San Diego professionally, was a member of Upland's Freshman team that year.

It was a warm day in April. Upland and Eisenhower had not met on the diamond

Rollie Fingers, the rookie,
observes umpire "Scotty's"
strict rules interpretation.

that year. We were tied for first in our Tri-County League. As it turned out, the winner of this game that day won the league.

We played four innings of a seven-inning game. We were behind 4-3. The bases were loaded in the bottom of the fourth. My big catcher, Wayne Haggard, was at the plate, a bad curveball hitter.

Our only umpire was behind the plate. His name was 'Scotty', a real good guy and a 'character'. A clown with a sense of humor.

Wayne worked the count to 3 and 2. The pitcher, with bases loaded, and all the runners going hard to the next bases, threw a hard curve that broke down. The Upland catcher caught the ball after Wayne swung and missed for strike three. The catcher for Upland rejoiced. Yelled and excited, he tossed the ball slowly out on the ground at the base of the mound. All the Upland players were congratulating the Upland pitcher for striking out the man with bases loaded.

Suddenly, my rightfielder yelled at the runners "circle all the bases and come home." I looked at him, Harry Brehm, and didn't know what he was doing. All the runners obeyed him and came home, touching every base in order. He said to me, "Coach, that was a trapped third strike. The catcher has to touch the runner who struck out, or throw down to first base. He did neither. The inning hasn't ended."

I told my team to stay in the dugout. No team went out and took the field. I strolled up to Scotty, the umpire, and I said, "Scotty, I appeal that last play....That was a trapped third strike, not a caught third strike. Therefore, all the runners' runs count. They all touched home plate. The third out of the inning has never been made. The score is now 7-4 in our favor. Upland has to return to the field." Scotty said to me at the top of his voice, "Coach, you are absolutely right. The appeal is awarded to you."

About this time the whole Upland team came out of the dugout to find out just what was wrong. Scotty told the Upland coach that the 1/2 inning was not over. I won't repeat in writing the words that transpired between Scotty, the Upland coach and the Upland players. Finally, the "rhubarb" ended. My team sitting in the dugout was taking it in and enjoying the scene, but not rubbing it in.

Would you believe that there were no more runs scored that inning or the rest of the game?

We won the game 7-4, scored 4 runs on that one play (incidentally, the catcher who ko'd on the third strike curve circled all the way around the bases and scored, too).

We beat Upland again, won the league by three games, and no one came close to beating us from that point on.

I'll bet that, wherever those kids are now, they still remember that day, that inning, that "good call by Scotty" at home plate. He was correct and had the courage to call it.

The moral of this story, of course, is that failure to know even one of the rules of defensive play from the rulebook is costly. The penalty for this was terrible. I happened to have a sharp, alert boy in the dugout who "picked up their error." I didn't pick it up. He did. But I sure learned a lesson that day.

Finally, I have to tell you readers that exactly the same thing happened the next season - at Colton High School. I appealed the play, that time we just got two runs on the appeal. The umpire again saw it, but was waiting for my appeal.

So, you see, these "unusual" rule occurrences sometimes crop out more frequently than you would think, eh?

Finally, Orange County, California, the city of Anaheim, and owner Gene Autry and others, all helped to make the new home of the California Angels, Anaheim Stadium, a reality. Now the thousands of baseball fans in the Los Angeles basin could see both National and American League ball.

The early Angels teams in their new stadium were fun to watch, and less than an hour's drive from Stu's home in San Bernardino. Now to be able to see every big league player in the game, yearly, was indeed a treat for the coach and fan.

Stu Southworth recalled those great boyhood stories told by his dad and granddad of seeing the St. Louis Browns one week and the St. Louis Cardinals the next week - in the same ball park. And how about that 1944 World Series - all St. Louis - won by the Cardinals after a tough intracity struggle? Stu and all of the Los Angeles basin fans are wondering when that area will see their first "Freeway Series"? (Dodgers versus Angels in the "Fall Classic.") Very soon, they are hoping.

Stu took his family (Liane, Mike, John, Kathy) to Angels Stadium in those early years. One game in particular he remembers. Those talented Baltimore Orioles of that era (Boog Powell, Frank Robinson, Eddie Etcheberran, Brooks Robinson - what a crew of ball players).

That year, as usual though, Stu's eye was caught by the great base runners of the American League. In particular a Kansas City Royal, Amos Otis. For many years Amos was second in one category of base running, the "stolen base percentage," steals divided by attempts. Bobby Bonds, the Riverside Poly High School star, mentioned a few stories ago in this volume, a major leaguer whom Coach Stu and has teams competed against in earlier years, leads in the "stolen base percentage" department.

The baseball fan will enjoy the following description of some of the great base thieves of the 1960 and 1970 eras.

BASEBALL STORY NUMBER 45 - 1960-1980
AMOS OTIS AND THE PARADE OF OTHER GREAT
BASE THIEVES OF THE 1970 AND 1980 ERAS
OR
A REAL "ROGUE'S GALLERY" OF THE LATE
20TH CENTURY SPEEDSTERS

THE ABILITY TO STEAL BASES is a valuable asset in a player's arsenal. The threat of a stolen base can disrupt the strategy of both the pitcher and the catcher. The pitcher may concentrate more on the runner than on the batter, and catcher may be more inclined to call for fastballs so that he can get the ball away fast in the event the runner decides to steal. It all gives the batter a decided edge.

Ty Cobb, of course, was a master at upsetting the opposing battery whenever he got on base, which was quite often. In recent years, the best base stealer was Maury Wills, whose running was an essential part of the Dodgers' drives to the pennant in 1962, 1963, 1965, and 1966.

The best in this returning art today - Lou Brock of the St. Louis Cardinals and Bert Campaneris of the Oakland A's. Other fine base stealers include Joe Morgan and Bobby Tolan of the Cincinnati Reds, Willie Davis of the Los Angeles Dodgers, Bobby Bonds of the San Francisco Giants, Freddy Patek of the Kansas City Royals, Tommy Harper of the Boston Red Sox, and Cesar Cedeno of the Houston Astros. Before the 1973 season, Brock led the National League in six of eight. Both had exceptionally high stolen base percentages, but neither owns the highest percentage (of players in the last 40 years who have stolen 100 or more bases). (Stolen base percentages, steals divided by attempts, weren't recorded before 1930.) That honor belongs to Bonds, followed closely by Amos Otis of the Royals.

Otis gave no evidence of his base stealing ability during his apprenticeship with the New York Mets, but once he got the chance to play regularly, with the Kansas City team, there was almost no stopping him. In 1970, his first season with the Royals, the young outfielder failed only twice in 35 attempts. Not since Max Carey stole 51 bases in 53 tries for the Pirates in 1932 has a base stealer been as successful. In 1971, Otis stole 52 bases in 60 attempts, leading the American League in the number of steals as well as in percentage. That same year, Otis' team mate, Freddy Patek, stole 49 bases. (In 1972, the Reds' Joe Morgan, 58, and Bobby Tolan, 42, stole 100 bases between them, one less than the Otis-Patek total.)

A Real "Rogue's Gallery" of the Late
Twentieth-Century Speedsters.

Otis' greatest day on the base paths was September 7, 1971, against the Milwaukee Brewers in Kansas City. The fleet-footed center fielder excelled at the plate, too, hitting safely in all four appearances. He singled off Marty Pattin in the first, third, and fifth innings and stole second each time. Darrell Porter was catching for the Brewers. Otis capped his performance by scoring the winning run in the seventh. With Ken Sanders on the mound, he beat out an infield hit, stole second and third, and came home on an overthrow by Porter. The final score was Kansas City 4, Milwaukee 3.

Otis' five stolen bases in one game fell short of the major league record, set by Eddie Collins of the Philadelphia Athletics in 1912. Nonetheless, Amos was the first to steal five since Johnny Neun did it for Detroit in 1927. Dan McGann of the 1904 New York Giants and Clyde Milan of the 1912 Washington Senators are the only others since the turn of the century to steal five bases in a game.

The least impressed by Otis' base stealing exploits is Otis himself. "I never wanted to be known as a base stealer," he says. "I want to be known as an all-around player."

In the past few years some rather remarkable base stealers have emerged. Most noteworthy would be:

RICKEY HENDERSON - OAKLAND ATHLETICS
(Rickey set the season record for stolen bases with 130)

VINCE COLEMAN and WILLIE MC GEE - ST. LOUIS CARDINALS
(These two speed demons have terrorized National League teams for the past several seasons)

TIM RAINES - MONTREAL EXPO'S

With the importance of speed on the bases the 1980 - 1990 decade, it is expected that baseball will see even more base thieves and some which surpass the speed of all before them.

Stu Southworth was especially impressed by the strong Oakland "A" teams of the American League in the years of their three World Series appearances. Moving in from Kansas City and capturing the support of the Bay area fans, Charley Finley had really done a complete job with them.

That three year stint of the "A"'s was fun, and Stu and family enjoyed watching them at Anaheim Stadium competing against the California Angels. At that time the Angel's pitcher, Nolan Ryan, was incredible, and one evening, the year after Oakland had won one of their World Series rings, Stu and son (Mike) sat at Anaheim (in awe) as Nolan Ryan struck out the entire Oakland lineup their first time at bat. For the first three innings those Oakland Athletics were either swinging at air or watching the strikes go by in a blur. Nine K's and not one Oakland hitter even scratched the ball. You couldn't even hear a foul tip. It was in that game that Ryan broke an all-time American League strikeout record, for total number of strikeouts, set decades before that night by the famous Rube Marquad. What a thunderous applause, lasting many moments, were given to Nolan as he K'd the final hitter for the new record. No one realized that evening, in the early 1970's, that Nolan Ryan would still be mowing 'em down in the 1991 season and getting five or six near misses at no-hitters in the 8th or ninth innings. YOU ARE TRULY UNBELIEVABLE, NOLAN RYAN. I wonder what the famous "Murderer's Row" (Yankees of the 1920's) would have done to Ryan?

Eventually that great Oakland Athletic team had to meet the Cincinnati Reds and their great Johnny Bench, recent Hall of Famer, in the 1972 World Series. An outstanding and unusual play was pulled in one of the series games by that wily old fox, Manager Dick Williams - against none other than the batter, Johnny Bench. Poor John and the Reds fell for this one. The play to which we allude had been performed before, on unsuspecting hitters.

What makes this such a memorable moment was that the play occurred at a crucial time in a World Series game and to such a dangerous hitter. It appeared that the momentum was clearly swinging in the Red's favor. The execution of this dastardly trick to Bench absolutely swung the game momentum back to the Oakland team.

Now enjoy, savor the brief World Series moment which shocked the Reds from the Cincinnati "Big Red Machine." Surely Johnny Bench and Sparky Anderson were the most surprised. It was clever, but the timing was the thing. What a moment to pull it off!!

Oh, we almost forgot to mention that the little substitute who was sitting on that Upland High School bench (while Stu's Eisenhower Eagles were executing that "trapped third strike" appeal play, a few tales ago) - it was Rollie Fingers - who was called in to relieve by Manager Dick Williams of those Oakland A's, and throw that fateful pitch to Johnny Bench. He was Oakland's number one "fireman," and what a "sinkerball" he had at the time!! The pitch that Fingers threw was a hard slider.

BASEBALL STORY NUMBER 46 - 1972
THE GREAT WORLD SERIES "INTENTIONAL STRIKEOUT"
OR
ANYONE BUT JOHNNY WOULD HAVE BEEN "BENCHED" FOR FALLING FOR THAT ONE

SOMEONE ONCE SAID THESE WORDS about our great national pastime - "The great American game of baseball is a fraud, a treachery and is un-American. It offers a regrettable example to the nation's youth, is populated by cheats, thrives on sneaky tricks and teaches "Fagin values" to thousands of Little Leaguers. It is corruptive and should be repressed. And sometimes, as played by major leaguers....it is fascinating." My how true it is! Has there ever been such a game invented by the mind of man in which so many types of "skullduggery" have crept in?

For those who are impressed by the chicanery of major leaguers, if you missed the third game of the 1972 World Series at Oakland Coliseum, you missed a trick equalling the "Brink's Heist" or the "Great London Train Robbery." With absolutely perfect execution (of a long practiced deception) those mustached green and gold Oakland A's, led by their Charlie Finley and Manager Dick Williams pulled it off for the TV audience to gasp about.

To make matters worse, this long saved debauchery was saved for none other than the great Johnny Bench, now the Hall of Fame catcher. He was the National league's home run king and Most Valuable Player - but he temporarily forgot that he was not competing against "men of honor."

This is how Washington Post columnist Shirley Povich described the "magnificent deception of October 20, 1972."

In the top of the eighth inning, the Cincinnati Reds were threatening to add to their skimpy 1-0 lead at the expense of Vida Blue, who had replaced John ("Blue Moon") Odom. With one out, Blue walked Joe Morgan, who raced to third on Bobby Tolan's single up the middle. In came Rollie Fingers, the A's relief specialist. Tolan easily stole second as Fingers worked carefully to Johnny Bench. The count went to three and two.

Enter Dick Williams, stage left. The A's manager called time, walked to the mound, and belabored the obvious: With first base open, the A's would not risk a good pitch to the Red's dangerous clean-up hitter. Catcher Gene Tenance and their baseman Sal Bando joined the discussion. Then, with the subtlety of a mustachioed villain in a

Anyone but Johnny would have been
"benched" for falling for that one.

silent movie, manager Williams twice pointed to first base, apparently instructing Fingers to walk Bench on the next pitch.

Impresario Williams could not resist an additional flourish. He pointed to the next hitter, Tony Perez, in the on deck circle. The "charade" anesthetized Bench, but the A's had not yet finished introducing the small town Oakie man to big city theater. Catcher Tenance trudged dutifully back to home plate, waited for Bench to step back into the batter's box, and not only held his mitt at arm's length in anticipation of the fourth ball, but also began the ritual of moving a step toward first, as catchers always do when a deliberate pass is coming.

Too late, Bench's teammates discovered the ruse. As Fingers delivered the ball, Joe Morgan yelled to Bench from third, "Be ready, John! They're gonna pitch to you."

Alex Grammas, the Reds' third base coach had seen the play in the minors, as had Morgan. "I started to holler, but all I got out was 'uh,'" Grammas says, "and by that time, the ball was on the way."

The denouement was crushing and swift. Tenance quietly eased into his regular catching position, and Fingers, without much windup, delivered a splendid slider that clipped the strike zone about knee high. Bench stood there transfixed, his bat on his shoulder. "I guess that made me look like the goat," he said sheepishly.

It could have been worse. Though the Reds failed to score in the inning, they held the A's and won 1-0. Still Fingers relished his dramatic debut. "I tried to be relaxed," he explained later. "I just came up real nonchalant and let the ball go....I couldn't have thrown it better if I had taken fifteen minutes."

Stu's attempt to get back into baseball coaching after his wife's death was not accomplished until the following spring of 1975. At that time he was asked to coach the Sophomore baseball squad at San Gorgonio High School until their regular coach, Willie Hasson, could be free from his basketball coaching. His season had been extended two weeks by the C.I.F. playoffs. Stu didn't know the sophomore personnel too well, so he practiced with them quite a few days before attempting an intersquad game.

On the day of that practice game, the coach divided his number of players into two fairly equal squads. Now remember that during Stu's long tenure as high school baseball coach, Coach Southworth observed many inept kids try out for a squad, but one stands out in his mind as actually "being a real danger to himself" on a ball diamond. (A sad tale of a high school Sophomore who had the greatest desire but no tools for the game). This lad was just about as "blind as a bat." A very dangerous situation!

This following account of tryouts that day in the practice game is in no way "funning" this young man, but his lack of good eyesight did lead to an incident which Stu wonders ever occurred in baseball at any level. It was the first and last time Coach Stu saw it occur.

BASEBALL STORY NUMBER 47 - 1975
THE LITTLE BLONDE BATTER WITH THE "COKE BOTTLE" GLASSES
OR
HE WONDERED WHY HE NEVER HEARD THAT BALL "POP" IN THE CATCHER'S MITT

HERE IS A STORY NO one will believe, but it happened just as I tell it. The moral of the story is, "Don't let anyone who has terrible eyesight ever get up to bat in baseball." He is a menace to himself.

One young Freshman, blonde and wearing the thickest "Coke Bottle" glasses that I have ever seen, stepped up to the plate. I noticed that he would swing at anything thrown. As the pitcher delivered, he seemed to have no idea where the ball was. I questioned him about his eyesight, and he said that with his thick glasses, he could see the ball all right. I doubted that, but he was fiercely competitive, and I later learned that his mom and dad were pushing him to land a position on our team, for we had won the league title the season before, and we were highly regarded.

After several days of watching this boy perform in the field (he wasn't a bad thrower and fielder) and swing at bad pitches at the plate and never hit one, it was time for our intersquad game. After this game, of course, we would decide who to cut for the season.

During this game, we had a very good left handed pitcher for one squad, and this little blonde boy came to the plate, determined to get his first hit of the season.

The pitcher fired two pitches so fast over the plate, the boy with the "Coke bottle glasses" swung each time, after the ball was in the catcher's mitt. Everyone present chuckled some.

There was a runner on first base, and the pitcher had an excellent pickoff move to first. On the third pitch, the lefty took his stretch, looked toward first base, and threw a very fast pickoff throw to the first baseman. The runner got back safely.

Just as the ball was released to first by the pitcher, the little blonde batter saw only the blur of the ball with those poor eyes, and he brought the bat around, swinging with all of his might. He actually thought the ball had been thrown to him, and he had struck out again. So the dejected fellow walked to the dugout.

The poor plate umpire laughed out loud, stopped the game, and said to himself and for all to hear, "What should I call that one?" He looked over at me, the coach of the boy.

The little blonde batter wondered why he never heard the
ball "pop" in the cather's mitt?

Everyone on both teams were so stunned by that incident, no one knew what to say, or think, or how to react. Who had ever seen a batter swing at a ball thrown to first for a pickoff? I called the boy away from the plate and let another batter step up, warning the original batter that he was a danger to himself at the plate.

After the day's practice was over, I convinced the little blonde boy that baseball was not his game, and he quit. He still did not understand, though, why he couldn't hit a baseball.

Really, I probably saved the young boy's life that day.

During his first 25 years of coaching high school and American Legion baseball in three western states, Stu Southworth was learning the game, carefully collecting and preserving team statistics, changing some of his strategy; for he felt that someday, near retirement age, he would write a baseball test - on base running and/or signals.

It was not until the summer of 1981 that Coach Stu was able to block off enough time to compose his "THE MANUAL OF BASERUNNING PLAYS IN BASE-BALL," a 104 page collection of all 28 of baseball's base running plays used since 1869. With this initial introduction into the writing field, Stu waited until the summer of 1984, the year that he retired from the teaching field from the San Bernardino Unified School District.

His next attempt would be toward a more complete volume, much longer and wider in scope. Actually, it was an attempt to incorporate into one book all that had ever been learned about both base stealing and base running. The eleven chapter text was a very successful venture. He sold it the Summer of 1986.

In one of these eleven chapters mentioned, Coach Southworth wrote to many coaches of the Southern California area, asking that they submit examples of either "bizarre or outlandishly humorous incidents" which they had seen or heard of, occurring in baseball at any period of time.

The following account is one sent in from a Coach Don Monger, Head Football Coach and physical education teacher at Don Lugo High School in the city of Chino, California. Before reading this most bizarre ending to a baseball game which this author has ever heard, we have to ask ourselves these two questions: (1) What is the greatest damage than an offense can cause a defense in baseball - in one play? (2) What is the greatest damage that a defense can cause an offense in one play? And the answer to these two questions are: Question One - THE GRAND SLAM HOME RUN, and Question Two - THE TRIPLE PLAY. The reader will be stunned to realize that a play in baseball can contain both of these unusual elements. Read on.

Baseball Story Number 48
Sometime in the 1960's or 1970's
"The Grand Slam Triple Play"
or
Four "Sure Runs" Quickly Converted To
Three "Sure Outs"

ONE YEAR IN THE CONSOLATION finals of the Citrus Junior College Baseball Tournament, I was pitching for Mount San Antonio College. It was the bottom of the ninth inning with our team leading 10-8, bases were loaded, with Golden West at bat. The count was 2-0 and the batter hit a deep shot to left field that had "grand slam" written all over it.

The runner on third base crossed home plate, the runner on second was about five feet from home plate, the runner on first was half-way between second and third, and the batter was in his home run trot. The left fielder, Kelly Godfrey, currently the Activities Director at Los Altos High School, turned his back and raced to the fence; making the catch, he turned and threw the ball to the shortstop, Ron Opatkiewitz, who threw it to the third baseman, Tim Feldhaus, for out number two, who threw the ball to the second baseman, Mike McClure, for the third out — (triple play to win the game 10-8).

The funny thing was that when the ball was caught, all of the runners stopped, in a state of shock, or as if their feet were set in cement.

By the summer of 1989 Stu Southworth, ex-baseball coach and by now an author of four baseball texts on base running in the game, was spending some of his time watching San Bernardino's Class "A" professional ball club, the San Bernardino "Spirit," set an all-time California League record for attendance, three years in a row. Stu was also writing some each day and paying a lot of attention to his lovely wife, Thelma, and his two children. Michael had turned 40 and Stu's daughter, Kathy, was nearing 36. A retired coach gets to read more and watch much more television. Stu was seeing more baseball now, in person and on TV.

One day that summer of 1989 Stu was watching a Cub-Phillies game. He watched a batter drive a double just inside the first base line. The ball suddenly disappeared. Let's find out what the bewildered outfielder discovered when he got to the ball.

Four "sure runs" converted to
three "sure outs."

BASEBALL STORY NUMBER 49 - 1989
"FOLLOW THE BOUNCING BALL" -
INTO THE BULLPEN
OR
MAGICIAN BEDROSIAN DOES HIS SUDDEN
DISAPPEARING ACT ON THE BALL

EVERY MAJOR LEAGUE BALLPARK has a different configuration and various distances to various points. No two are alike. This makes it interesting for visitors, for they not only have to remember the home field ground rules, but they also must recall how to play difficult balls hit to various fields, barriers, bullpens, and any other areas which either jut out into the playing area or are a nearby hazard. Very interesting.

One summer night in 1989 the Cubs-Phillies game was progressing nicely until a Cubbie hit a hard shot down to first base. It apparently hit the bag slightly, then the ball angled over into foul ground and headed toward the visitor's bullpen. Phillies pitchers and catchers were in their warmups. As the ball veered directly toward the bullpen, the gate was swung open. Steve Bedrosian, Philly pitcher, then closed the gate as the hard grounder entered. Some one in the bullpen area must have put the ball in his pocket, for when the fielders (giving that fair ball chase) came to the place where the ball should be rebounding back to them to be relayed in to the cutoff man, there was no ball. It had disappeared. Shall we call this "the case of the hungry bullpen?" The area had just "devoured" the ball. This could occur, of course, because, as men chase an errant ball on foul ground, away in front of them, they often take their eyes off the ball for a second or two, having located the ball and where it should be when they get to that point. Apparently this is what occurred to the collective Philly chasers. They searched and searched for the ball, then realized what those naughty bullpenners had done to them. I suppose the next thing to do was to throw one's arms straight up into the air to show interference, and a ground rule double.

Who says baseball hasn't changed over the years, that there is never any "new thing under the Sun" in the game? Here is a true and hilarious act about modern players, fields, and tactics. It was such a funny moment that the ESPN channel showing it on TV - replayed it a number of times.

To say that a baseball coach's life changes during retirement is an understatement. During a coach's active life on the diamond, he wishes so often that he could attend

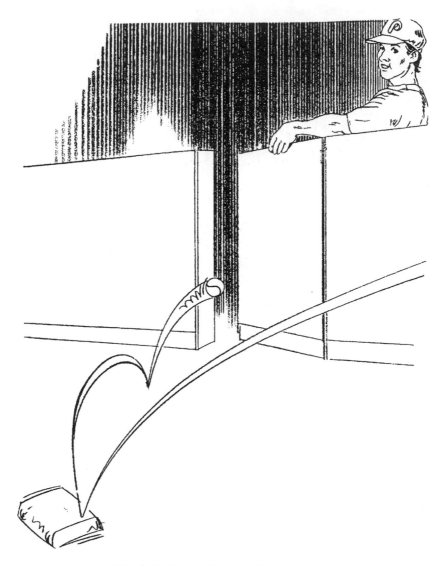

Magician Bedrosian does his sudden
disappearing act on the ball.

the big national playoffs at the end of the season. NCAA, NAIA, NBC, WORLD SERIES, AMERICAN LEGION WORLD SERIES, and many others. But alas. There are always held during school weeks. The NCAA DIVISION I WORLD SERIES, for instance, is always held the first week of June, just as teachers and coaches are getting ready to close the schools.

The purpose of retirement is to be able to do the things one had not the money to do, the time to do, or the experience to do. You can bet that Stu and wife Thelma attended the NCAA College World Series at Omaha, Nebraska three of the first four years retired. Thelma and Stu agreed to retire the same year from teaching. So, in 1985, 1986 and 1988, both were there at Omaha.

Miami University's "Hurricanes," under their great Coach Ron Fraser, won the 1985 series, beating a great Texas University squad, and Greg Swindell. A very tall order. Miami University returned the next year with a new "trick play" rehearsed. This squad had invented a "trick first base pickoff play" in which the pitcher initiated the action of the play. This crafty coach and team just waited for the perfect time to execute it. The opportunity finally came.

Fans, players, coaches - follow this play and enjoy some real deception.

BASEBALL STORY NUMBER 50 - 1987
MIAMI UNIVERSITY'S NEW FIRST BASE PICKOFF PLAY
(THE CASE OF THE "MISSING OVERTHROW")
OR
THE FIRST BASEMAN AND SECOND BASEMAN FAKE-CHASE

WOULDN'T YOU KNOW IT? AFTER seeing the 1985 and 1986 College World Series at Omaha, Stu and Thelma missed this gem which we're about to recap for the readers. Several times they saw the rerun on the ESPN channel covering the Series.

Miami University was in the middle of one of the tough ball games they had to play that year, and the opponent got a man on first base. The play is executed thusly:

1. Have the pitcher throw over to first three times in a row, chasing the daring runner back. Each time he gets up and dusts himself off.
2. Have the same pitcher fake a hard pickoff to first a fourth time, just using the same timing and motion he used before.
3. Instead of first baseman taking the throw, he waits a time equal to the time it takes the ball to reach his glove, then he races at top speed to the "Phantom ball," away back of first, in the foul line.
4. To make the play the more realistic, the right fielder and the second baseman join the chase. All three of the men hustling after the "throw that never was" are converging on an imaginary point where the ball would bounce off the low wall in front of the stands.
5. Now both the diving first base runner and the first base coach are confused. The greedy runner is not about to let this opportunity escape to advance to second base on a bad pickoff overthrow. Even if the base coach realizes it is a trick, the runner will probably go.
6. The shortstop comes over to cover second base now.
7. The pitcher (who threw the ball away, supposedly) is fussing and fuming off the mound area, kicking dirt, mad at himself - or so it would seem.
8. After the pitcher goes through the fake act briefly, he moves over to intercept the

The First Baseman and Second Baseman
Fake-Chase.

first base runner and puts the tag on him. He had the ball in his glove all the time. The pickoff throw was so realistic to crowd, defense, runner, first base coach - he had them all fooled. The pitcher actually had hypnotised everyone.

We wonder if coach Ron Fraser hired a professional choreographer to rehearse that one? It must have taken hours to perfect that (among all the possible pitchers, first and second basemen, and the shortstop and right fielder). Probably a special "oral sign" or obvious "hand signal" was given by the coach to tell everyone that the play was to be pulled on a certain pitch. The Miami University bench would also have to be choreographed to shout, yell, create havoc, at exactly the time the ball was supposed to have passed the first baseman and his glove. (SO IT WAS A TOTAL TEAM EFFORT).

This play would probably work best against a runner on first base who is a real speed demon, one who is a daring, aggressive runner.

Stu wondered how many times Miami University used this play during their regular season or regional playoffs, just saving it for the Omaha NCAA College World Series, waiting for the right moment?

If an Academy Award were given for the "best college baseball acting performance of 1987," shouldn't the Miami University "Hurricanes" win it, hands down?

It is not to say that every strange event seen in a baseball game has probably occurred before, somewhere, sometime, since the game began. There are at least four times, in the annals of baseball literature, recording some player's ingenuity in using an ordinary white potato, exactly the size of an official baseball, peeling it, painting it to look exactly like the real thing, then introducing that artificial sphere to confuse an opponent at some point in a baseball game. Let the reader hear the latest, the 1987 version of this chicanery, for it did occur at the professional level.

BASEBALL STORY NUMBER 51 - 1987
"THE GREAT POTATO PICKOFF PLAY OF 1987"
OR
THIS "SPUD'S FOR YOU," ORLANDO. AND, OH YEAH, I LEFT ONE FOR EACH OF YOUR GREAT TEAMMATES, TOO. JUST LOOK UP ON YOUR LOCKER SHELVES

NOW WILLIAMSPORT, PENNSYLVANIA, IS THE home of American "LITTLE LEAGUE." In fact, Little League celebrated its 50th anniversary this past summer, in 1989. This good sized city also has a Class "AA" professional baseball team, "The Bills," members of the Eastern League. In the summer of 1987 this club had reached a despairing point - they were 28 games out of first place. Baseball games were no longer fun - just a long, grim daily duty. Manager, Orlando Gomez, a veteran minor league skipper of ten years tenure, was very unpopular then.

When he sent catcher Dave Bresnahan, his first team receiver, back down to Class "A" baseball, he became even more unpopular. Bresnahan was that kind of "character" who seemed to be the "glue" holding a group together in troubled times. He certainly had that charisma. This Bresnahan had a long history of high school and college baseball accomplishments, a talented defensive man. But the 25 year old blonde young man had run smack dab into "that grim reaper of all hitters," the professional pitcher. He couldn't hit water if he fell out of a boat.

Bresnahan approached a game with a sense of fun - every game. It was sure a refreshing outlook for a losing club, which trait endeared him to every club member. "Brez" motivated that team in countless ways which any manager should have realized. After this leader was sent down to Class "A" ball by Manager Gomez, it was necessary to bring him up to Williamsport again, for the alternate receiver got injured soon after reporting. There he was with his old teammates again, but also with Manager Orlando Gomez.

Soon after his re-entry into the old locker room at Williamsport, "Brez" started talking to everyone about "the potato." The "potato"? Well, now what was he going to do with a potato in baseball? This intrigued all of his teammates. Potatoes were usually seen at home or in the markets.

While Bresnahan was in college, a few years earlier, he was sitting on the bench in front of his locker one day. In a moment of blinding inspiration he thought, "Wouldn't it be hilarious to use a potato in a baseball game? Carve up one which looked exactly like a baseball, a perfect imitation."

At this point in that season, 28 games out of first place, the time had come to try it. "Brez" told the pitcher Mike Poehl, "I've always wondered if it would work in a game?" This is the Scheme which the catcher had conjured in that brain of his:

A third base runner would see a baseball (really a potato) sail over third base wildly, on an attempted catcher pickoff throw, into left field. Surely the runner would get up and hurry home after seeing the bad throw. This runner would then be tagged out with the real ball just as he was ready to touch home plate. He would stand at home, gaze bewilderly at left field, then the real baseball. Pitcher Poehl laughed, but he asked "Brez" not to do it in a game that he was pitching. all the other Bills from Williamsport loved the idea. They couldn't wait for anything to liven up that season. It was agreed. August 31, 1987, would be the long-remembered "Williamsport Potato Day."

Then a sudden chill ran through the losing team. "What if the umpire gets real angry and lets the run count?" It was agreed among the players that the umpire should eject the catcher for pulling the trick, call all runners back to their original bases, and proceed with the game from there. They all began to worry about the rules governing this illegal act. Some of them called up a major league umpire to double check what would be done. That arbiter said that there was no clear recorded rule to govern such a situation. He said that probably the umpire would not count the run, he would send the runner back, then have a great laugh about it later. Maybe eject the catcher from the game. (Actually, if any umpire wanted to enforce it, baseball rules clearly state that any game can, at that point, be forfeited to the other team for "even one player purposely making a farce of the game of baseball." A potato could certainly be construed as a "farce," eh?

Monday before the big game, four potatoes were purchased at the local market. Each of them was selected for size. Of course, a potato is very white, like a baseball. "Brez" drew in two sets of seams on each ball, using a red felt pen. Some of the players had a game of catch with one of them. The fake ball did look very realistic in flight when it was thrown very hard.

Bresnahan had a knot in his stomach on his way to the ball park. He set up his four "carved spuds" high above his locker on the shelf. They were well hidden behind some other gear there. All the Bills saw the four balls resting there, and they shouted with joy, "Whoopee, it's Potato Day." They asked him, "Hey, are you really going through with this?" Again the starting pitcher worried that the plate umpire might let the "potato run" count. What if they were, at that moment, in a real tight ball game? They might lose the game on that play. It could happen.

Sure as shooting. Wouldn't you know it? The Bills were down 1-0 to the opponent from Reading, Pennsylvania, as the fifth inning approached. The Reading catcher got on base with a solid single, was sacrificed to second. A grounder to the second baseman moved the runner to third base. The stage had been set. Perfect setting. The time had come. It was "D-Day" for Bresnahan and the Bills. "It's now or never," thought

This "spud's for you," Orlando.
And, oh yeah, I left one for each of your
great teammates, too. Just look
up on your locker shelves.

catcher Bresnahan. After the first pitch to the following hitter, Bresnahan yelled to the plate umpire, Scott Porter, "My webbing in the catcher's glove busted. I'll run get my other glove."

The Williamsport Bills' third baseman turned to the pitcher, Poehl, and they both had to bend over some (to hide their laughing) while "Brez" hustled into the team locker room and got his other catcher's mitt (plus one carefully selected potato) from the shelf.

Manager Orlando Gomez was totally oblivious to the potato being sneaked inside the glove's deep pocket, but all the players on the bench stared with either disbelief or hilarity as catcher Bresnahan trotted back to his place behind the batter, grinning to all the bench.

In his crouch now, Bresnahan carefully signalled his pitcher with a right hand that was draped over his right knee - with the potato in it, hidden from anyone's view. Pitcher Poehl threw a low inside ball on purpose.

As "Brez" received the real baseball, embedded firmly in the mitt, he jumped up quickly and threw the apparent pickoff throw to third baseman Swain. It was thrown high and wide so that the "actor-third baseman" made a lunge to reach it, but he deliberately missed it. Of course, it was the potato which was thrown wildly then. Just after the bad throw, Bresnahan threw his catcher's mitt to the ground and swore theatrically, and he was kicking the dirt, mad at his blunder. Of course, the Reading third base coach had his runner head for home, so the play worked perfectly. The runner made no effort to slide. Just as catcher Lundblade, the Reading runner, was about to lumber across home plate, "Brez" had the real baseball in his right hand, and the tag was applied to the catcher's ribs. "Brez" grinned as he yelled to his opponent, "Hey, runner, you're out." He finally rolled that real ball toward the mound and walked off the field, for the tag was the final out. the entire crowd, players, umpires, and certainly runner Lundblade, were silently stunned.

In the meanwhile, the third base umpire went out and retrieved the round potato. Plate umpire Potter saw it and said, "Hey, you can't have two balls in play in a baseball game." "Brez" barked back to Potter, "Ump, it's not a ball. It's a potato." By this time umpire Scott Potter was fuming. He yelled instantly, "Say, this is professional baseball. Are you trying to show me up. THAT RUN COUNTS." He repeated that last message to the official scorekeeper. The Bills' fears were well-founded!

Third baseman Swain ran in, yelling, 'Hey, you can't do that, ump. It's a joke. Just do the play over."

"Nope, the run counts." "Aw, come on, ump." And so on for a brief while. The final decision was "The run counts." The score at that point stood Reading 2 - Williamsport 0.

Manager Orlando Gomez took this tricky act very personally. He felt that "Brez" was "thumbing his nose at him" for sending him down to Class "A" ball earlier. Gomez removed Bresnahan from the game, but the whole incident so fired up the rest of the Bills, they rallied to beat Reading 4-2. All of the squad wanted to win it for "Brez." Manager Gomez fined the innovative catcher $50.00. The team took up a collection of $50.00 and gave it to Bresnahan later.

The next morning's news article failed to see any humor in the prank, claiming it "Very unprofessional." The same day, Gomez fired Bresnahan from the club. Gomez's decision really floored the "prankster-catcher." He did not think that his manager would go that far.

"Brez" composed himself, then phoned home to break the news. His dad at home and "Brez" ended up coughing and crying with laughter (over the phone in the clubhouse).

The next day Bresnahan cleaned out his locker. On his way out of town, he stopped at the nearest market and bought a big bag of potatoes. He went backed and placed one round potato up in each team mates' locker shelf.

Catcher Bresnahan dumped the last potato on Gomez's office desk, with this note: "ORLANDO - THIS 'SPUD'S FOR YOU' - BREZ"

Stu was reading a local news account in the sports page, Summer of 1989. He saw the same incident on the late TV sportscast that evening.

We wonder if this has ever happened before in major league ball, at least? The newsclip carried an account of an umpire who was undressing in the umpire's room, after a New York Yankees - Milwaukee Brewers ball game. The ump interrupted his undressing routine, stopped to think of that last play of the game, one in which a runner was crossing home plate before the third out of the ninth inning, ending the game, had been made on a slow pitcher's throw to the first base. THE LAST OUT WAS MADE DURING THE SCORING OF THE RUN. IN FACT, THE UMP REMEMBERED THAT THE RUN HAD SCORED BEFORE THE OUT HAD BEEN MADE AT THE BASE. THIS EXTRA RUN MADE NO DIFFERENCE IN THE OUTCOME OF THE GAME, ONLY THE FINAL SCORE.

The umpire put his clothes back on, hurried up to the Official scorer's table, told the scorer the story, changing the final score from 4-1 to 5-1.

BASEBALL STORY NUMBER 52 - 1989
"UMPIRE UNCOVERS AN EXTRA HIDDEN RUN" -
I'VE HEARD OF THE "HIDDEN BALL TRICK"
BUT NEVER A "HIDDEN RUN TRICK"
OR
HOW TO GET AN EXTRA RUN AFTER
THE GAME IS OVER

A STRANGE THING HAPPENED ON the way from the ball diamond to the shower room the eveningof July 3, 1989. It was at a major league game between the New York Yankees and the Milwaukee Brewers.

What actually happened was that the crew chief, Larry Barnett, changed the final score of the game, long after it was over. Not that this did change the game's outcome at all, for the Yankees had beaten the Brewers 5-1. But the official scorer had recorded the outcome as an official 4-1 score.

How could such a change ever happen in baseball? How could an umpire suddenly find an extra run and award it to the winning team? It was a rare play, indeed. The winners didn't even realize that they were entitled to that extra run (that was not really needed for the win). It could have been called a rarer "fourth out call," too. Even the umpires didn't realize the extra run was to be awarded until they huddled inside the dressing room shortly after the game's completion and were discussing the weird events. Some umpire in that group suddenly caught the obvious error from that postgame discussion.

We will lay out the details to the reader and see if he would have caught this error in scoring the extra run. With one out in the eighth inning, with New York leading 4-1, the Yankees had two base runners on. Mike Pagliarulo was at third base while the first base runner was Bob Geren. Wayne Tolleson was the hitter when Yankee manager, Dallas Green, flashed to him to the suicide squeeze bunt sign, from the dugout area. Even with just one out, both runners broke with the pitch. They were stealing all the way, figuring on a bunt on the ground. Poor Tolleson's bunt try, however, sailed softly into the air and was quickly caught by pitcher Jay Aldrich. Aldrich grabbed the fly not too far from first base. He could see there that it was a sure double play throw to first, for the runner had broken for second base.

The pitcher took his sweet time, knowing that his toss to first base would end the

How to get an extra run
after the game is over.

inning and the third base runner's score would be nullified. Right? No - wrong! He threw the ball to first base, the third out was made, and both teams were satisfied that the inning was over. The Brewers ran off the field ready to start the ninth inning.

Two appeal plays could have been made here by the Yankee manager, Dallas Green, but neither were made. After the bunt was caught, while the pitcher took his time on the throw to first base, the third base runner scored before the third out was made. The Yankee manager Green should have appealed to the plate umpire to count that added run scored on that play. He did not, so he lost his only real opportunity to ask for that extra run at that time.

Also, the Brewer's manager could have yelled at the pitcher who caught the bunt fly, "throw the ball to third base (doubling up that runner instead of the first base runner). That runner left the base on a fly and did not return. An appeal play situation. Had that appeal been made, the extra run would never have been awarded, and we wouldn't be telling this story.

So, as it turned out, neither manager caught the error, and neither of them appealed, as they could have.

Umpire Larry Barnett cited the Official Rulebook rule number (Section 7.10) as the reason for awarding the fifth run - the third base runner crossing the plate before the third out was executed at another part of the diamond.

Some umpires are so nice. He really didn't have to do that, did he? How generous, Larry.

EPILOGUE

"THE GRAND FINALE OF BASEBALL'S UNUSUAL HAPPENINGS" FROM 1860 TO 1990

THE FAITHFUL BASEBALL READERS OF this volume have experienced the fun and excitement of reliving this potpourri of varied experiences on the baseball diamonds of America for the past 130 years. The author thinks it more than fitting that he saves the very best until last - that being the final narrator of the three - Sam, Will, and Stu - and being the one of the three baseball story tellers who coached young men to play the game, he unveils "his most memorable day on a ball diamond," either as a player, coach, or spectator. It is hoped that the reader will find this bizarre game truly the climax of this book's stories.

One day in 1974 Stu was running some errands around downtown San Bernardino, and he was pretty tuckered out, so he ducked into the little coffee shop next to the Main Post Office at 5th and D Streets. There, had been opened an eatery called "THE YUM YUM."

As Stu Southworth was entering the "YUM YUM" and was stepping down to the main floor level, his eye was caught by the outline of the hulk of a young man, the chef there, busily hustling breakfast orders out to some impatient customers. The profile of the man was familiar to Stuart, even seeing him in the tall chef's hat. The next moment that chef turned toward Stu and said loudly, "Hey, coach." No sooner had Stu replied with a "Hi, Brian" than the two were facing each other, Stu and Brian, started laughing hilariously at something. What could it have been that amused the two, simultaneously? Customers stared at the two, waitresses stopped their serving. Every soul in the "YUM YUM" must have thought these two men to have been seized by a form of temporary insanity. (Actually they were), Chef Brian really bent over double with uproarious laughter. Tears came to his eyes, the chef's tall cap fell off, he dropped his egg spatula on the counter.

Coach Stu Southworth reacted in like manner. He hardly made it to the first booth, for the two guys were reminiscent of a day, not too long past (seven years, to be exact) when this coach and Brian, his player, shared (and were two of the main characters in) what is possibly the most unusual parade of "continual plays" ever witnessed on an American baseball diamond.

Stu did get over to the booth, sat down, the waitress delivered his cup of hot black coffee. Chef Brian Smith and his Coach Stu Southworth spent most of an hour rehashing the exact events in order. Actually it was the account of a baseball team who scored six consecutive runs one inning on the same play - executed six different ways. What is more amazing about the six runs is the fact that a batter never got his bat on a ball, not one pitch was batted or bunted, each play started with runners on first and third bases, and every run scored from the throwing errors of the defense.

The chef, Brian, however, really made that day, that inning, by performing a most unusual act during one of the plays. It is too bad that the reader cannot also enjoy a movie or a video tape of this last tale.

Baseball Story Number 53 - The Finale My Most Hilarious Day In Baseball - 1966 At Centreville
OR
Brian Smith, The Big Clown, Goes Into His "Roman Banquet Act" Between First And Second Bases

MY MOST HILARIOUS DAY IN BASEBALL
(an afternoon at Centreville, California)
(An Object Lesson In The Effect Of Good Base Running On An Opponent)

"Even as I am sitting down to relate this baseball game of the past to you, I am chuckling to myself. This is an account of not only the most hilarious baseball game I ever coached, but it is also one of my most memorable days I spent in the game. Unfortunately, as in most funny events of this nature, someone has to be the victim of the humor. For this I apologize.

It was in the Spring of 1967. I was Junior Varsity coach at San Gorgonio High School in San Bernardino, California. We had a team that was composed of players who could do everything well, but especially did they love to run the bases. They delighted in pulling the most "outlandish plays" on our opponents at the most unusual times.

One afternoon in April, about our 15th game of the year, we journeyed by bus to a high school in our league, located in Centreville. Both teams took the infield and outfield practice, and the game began. We could see that their team was not too sharp, and their tall, right handed pitcher was not too fast. Perhaps this made us over-confident. Each inning we went to bat and hit the ball hard and deep, but always right at someone. We made an error or two and suddenly we were behind 3-1 going into the top half of the sixth inning.

The spectators were many, and they were watching a hard-nosed, close ball game. We had had only two scratch hits up to this point, and so, before we went to bat in the sixth, I told them (in a huddle) that we weren't going to play straight "hit away type baseball" any more. I let the team know that they would be going into our "running game" and for them to watch for signs to execute the unorthodox plays we had practiced.

The inning begins. My first batter walked. I game him the steal sign, and he broke. The catcher threw the ball five feet over the shortstop's head at second base, and my runner was on third. The pitcher was not too happy, and he threw two balls to the batter. I called time out and we had the old "Double Steal with a man starting at home plate" ready to go. I told my runner that, if he walked, he was to trot to first base and stop, count a slow "1001," adjust his belt, then break for second at high speed. The pitcher had the ball when he broke, and he hesitated too late to throw to second, but he did throw. My third base runner was edging off third. The second the pitcher threw to second base, he broke for home. When the second baseman received the throw, he threw home too late and the ball caromed off the catcher's mitt about twenty feet. The second base runner came on to third.

Now the score stood: San Gorgonio 2, Centreville 3. A runner sits on third base.

This upset the pitcher so badly that he walked the next batter. Where are my runners now? Again at first and third. I gave the first base runner, on the second pitch, the sign to steal. He broke for second base on the pitch and the catcher threw to second, but too late. On the catcher's throw the runner on third base broke for the plate and beat the throw home. Now the score stood: San Gorgonio 3, Centreville 3. I tried a different tactic with the next batter. We sacrificed the winning run to third, but the pitcher fumbled the ball, firing too late to first.

Again, where are my runners? On first and third. This time I called a "Delayed Double Steal" The batter "took" the pitch and the catcher had the ball. As he tossed the ball back to the pitcher rather softly, the first base runner took off for second base but stopped halfway to second. The pitcher threw to the second baseman and he started to run down the runner. My third base runner broke for the plate when the second baseman was tossing to the first baseman. the poor first baseman was so startled that he threw wide in the dirt past the catcher, and the stealing second base runner went to third.

By this time the Centreville team was "fuming." Their coach and players were barking at each other. I looked over at the glum expressions on the faces of the Centreville crowd.

We were now ahead 4-3 and had done it on three consecutive first and third Double Steals, but the timing had been run differently in all three.

I glanced over at our stands and the spectators were laughing so hard we could hardly hear ourselves in the dugout nearby.

Situation now is man on third base. By this time their pitcher has "gone into shock." He walks the next batter on four pitches. I called time out and told the runner to walk off first base slowly to see what the pitcher would do. He did as I bade, and the pitcher was so mad he charged at the runner. He got close to him in the baseline and held the ball up and tried to outrun the base runner. The base runner out ran him to second. The pitcher never released the ball. He just stood as the runner slid into second base and the third base runner had broken for the plate and scored.

Score how is 5-3. We have worked the same play now four consecutive times for four runs. Runner is now on second base.

Brian Smith, the big clown, goes into
his "roman banquet act" between
first and second bases.

I look at both stands and people are laughing so hard they are leaning on each other and holding their sides.

My team in the dugout has become completely "unglued." Two or three are leaning on the screen fence to hold themselves up from laughing so hard. Some are actually falling off the bench.

If they had only known what was coming next. The Centreville coach goes to the mound now and tells his team to completely ignore the runner off first base on future plays we pull with men on first and third.

Up to bat steps our biggest clown of all, Brian Smith, a football player who was huge, a left-handed pitcher. I told him if we got the first and third situation again, to walk off the base and go halfway but not to go to second base, just to see what they would do.

On the first pitch I have Brian take and the second base runner stole third base. The catcher threw miles late. This upset the pitcher so that he walked Brian. Men were again on first and third bases. The pitcher is so stunned by all this, he is in a trance. Brian walks off the base, gets halfway from first to second and says something to the pitcher. Their pitcher ignored him. Then Brian did something I have never seen anyone in baseball do. To our utter amazement, that clown laid down on the ground, facing the pitcher, cocked his hat over his eyes, and he put his head up on one hand, holding his head up by one arm. He resembled a "Roman reclining at a banquet lying on a soft couch." He took his other hand, with his index finger, beckoned to the pitcher to "come on and get me." You could not hear yourself think, the screaming and laughing was so loud. Everyone in the ball park was hooting and guffawing. Centreville's bench was now laughing, as well as their crowd. But our spectators were gasping for air. The bus driver who drove us over was trying to hold up Mr. and Mrs. Crabtree, two of our parents, who were holding each other in tight embrace. They were both kneeling on the ground. Another parent was on the grass rolling over and over holding his side, gasping for a breath.

By this time I broke out laughing and was hanging onto the cyclone fence in uncontrollable laughter. Just then, the pitcher "went berserk." He charged off the mound and, enraged like a mad bull, went after Brian Smith. He had Brian one third of the way to second base and was gaining on him. The third base runner broke for the plate just as the ferocious pitcher tripped and fell flat on his face, and the ball shot out of his hand to shallow right field. By the time the ball was retrieved, Brian was into third base sliding. But now the two umpires are laughing. They have to stop the game a few seconds to compose themselves. Situation is now a man on third base and we lead 6-3. We have worked our famous "first and third double steal" five times in a row, and each time something different has happened.

Their coach would not change pitchers. He said they had only one pitcher that day. So, he walks our next batter to the delight of our bench and our fans.

Same situation. Men on first and third. This time we go back and repeat our first option of the play. On the next pitch the first base runner breaks for second base, the pitcher whirls and fires to second and they finally get the first out of the inning. But as he is tagged, Brian edges off and breaks for the plate. He makes it under the late throw to the catcher.

Score is now 7-3 and we have executed the first and third play six consecutive times for six runs. My kids came over and talked. We decided to take the running plays off, let the batters hit the rest of the inning. Would you believe we scored no more runs that inning or in the seventh inning? Neither did they. Game score was 7-3.

Why am I telling you this story? Certainly not to embarrass the opponent.

1. See what can happen to a tight ball game when you "push the button" and say "run"? The game became a "circus."
2. A good running team runs a play "into the ground" until the opponent proves that he can stop it.   3.   We would probably not have beaten that team that day by straight hitting. They had momentum. We took it away from them by the "element of surprise."
4. Running is a "spectator sport." I doubt that anyone on that ball field was not entertained by hustle and clever technique.

Why don't more coaches depart from the old "traditional patterns of play" and try something innovative? Are we to say that baseball coaches are not experimental and are unimaginative??"

BIBLIOGRAPHY

1. DANZIG, ALLISON, and REICHLER, JOE, THE HISORY OF BASEBALL - ITS GREAT PLAYERS, TEAMS AND MANAGERS, Englewood Cliffs, New Jersey, Prentice-Hall, Incorporated, 1959.

2. ENCYCLOPEDIA BRITTANICA. 1968 edition.

3. HONIG, DONALD, THE BROOKLYN DODGERS - AN ILLUSTRATED TRIBUTE, New York City, St. Martin's Press, 1981.

4. KINDALL, JERRY, BASEBALL, Head Baseball Coach, University of Arizona, Arizona, New York City, Harper and Row, Inc. SPORTS ILLUSTRATED BOOKS, 1983.

5. KUHN, BOWIE, THE OFFICIAL BASEBALL RULEBOOK, REVISED EDITION, MAJOR AND MINOR LEAGUES, Commissioner of Baseball, 1984.

6. LEIB, FRED, BASEBALL AS I HAVE KNOWN IT, New York City, Coward, McCann, and Geoghegan, 1977.

7. OLAN, BEN, and REICHLER, JOE, BASEBALL'S UNFORGETTABLE GAMES, New York City, The Ronald Press Company, 1980.

8. REICHLER, JOE, BASEBALL'S GREAT MOMENTS, New York City, The Crown Publishers, Inc. 1979.

9. SMITH, IRA and SMITH, H. ALLEN, LOW AND INSIDE, New York City, McGraw-Hill Publishers, 1947.

10. SOUTHWORTH, HAROLD S., MANUAL OF BASE RUNNING PLAYS IN BASEBALL, San Bernardino, California, self-published, Crown Printers, 1981.

11. TYGIEL, JULES, BASEBALL'S GREAT EXPERIMENT - JACKIE ROBIN-SON AND HIS LEGACY, New York City, The Oxford University Press, 1983.